Thoreau in the Human Community

Thoreau in the Human Community

Mary Elkins Moller

The University of Massachusetts Press   Amherst, 1980

Copyright © 1980 by The University of Massachusetts Press.
All rights reserved
Library of Congress Catalog Card Number 79-22549   ISBN 0-87023-293-2
Printed in the United States of America
Library of Congress Cataloging in Publication Data appear on the last
printed page of this book.

A few portions of this book have appeared earlier: parts of chapters 2 and 4,
with additional material, in "Thoreau, Womankind and Sexuality," and a
somewhat different and fuller version of chapter 9 (under the title, " 'You
Must First Have Lived' "), in *ESQ: A Journal of the American Renaissance*,
vol. 22 (third quarter), 1976, and vol. 23 (fourth quarter), 1977 respectively.

Acknowledgment is made to the following for permission to reprint copy-
righted material:
   Houghton Mifflin Company, for material from Perry Miller, *Consciousness
in Concord: The Text of Thoreau's Hitherto "Lost Journal," 1840–41,
Together with Notes and a Commentary* (Boston: Houghton Mifflin, 1958).
Copyright © 1958 by Perry Miller. All rights reserved.
   Random House, Inc., for selections from William Faulkner, "The Bear,"
in *Go Down, Moses* (New York: Random House, 1942). Copyright, 1940,
1941, 1942, by William Faulkner, Copyright, 1942, by The Curtis Publishing
Company.

This book is dedicated to Cliff,

David, Cathy, and Jon.

Acknowledgments

My AWARENESS of Thoreau came first from my father, Frederick
Elkins, a lover of nature and of *Walden;* but the awareness was
not built upon for a number of years, not "improved," as Thoreau
would say, until in graduate school at Harvard I moved from a
preoccupation with British literature toward an ever-increasing interest in the literature of my own country, and especially that of
my adoptive region of New England. This general interest was
fed by courses with Kenneth Murdock, Perry Miller, Alfred Kazin,
Edward Carter, and Reuben Brower, and by F. O. Matthiessen's
American Renaissance. It was Perry Miller, with whom I have had
to quarrel in this book, who after all—in addition to nurturing
the overall concern with American studies—prompted me to in-
vestigate, and then to explore deeply, Thoreau's vast and fascinating *Journal.* When finally I got around to writing on Thoreau, I
was fortunate in having the counsel and encouragement of Kenneth Lynn and of Joel Porte. And I have profited from conversations with Patrick Quinn of Wellesley College.

The book has been read, and extremely useful suggestions
have been made, by Professors Walter Harding and Alexander
Kern, as well as by readers and staff members at the University
of Massachusetts Press. I would especially like to thank Ms.
Leone Stein, Director of the Press, for helpful commentary and
suggestions.

Megan Marshall has worked with me, skillfully and faithfully,
as editorial assistant and reader–sounding-board, as has Lyn Oliver
also. And thanks are due to Jeane Morris for patient and skilled
deciphering and typing.

The dedication records a long-standing and continuing debt of gratitude, to my husband and children—not always utterly patient with my preoccupations and complaints, but ultimately supportive, and much beloved.

Cambridge, Massachusetts
September 1979

Contents

Introduction

I N a letter of 1856, to Daniel Ricketson, Henry Thoreau developed a brief but very interesting character sketch. Ricketson had earlier reported to him an abrupt visit from Ellery Channing, who was now residing near the Ricketsons in New Bedford. "I am rejoiced to hear that you are getting on so bravely with him," Thoreau replied.

He and I, as you know, have been old cronies. "Fed the same flock by fountain, shade and rill. . . ." "But O, the heavy change" now he is gone!
The C[hanning] you have seen and described is the real Simon Pure. You have seen him. Many a good ramble may you have together. You will see in him more of the same kind—to attract and puzzle you. How to serve him . . . has long been a problem with his friends. . . . I suspect that the most that you or anyone can do for him is to appreciate his genius—to buy and read, and cause others to buy and read his poems. That is the hand which he has put forth to the world—take hold of that. . . . He will accept sympathy and aid, but he will not bear questioning—unless the aspects of the sky are particularly auspicious. He will even be "reserved and enigmatic," and you must deal with him at arm's length.[1]

The letter offers a useful illustration of Thoreau's capacity for friendship, and of his genuine talent, however seldom displayed, for expressing it. No one would deny that a real affection for Channing is expressed in this passage—at first hyperbolically ("You have seen him . . . the real Simon Pure"), then very earnestly. Readers who remember certain sardonic darts levelled at Channing in Thoreau's *Journal* will probably be impressed by his use here of the haunting lines from "Lycidas," which surely evidence a strong attachment. Also evident in the letter are Thoreau's affection for Ricketson, and his generosity in sharing his friendships.

But what I find most striking is the fact that Thoreau's sketch of Channing could serve very well to characterize Thoreau himself —as he is described by others, including Emerson and Channing, and as he sometimes depicted himself: his own refusal to be questioned, his own "reserved and enigmatic" quality, his having to be dealt with "at arm's length." Yet the metaphor of the hand put forth to the world also seems apt, for describing an effort apparent in much that Thoreau wrote—in his case, an effort more personal and intense than that implied by the mere fact of writing for publication, and not least apparent in the privacy of the *Journal*.

My aim in this book is to explore and analyze those passages in Thoreau's writings which reveal his varying attitudes toward other persons and toward Humanity, which reveal his need for communication and intimate relationships—for some means of reaching beyond the Self—and his varying degrees of success and failure in these domains.

My interest in these questions originated when I noticed a certain recurrent correlation in the *Journal*. Passages that displayed interesting linguistic peculiarities, and whose tone seemed more emotional than usual, were often the passages that revealed Thoreau's complex feelings about other people, or his wish to relate to some super-human entity. In this study I seek to arrive at the fullest possible understanding of such passages, in the *Journal* and elsewhere, through a close examination of their style and tone, and, by viewing them in relation to other passages, to arrive at a better understanding of this major writer.

Although the questions raised here are obviously of biographical interest, this is not a strictly biographical study. I have made relatively little use of sources outside Thoreau's own works, and the book's overall organization is topical rather than chronological. My interest is in Thoreau's writing, as it was shaped by what I take to be his most profound needs, and in the man as he is revealed in his work—especially in those passages that have seemed to me most intensely felt. I should add that (though I see how the *Journal*, especially, invites such analysis) I am not equipped to attempt a psychoanalytical study of the man. I operate, then, with no ambition to be either conventional biographer or lay-analyst, but simply as a reader fascinated by the passionate ambivalences of Thoreau.

The matter of chronology has been considered here only intermittently, where the dating and sequences of certain passages (chiefly in the *Journal*, occasionally in letters) would seem to have a bearing on their interpretation and on our understanding of some crucial chapter in Thoreau's experience. In the *Journal*, this matter of dating and sequence of composition poses certain problems. We know that the extant journals, especially those of the earlier years, represent an amalgamation, a gleaning, rather than an entirely free-flowing first-hand composition. The 1906 *Journal* editors provided many hints to this effect—in the form of references to presumed earlier notebooks which were discarded after their contents were transcribed, indications of pages deleted from surviving notebooks, notes regarding surviving loose manuscript sheets whose contents sometimes parallel material in the bound volumes, and notes on the extent to which Thoreau made use of *Journal* material in the *Week*, *Walden*, and other works published during his lifetime. An examination of the manuscript notebooks in the Morgan Library vividly bears out one's impression—formed from a long exposure to the published text and reinforced by those editorial hints—that the *Journal* is a very complex combination of therapeutic personal confession, literary workbook, and highly conscious work of art, lovingly shaped for its own sake.

In his 1958 edition of an early journal volume, Perry Miller took a memorable stand for regarding the whole *Journal* primarily as a literary workbook, whose contents were more often than not copied and reworked from scrappy notes, or other journals, and then "ruthlessly" rifled for contributions to Thoreau's books, essays, and lectures.[2] In documenting this view, Miller minimized the immediate, personal character of the journals, tending, in effect, to question Thoreau's sincerity at many points. He suggests—often sarcastically—that since Thoreau was capable of piecing together a "mosaic" paragraph for the *Dial*, the *Week*, or another work, from widely scattered passages in the *Journal*, those passages cannot be taken as expressions of genuine attitudes and feelings even when first set down.[3]

There are reasons for disputing so extreme a view, some of which are clearly supported by a reading of the original manuscripts. For example, in precisely those passages whose words are most passionate, despairing or exulting, there is often evidence of a marked rapidity or stress in the script which, together with small breaks or errors, suggests both the throes of first composition and, even more, the urgent venting of deep feeling. In any case the sincerity of the feeling is unmistakable. And rendering it in words clearly brought Thoreau more than relief: it also brought the pleasure, and the pride, of fulfilled creativity. That Thoreau himself came at times to regard his *Journal* more as an autonomous work of art than as a "workbook" is evident, for example, in a passage from 1852 in which he muses on the possibility of its being printed "thus . . . in [this] same form"—as it finally was forty-six years after his death.[4] Furthermore, other critics have responded quite differently from Miller to Thoreau's "mosaic" method of composition. Using that very word (it was originally Margaret Fuller's) ten years before Miller's essay, Joseph Wood Krutch—who had no difficulty believing in Thoreau's sincerity—had called the "brilliant" last chapter of *Walden* "a crystallization . . . a mosaic of crystals," and noted admiringly how fragments from the *Journal* "were . . . carefully selected and carefully fitted together in such a way that what looks like explosive brilliance was actually the result of a patient craftsmanship."[5] It is only Miller who sees such passages as "strung together," * "squeezed out," or "stuck into [later works] much as a cook sticks cloves into a ham."[6]

I feel it is necessary to call Miller's views into question because his judgment of the *Journal* and of Thoreau himself—a judgment which consistently ignores the generous, yearning, and communal impulses in favor of the sometimes perverse, misanthropic ones—has continued to exert an unfortunate influence.[7] Thoreau

---

* "Thoreau launches again and again into those celebrations of the wild which at the end of the decade [the 1850s] were strung together to form the belated 'Walking'" (Miller, *Consciousness in Concord*, pp. 78–79). In 1962 Kenneth Lynn saw fit to include this "strung-together" essay among his selections from Thoreau in *Major Writers of America*, and in his accompanying introduction he asserts that Thoreau's is "the most beautifully disciplined writing talent of the age" (*Major Writers of America*, ed. Perry Miller, vol. 1 [New York: Harcourt, Brace and World, 1962], p. 598). Note, by the way, Miller's word "belated." "Walking" was produced late in Thoreau's life, but why call it "belated"? The word suggests that he is being chided for some negligence or incapacity. But many readers have seen this essay as a final and fitting distillation of some of Thoreau's most important ideas. Frederick Garber is one of those; he treats "Walking" in the introduction and in the climax and conclusions of *Thoreau's Redemptive Imagination* ([New York: New York University Press, 1977], pp. vi, 211–20).

did at times draw back from intimacy. He did at times make impossible demands on other people; and, entertaining impossibly high expectations, he at times voiced bitter disappointment in the human race. But it is obvious that he did not merely "use" romantic-transcendentalist conventions about friendship; nor did he practice pretense or suffer self-delusion, as Miller suggests, indulging in fantasies of strong attachments only to withdraw from them, all the while anticipating failure. In passages I will be examining there is ample evidence of a very real desire for friendship and for love, as well as an impressive commitment to "serve the public." These passages show Thoreau's hand put forth, throughout his adult life, in efforts at direct personal contact and communication.

In my own exploration, I have assumed that Thoreau meant what he wrote, that it represented his sincere thought and feeling at whatever time he entered it into a manuscript or one of the journal volumes now available to us, no matter whether the version there found were the very first, set down smoking from his brain, or a second, or third, re-rendered from pocket notes or another notebook—and even if, with true transcendentalist freedom, Thoreau contradicted it elsewhere. It follows that the style, the diction, and the juxtapositions of material in these volumes must be taken seriously, as significant indications of Thoreau's state of mind at the time of their inscription.

Of course assumptions of this kind have been made by many critics and biographers before me.* But they have yet to be applied to the study of the one very complex and central aspect of Thoreau's life and writings which I am treating here: that involving his attitudes toward the rest of humanity. It has long been my impression that Thoreau the devotee and philosopher of Nature, the herald and epitome of self-reliance, the political nonconformist, is better known than the Thoreau I am here seeking to understand. I am also convinced that all these other roles were profoundly conditioned by the intensity of his feelings about other people and about the problem of relationships.

Finally, one sees throughout Thoreau's writings a desire for

---

* As Stanley Cavell put it in *The Senses of Walden,* "My opening hypothesis is that this book is perfectly complete, in that it means every word it says, and that it is fully sensible of its mysteries and fully open about them" ([New York: Viking Press, 1972], p. 3).

still another kind of relationship, which seems to me at least as significant as his desires and his difficulties in the area of human relations. That is his desire for the ecstasy of feeling himself mystically related to Nature, to the Universe, to some super-human power. It is also my belief that this need in Thoreau for mystical experience is closely related to the complex patterns of attraction and repulsion in human relationships on which this study is focused.

Thoreau in the Human Community

One

Thoreau, le Misanthrope

M ANY casual readers of *Walden*, and even some of its more serious readers who may also have dipped into the *Journal*, share a popular impression that Henry Thoreau ("the hermit of Walden woods") was a conscious and confirmed misanthrope.

It was a judgment rendered by several of his contemporaries, among them Lowell and Holmes, and supported to some degree by Emerson's portrait of him as a Nay-sayer, "but rarely tender," in the "Biographical Sketch," and by his very selective posthumous edition of Thoreau's letters.[1] Later readers of Emerson's *Journal* could find support for it in his frequent complaints of Henry's perversity and coldness.[2] And the judgment has persisted. A distinguished professor of American literature, who himself has written perceptively about *Walden*, was recently reported to have said (in conversation with a student) that "It's hard to empathize with Thoreau, unless you happen to like muskrats and shrub oaks better than people."

Before examining evidence of Thoreau's warmer feelings for humanity we must take full measure of this notorious misanthropy. It can indeed be found in *Walden*, in the "sunny" *Week*, in the letters, and above all in the *Journal*.

In *Walden*, clear-cut expressions of misanthropic feeling are relatively few. At times a quite hostile statement is (seemingly) undercut by a merely mischievous-sounding addition: for example, "The greater part of what my neighbors call good I believe in my soul to be bad, and if I repent of anything, it is very likely to be my good behavior." That mischief is insisted upon, however ("What demon possessed me that I behaved so well?"), and we sense that both declaration and question are to be taken seriously. Still, here and elsewhere, the tone is so relaxed, even genial, that the negative force of what is being said is not immediately felt.

I have lived some thirty years on this planet, and I have yet to hear the first syllable of valuable or even earnest advice from my seniors.

Commonly men will only be brave as their fathers were brave, or timid.

Why level down to our dullest perception always, and praise that as common sense? The commonest sense is the sense of men asleep, which they express by snoring.[3]

In a few instances the tone is much more biting, and what in other passages was a criticism of other men sounds very much like a rejection:

I have never felt . . . in the least oppressed by a sense of solitude, but once, and that was a few weeks after I came to the woods, when, for an hour, I doubted if the near neighborhood of man was not essential to a serene and healthy life. To be alone was something unpleasant. But I was at the same time conscious of a slight insanity in my mood, and seemed to foresee my recovery.

I live in the angle of a leaden wall, into whose composition was poured a little alloy of bell metal. Often, in the repose of my mid-day, there reaches my ears a confused *tintinnabulum* from without. It is the noise of my contemporaries.[4]

But that tone is rare in *Walden*. It is heard with some regularity in the *Journal*, which can furnish evidence of Thoreau's misanthropy in any one of its fourteen volumes:

Such is man,—toiling, heaving, struggling ant-like to shoulder some stray unappropriated crumb and deposit it in his granary; then runs out, complacent, gazes heavenward, earthward (for even pismires can look down) . . . there seen of men, world-seen, deed-delivered, vanishes into all-grasping night. (*J*, I: 34; 1838.)

Society is always diseased, and the best is the sickest. (*J*, I: 306; 1841.)

Sometimes, by a pleasing, sad wisdom [note the first adjective], we find ourselves carried beyond all counsel and sympathy. Our friends' words do not reach us. (*J*, I: 452, written sometime between 1837 and 1847.)

When I have been confined to my chamber for the greater part of several days, . . . I have been conscious of a certain softness to which I am otherwise and commonly a stranger, in which the gates were loosened to some emotions; and if I were to become a confirmed invalid, I see how some sympathy with mankind and society might spring up. (*J*, III: 106; 1851.)

It appears to me that, to one standing on the heights of philosophy, mankind and the works of man will have sunk out of sight altogether.

This sentence begins a long passage (*J*, III: 381–82; 1852) which probably represents Thoreau's most sustained effort to formulate a "philosophical" statement of his misanthropic feelings: "The poet says the proper study of mankind is man. I say, study to forget all that; take wider views of the universe. That is the egotism of the race. . . . When another poet says the world is too much with us, he means, of course, that man is too much with us. . . . In order to avoid delusions, I would fain let man go by and behold a universe in which man is but a grain of sand. . . . I do not value any view of the universe into which man and the institutions of man enter very largely. . . ." The numerous rephrasings of its one idea clearly mark this as a highly conscious formulation. The following passages seem more immediately felt and personally acrimonious:

I know two species of men. The vast majority are men of society. They live on the surface; they are interested in the transient and fleeting; they are like driftwood in the flood. . . . They dwell, they are ever, right in my face and eyes like gnats; they are like motes, so near the eyes that, looking beyond, they appear like blurs; they have their being between my eyes and the end of my nose. (*J*, III: 460; 1852.)

I love Nature partly *because* she is not man but a retreat from him. . . . If this world were all man, I could not stretch myself, I should lose all hope. (*J*, IV: 445; 1853.)*

Yesterday I was influenced with [*sic*] the rottenness of human relations. They appeared full of death and decay, and offended the nostrils. (*J*, IV: 472; 1853.)

I despair of ever getting anything quite simple and honest done in this world by the help of men. They would have to be pressed through a powerful press, *à la* cider-mill, that their old notions might be thoroughly squeezed out of them, and it would be some time before they would

---

* This passage includes the couplet, "Man, man is the devil / The source of all evil."

get upon their legs again. . . . I could cry, if it were not for laughing. (J, VI: 70–71; 1854.)

I have seen many a collection of stately elms which better deserve to be represented at the General Court than the manikins beneath. . . . I find that into my idea of the village has entered more of the elm than of the human being. . . . A fragment of their bark is worth the backs of all the politicians in the union. (J, VIII: 139–40; 1856.)

There sits one by the shore who wishes to go with me, but I cannot think of it. . . . Why, I am *going,* not staying, I have come on purpose to sail, to paddle away from such as you. . . . Why, if I thought you were steadily gazing after me a mile off, I could not endure it. (J, IX: 46–47; 1856.)

(Even though Thoreau had, evidently, made his escape into solitude, he nevertheless carried on this last complaint for the better part of two pages.)

In the street and in society I am almost invariably cheap and dissipated, my life is unspeakably mean. . . . I wish to get the Concord, the Massachusetts, the America, out of my head and be sane a part of every day. . . . I wish to forget . . . all mean, narrow, trivial men (and this requires usually to forego and forget all personal relations so long). . . . (J, IX: 208–9; 1857.)

The gregariousness of men is their most contemptible and discouraging aspect. See how they follow each other like sheep, not knowing why. Day and Martin's [shoe] blacking was preferred by the last generation and also is by this. They have not so good a reason for preferring this or that religion as in this case even. . . . Men are the inveterate foes of all improvement. (J, X: 350–51; 1858.)

The preachers and lecturers deal with men of straw, as they are men of straw themselves. Why, a free-spoken man, of sound lungs, cannot draw a long breath without causing your rotten institutions to come toppling down by the vacuum he makes. Your church is a baby-house made of blocks, and so is the state. . . . Look at your editors of popular magazines. I have dealt with two or three the most liberal of them. They are afraid to print a whole, . . . a free-spoken sentence. They want thirty thousand subscribers, and they will do anything to get them. . . . One of our New England towns is sealed up hermetically like a molasses-hogshead,—such is its sweet Christianity. . . . On the one side you will find a barroom which holds the "Scoffers," on the other a vestry where there is a monthly concert of prayer. There is just as little to cheer you in one of these companies as the other. It may be often the truth and righteousness of the barroom that saves the town. There is nothing to redeem the bigotry and moral cowardice of New Englanders in my eyes.... (*J*, XI: 324–26; 1858.)

The mass of men, just like savages, strive always after the outside, the clothes and finery of civilized life, the blue beads and tinsel and centre tables. (*J*, XII: 332; 1859.)

("The mass of men" is a phrase which pervades the *Journal.** Within a period of a few weeks in 1853, for example, Thoreau had written: "The mass of men are very unpoetic...." (July 30.) "I saw that it was as impossible to speak of marriage to such a man —to the mass of men—as of poetry.... The marriage which the mass of men comprehend is but little better than the marriage of the beasts." (August 11.) "The mass of mankind, who ... are *bent* upon their labor ... know nothing [of the beauty of nature.]" (August 19.) "The fact for the savage, and for the mass of mankind, is that it is better to plant, weave, and build than do nothing or worse...." (September 1) (*J*, V: 347, 369, 383, 410).

But, for Thoreau, 1859 was pre-eminently the year of John Brown, and here is his view of "the mass of men" in that crisis:

The brutish thick-skinned herd, who do not know a *man* by sympathy, make haste home from their ballot-boxes and churches to their Castles of Indolence, perchance to cherish their valor there with some nursery talk of knights and dragons.... Another neighbor asks, Yankee-like, "What will he *gain* by it?" as if he expected to fill his pockets by this enterprise. They have no idea of gain but in this worldly sense. If it does not lead to a surprise party, if he does not get a new pair of boots and a vote of thanks, it must be a failure....

This event advertises me that there is such a fact as death,—the possibility of a man's dying. It seems as if no man had ever died in America; for in order to die you must first have lived. (*J*, XII: 405–6, 437.)[5]

(This idea had been present as far back as 1853: "Methinks that many if not most, men are a sort of natural mummies. The life

---

* When first encountered there it has a familiar ring, and we remember "The mass of men lead lives of quiet desperation" (*Walden*, chapter 1).

having departed out of them...they still keep up a dry and withered semblance of life." [*J*, V: 10].) And similarly negative utterances continue intermittently in the *Journal*'s final volumes.

Always you have to contend with the stupidity of men.... The stupid you have always with you. Men are more obedient at first to words than ideas.... Read to them a lecture on "Education," naming that subject, and they will think they have heard something important, but call it "Transcendentalism," and they will think it moonshine. (*J*, XIII: 145; 1860.)

Many people have a foolish way of talking about small things and apologize for...having neglected their ordinary business and amused or instructed themselves by attending to a small thing; when, if the truth were known, their ordinary business was the small thing, and almost their whole lives were misspent, but they were such fools as not to know it. (*J*, XIV: 104; 1860.)

Altogether, this fairly random culling seems to exhibit a thorough-going, unqualified misanthropy, expressed in a variety of characteristic ways. Two passages have a somewhat self-conscious, academic quality, but of these the long "philosophical" statement of April, 1852, is patently more serious than the "Such is man" sentence of 1838, whose tone and rather elaborate rhetoric are more suggestive of youthful posturing than of deeply felt cynicism.* Other passages appear, by contrast, much less finished, much more hurriedly and heatedly written—for example, those on "men of society," and "the rottenness of human relations," that of 1858 about "men of straw," and the 1859 passage on the infrequency of death.

The entries which show Thoreau weighing man against Nature, to man's hopeless disadvantage, are typical of many in the *Journal*. At times he ponders this conflict, or incompatibility, even more directly: "Nature and man; some prefer the one, others the other; but that is all *de gustibus*. It makes no odds at what well you drink, provided it be a well-head" (*J*, II: 170; 1851). "It appears to be a law that you cannot have a deep sympathy with both man and Nature" (*J*, III: 400; 1852). "By my intimacy with Nature I find myself withdrawn from man" (*J*, IV: 258; 1852). And when,

---

* We find, in fact, that Thoreau pencilled one word in the margin opposite this passage—"Carlyleish," which suggests that he himself came to see it as artificial, a literary exercise.

in his surveyor role, he has been "preambulating the bounds" of the town (verifying its boundaries), he even finds his customary delight in Nature undercut by association with the "mean and narrowminded men"—selectmen and landowners—with whom he has had to confer: "What can be uglier than a country occupied by grovelling, coarse and low-lived men? No scenery will redeem it." Such men are a greater "curse" than "hornets, hyenas and baboons" (*J*, III: 23–24; 1851). Elsewhere, at the end of a diatribe on "politics, society, business and . . . the whole outward world," he asserts that "I come from the funeral of mankind to attend to a natural phenomenon" (*J*, III: 103–4; 1851).

Typical also, in this series of misanthropic passages, are the outbursts on human "stupidity," gullibility, superficiality, bigotry, and hypocrisy. Despite its furious tone, however, and our sense of some compulsion that kept Thoreau's pen driving through five indignant pages, we are likely to find the "men of straw" passage, of November, 1858, somehow less misanthropic, less disturbing, than others in this series. In fact, it is partly *because* of the "temperature" of the passage that we feel this. We recognize that it was written in anger; and because its targets are specific, and treated in some detail, this anger seems largely justified. It is known, in fact, that Thoreau had an unhappy confrontation with the press at about this time, when Lowell at the *Atlantic* surreptitiously deleted a "pantheistic" sentence from one of his essays.[6] In any case, the timidity and hypocrisy of the church, politicians, the press, and lecture committees—these are surely legitimate objects of indictment and satire. So also is the human tendency to care more for labels than ideas, or to accept traditional attitudes and values without question.

All this points up an obvious and essential distinction. In many passages, though the tone may be bitter, and though the bitterness may issue in such generalizations as "There is nothing to redeem the bigotry and moral cowardice of New Englanders in my eyes," still we see that, basically, Thoreau is deploring, and *satirizing*, "institutions" (almost always a pejorative word in his writings), or specific human foibles. We remember "I could cry if it were not for laughing"; and we recognize that satire, however savage, usually has an ameliorative motive.

But in many other instances one can detect no particular occasion for disappointment or scorn, no specific object of satire. Instead, Thoreau seems gratuitously to be attacking, or dismissing, the whole of mankind. Such a passage is that of January, 1856, in which a response to the beauty of an elm grove evolves into an outburst of contempt for "the manikins beneath," "the human being." Or this: "It is pleasant to meet the dry yellowish-colored fruit of the poison dogwood . . . , it has so much character relatively to man" (*J*, II: 128, 1850). There are many such instances in the journals, where, in a passage of quite cheerful nature observations, or poetic reflections, one suddenly comes upon a concealed bombshell of misanthropy. In one of the celebrated "nocturnes," for example, a rhapsodic paragraph on moonlight and "the antiquity of night" comes to focus on night as a landscape "where men are not": "The farmer and his oxen now are asleep. . . . The human slumbers. There is less of man in the world" (*J*, II: 483; 1851).

Clearly, these expressions of misanthropic feelings must have been quite conscious and deliberate on Thoreau's part, however startling and abrupt they may appear to his reader. There are other instances in which such a feeling, though unmistakable, is more subtly suggested, so that one wonders whether Thoreau himself was fully conscious of it: "In the fine flowing haze, men at a distance seem shadowy and gigantic, as *ill-defined* [my italics] and great as men should always be" (*J*, I: 338; 1842). "I saw an old bone in the woods and covered with lichens, which looked like the bone of an old settler. . . . It was quite too ancient to suggest disagreeable associations. It was like a piece of dry pine root. It survives like the memory of a man. With time all that was personal and offensive wears off" (*J*, II: 93–94; 1850).

Such subtle, perhaps unconscious slurs seem to suggest a deep vein of misanthropy in Thoreau. But many readers will find more shocking (because it seems more intimately personal) one of the most explicit statements in the series quoted at the beginning of this chapter. That is Thoreau's reflection in 1851 that, for him, sickness begat "a certain softness to which I am otherwise and commonly a stranger," a "loosening" of emotional "gates," so that "if I were to become a confirmed invalid, I see how some sympathy with mankind and society might spring up." "I laughed at myself the other day," he went on, "to think that I cried while reading a pathetic story. I was no more affected in spirit than I frequently am, methinks. The tears were merely a phenomenon of the bowels, and I felt that that expression of my sympathy, so unusual with me, was something mean, and such as I should be ashamed to have the subject of it understand. I had a cold in my head withal, about those days. I found that I had some bowels, but then it was because my bowels were out of order" (*J*, III: 106; 1851).

One senses a kind of complacency, even arrogance, in Thoreau's initial insistence upon his usual immunity to feelings of sympathy and pity. The first sentence dwells on the idea that he enjoys such an immunity when he is in health, when most himself. The misanthropic climax of the passage lies in his subsequent statement that if he were to become an invalid "some sympathy with mankind . . . might spring up." The words are "mankind and society," but here no distinction is drawn between "society" (hollow worldliness, corrupt institutions) and "mankind." And the grudging "*some* sympathy *might* spring up" would seem to deny the remote possibility of any sympathy when he is in normal health. There is, however, a following sentence (ending with a period, not a question mark), which introduces a complication: "yet what is my softness good for, even to tears." Despite the punctuation, this is a question. It recalls other *Journal* passages in which Thoreau questions the effectiveness of "mere pity" and of the little "charities" practised by complacent people, in which he suggests that much of our "sympathy" is mere self-indulgence. At this point, in other words, a slight countercurrent enters the passage, an acknowledgment that sympathy might be a worthy emotion if it could be turned to some practical good. And, at about this point, the reader may become conscious of the *subversiveness*, the perhaps healthy rebelliousness, of this passage, written in 1851, in the America of sentimental "gift-books" and innumerable pathetic stories, in the heyday of Dickens and his many tearful imitators. But the question has no question mark, and the "softness" is wholly dismissed in a succeeding sentence: "It is not I, but nature in me." Here "nature" is definitely not the Nature habitually glorified by Thoreau, nor yet the essential element in himself—sometimes in "man" —which is capable of achieving a meaningful rapport with that Nature, but "nature" in a more common, colloquial sense—bodily functions, which he cannot control, but which He, his essential Self, transcends. Thus, Thoreau is now asserting that even in illness he —the real He—is immune to feelings of sympathy. Such feelings are merely simulated, as upon his reading of the pathetic story, by the appearance of tears, which are due to a bowel disorder: "I was no more affected in spirit than I frequently am. . . ."

In this context the word "expression" takes on some of its

original significance: the tears are "pressed out" very much against his will. But the larger phrase, "expression of my sympathy" might be taken as suggesting, after all, the existence of a real sympathy in Thoreau, however "mean" and shameful he feels his tears to have been. Here is an added complication. And he would be "ashamed to have the subject of it [this "expression of my sympathy"] understand." Is it because this would reveal a crack in what Emerson called his "perfect . . . stoicism"? Or because "softness" is no "good," ineffectual? Or because the tears are spurious and do not represent true feeling? At this point, I want simply to emphasize that the phrases "expression of my sympathy" and "What is my softness good for"—since in both he seems momentarily to acknowledge these emotions as truly his—introduce an element of ambivalence into a passage which at first seems completely misanthropic. As I have indicated, my study will concern itself throughout with this kind of ambivalence. But in this particular passage Thoreau returns, with a wry pun, to his original assertion: he appeared to have "some bowels [of compassion]" only "because my bowels were out of order."

2

If in Thoreau's warning to Ricketson that Channing must be "dealt with at arm's length" we recognize a partial portrait of Thoreau himself, we may be reminded of Emerson's remark that he would as soon think of linking his arm to a tree branch as of taking Thoreau's arm when they walked together.[7] This suggestion of an extreme physical fastidiousness in Thoreau—a reluctance to be touched—is borne out by evidence from his own writing.* There is a hint of it in the passage quoted above on "men of society," in the bitter complaint that "they dwell, they are ever right in my face and eyes like gnats; . . . they have their being between my eyes and the end of my nose." It becomes hilariously overt in an outburst against "three ultra reformers" who were visiting Concord and boarded with the Thoreaus.

---

* "One of the most persistent activities in Thoreau's life was the putting of spaces between himself and other men. . . . 'I love a broad margin to my life. . . .' [*Walden*, p. 111]" (Frederick Garber, *Thoreau's Redemptive Imagination* [New York: New York University Press, 1977], p. 17).

They addressed each other constantly by their Christian names, and rubbed you continually with the greasy cheeks of their kindness. They would not keep their distance, but cuddle up and lie spoon-fashion with you, no matter how hot the weather nor how narrow the bed,—chiefly [H. C. Wright, "who shocks all the old women with his infidel writings"]. I was awfully pestered with his benignity; feared I should get greased all over with it past restoration; tried to keep some starch in my clothes. . . . It was difficult to keep clear of his slimy benignity, with which he sought to cover you before he swallowed you and took you fairly into his bowels. It would have been far worse than the fate of Jonah. I do not wish to get any nearer to a man's bowels than usual. They lick you as a cow her calf. They would fain wrap you about with their bowels.

There follows about half a page of anecdote and analysis, in which Thoreau praises the "beautiful reserve" of flowers, and in which, at one point, he seems to consider the offender redeemable: "I wanted that he should straighten his back, smooth out those ogling wrinkles of benignity about his eyes, and with a healthy reserve, pronounce something in a downright manner." But then revulsion recurs: "I do not like the men who come so near me with their bowels. It is the most disagreeable kind of snare to be caught in. Men's bowels are far more slimy than their brains. . . . They lay their sweaty hand on your shoulder, or your knee, to magnetize you." (*J*, V: 263–65; 1853.)

No doubt the ultra-reformers were a sorry lot. When the particularly obnoxious one is quoted as saying, "with drawling, sultry sympathy, 'Henry, I know all you would say; I understand you perfectly; you need not explain anything to me;' and, to another, 'I am going to dive into Henry's inmost depths,' " we laugh our approval of Henry's rejoinder: "I said, 'I trust you will not strike your head against the bottom.' " Still, the choice of images ("they would not keep their distance, but cuddle up and lie spoon-fashion with you, . . . rub you continually with the greasy cheeks of their kindness . . . lay their sweaty hand on your shoulder . . .") seems to evidence an habitual recoil on Thoreau's part from physical contact with other people. Again we find "bowels" associated with the idea of sympathy—in this case, an unctuous pseudosympathy—presumably by way of the biblical "bowels of compassion." And here, again, the figurative "bowels" becomes literal, and the word is dwelt upon to a degree that can only be called obsessive.

Thoreau's revulsion from physical contact is hinted at also in the metaphorical twist given to this well-known complaint: "Wherever a man goes men will pursue and *paw him* [my italics] with their dirty institutions" (*J*, II: 40; June 21, 1850).[8] And it is generalized in this acid assessment of 1852: "What men call social virtues, good fellowship, is commonly but the virtue of pigs in a litter, which lie close together to keep each other warm. It brings men together in crowds and mobs in barrooms and elsewhere, but it does not deserve the name of virtue" (*J*, IV: 397). Some readers may assent to the analogy but dispute the judgment. "Perhaps so," they may say, "but . . . what is so reprehensible, after all, about keeping 'warm,' literally or figuratively?" Loneliness, isolation, and alienation are key words, central problems in twentieth-century literature; but Thoreau (who undoubtedly experienced them all) would have denied their validity. While this in part reflects attitudes of his time—Romantic Individualism, Transcendental Self-Reliance—Thoreau habitually intensified these attitudes in terms more extreme and compelling than those of any other writer. The above passage is one of the many which bear out Emerson's description of him as a "perfect piece of stoicism," or which show him impatient with—as a student put it—"the mereness of being human!"

It also serves to illustrate his habitual response to men in the aggregate, and hence to cities. We have seen that "the mass of men" is a consistently derogatory term—although a rather abstract one, meaning "most of humanity." Confronted by the concrete—a "mass of men" in the flesh—Thoreau's reaction is predictably negative. And, to describe it, he uses the terms "herd" (again, an animal analogy) and "mob" more frequently than the more neutral "crowd."

Thoreau's most crucial experience of city crowds came in 1843, during his sojourn with the William Emersons on Staten Island. His first reaction was that of the independent provincial who refuses to be awed by the splendors of New York, although he appears at the same time to have been fascinated by its masses of men. "Every thing there disappoints me but the crowd," he wrote to Waldo Emerson in Concord; "You don't know where any respectability inhabits.—It is in the crowd in Chatham Street. The crowd is something new and to be attended to. It is worth a thousand Trinity Churches and Exchanges while it is looking at them— and will run over them and trample them underfoot one day." [9]

A few weeks later his discomfort is first hinted at in his generous account, to Emerson, of a meeting with Henry James: James "has naturalized and humanized New York for me." And in a later paragraph we find a full-blown statement of what was to become his stock response to the urban scene:

I don't like the city better, the more I see it, but worse. I am ashamed of my eyes that behold it. It is a thousand times meaner than I could have imagined. It will be something to hate,—that's the advantage it will be to me; and even the best people in it are a part of it and talk coolly about it. The pigs in the street are the most respectable part of the population. When will the world learn that a million men are of no importance compared to *one* man?[10]

To his mother he wrote several months later: "Seeing so many people from day to day one comes to have less respect for flesh and bones, and thinks they must be more loosely [joined], of less firm fibre, than the few he had known. It must have a very bad influence on children to see so many human beings at once—mere herds of men." [11]

There is little indication in these letters of what specific spectacles in the New York streets may have offended Thoreau to that degree suggested in his June outburst to Emerson. Whatever observations may have fostered it, the remark to his mother reveals a basic facet of Thoreau's temperament. Only rarely could he feel sympathy toward, or kinship with, any appreciable number of people. These were feelings easily achieved by Walt Whitman, of course, who at the same time celebrated the "simple separate person," and lovingly rendered individual character-sketches of an extraordinary range of diversity. As Carl Bode and Walter Harding remark in their edition of Thoreau's correspondence: "One measure of the stature of the two leading Transcendentalists, Emerson and Thoreau, is that both praised Walt Whitman. It would have been unusually easy for them to be repelled by so different a personality and so physical a poem as *Leaves of Grass*." And thinking of the enormous difference in their respective responses to the city, of that alone, one is impressed once again by Thoreau's generous, even extravagant estimate of Whitman.[12]

But let us look more closely at that letter to Emerson, where Thoreau's rather violent denunciations ("meaner than I could have imagined," "something for me to hate"), apparently prompted by observations of particular evils ("I am ashamed of my eyes that behold it"), give way to a resounding rhetorical question. This contains a statement which might at first be considered equivalent to the Christian assumption that, in the sight of God, a million men are of no *more* importance than any one man. But it is not quite equivalent. The statement that "a million men are of *no* importance [my italics] compared to one man" can be interpreted most charitably as meaning "a million conformists" compared to one "genius / hero / saint." But it can as easily be read "a million peasants / workers / slaves" compared to one "baron / billionaire / Caesar." And what is meant by the question? If "the world" should "learn" this dictum—then what? Presumably, cities would cease to exist; human beings would cease to multiply. All this is a far cry not only from Whitman, but also from certain other statements Thoreau made elsewhere. Furthermore, the question, "When will the world learn . . .?", conveys precisely that impression of a bright young man striking a loftily cynical, aristocratic pose which has been remarked in several early *Journal* entries. (Significantly, it occurs in a letter to an older man whom at this date he still wished to impress.)

The fact remains, however, that statements of this general character recurred, often, when Thoreau was subjected to the sight or nearer pressure of a "mass of men." *A Week on the Concord and Merrimac Rivers* can furnish a classic example. Thoreau's remark to his mother that "Seeing so many people from day to day, one comes to have less respect for flesh and bones" bears a strong resemblance to the conclusion of the October Fair passage in the *Week's* last chapter. Here the emotion expressed at first is enjoyment. There is a sympathetic description of the country people who are flocking to the fair—"the sober farmer folk," and especially of the eager boys: "Amos, Abner, Elnathen, Elbridge,—I love these sons of earth, every mother's son of them, with their great hearty hearts. . . ." Thoreau has an appreciative eye for "the inspired negro" singer, and even for "the supple vagabond," who "empties both his pockets and his character into the stream. . . . He dearly loves the social slush. There is no reserve of soberness in him." But the geniality of the first paragraph gradually gives way to a tone of condescension. There are premonitions of it in "social slush" and in the description of the farmers "jabbering earnestly," as well as in the first, fairly neutral use of the word "herds": the farm boys are "rushing tumultuously in herds from spectacle to spectacle."

An ultimate stage of condescension is reached in the last paragraph, where men are explicitly identified with cattle: "I love to see the herd of men feeding heartily on coarse and succulent pleasures, as cattle on the husks and stalks of vegetables." The cattle simile is dropped abruptly in favor of a horticultural one, which is sustained through two sentences and made to yield certain guarded affirmations: "Though there are many crooked and crabbed specimens of humanity among them, . . . yet fear not that the race will fail or waver in them; like the crabs which grow in hedges, they furnish the stocks of sweet and thrifty fruits still. Thus is nature recruited from age to age. . . ." But the passage ends on a note of undiluted misanthropy. "This is that mankind. How cheap must be the material of which so many are made!" [13] The final exclamation, with its forthright "cheap" (so like the "less respect for flesh and bones" in the 1843 letter) is less jolting than the demonstrative "that" of the quiet preceding sentence. With the phrase "that mankind," Thoreau for the moment placed himself on some detached observation point outside mankind.

Most of these citations belong to the forties, but we find specific indictments of the city, as of "the mass of men," throughout the journals. In 1852 it seemed to Thoreau ironic that his interest in "like-minded naturalists and poets" compelled him to visit the libraries in Cambridge and Boston. "If I would read their books I must go to the city,—so strange and repulsive both to them and to me,—and deal with men and institutions with whom I have no sympathy. When I have just been there . . . it seems too great a price to pay for access even to the works of Homer or Chaucer or Linnaeus" (*J*, III: 270). Almost two years later he contrasted the sight of "one-eyed John Goodwin" gathering driftwood on the riverbank—"simple and direct"—with "the pursuits of most men, so artificial or complicated."

Consider how the broker collects his winter's wood, what sport he makes of it, what is his boat and hand-cart! Postponing instant life, he makes haste to Boston in the cars and there deals in stocks, not quite relishing his employment,—and so earns the money with which he buys his fuel. And when, by chance, I meet him about this indirect and complicated business, I am not struck with the beauty of his employment. It does not harmonize with the sunset.

Here Thoreau's displeasure with the city is only part of a larger impulse: what amounts to a rejection of the basic economic organization of nineteenth-century Western society. The twentieth-century commuter may find himself profoundly in sympathy with this passage, especially with the phrase "postponing instant life." Yet we recognize the futility, for Thoreau as for us, of the implied wish for a return to pure agrarianism or to some pastoral or nomadic age.

In the next paragraph Thoreau tends more toward the utopian communitarianism preached by his friend Bronson Alcott: "No trade is simple, but artificial and complex. . . . If the first generation does not die of it, the third or fourth does. In face of all statistics, I will never believe that it is the descendants of tradesmen who keep the state alive, but of simple yeomen or laborers." But instead of developing this in political-economic terms, Thoreau merely used it to underline his anti-urban bias: "This, indeed, statistics say of the city reinforced by the country." And the passage returns to its wistful beginning: "As for the complex ways of living, I love them not, however much I practise them. In as many places as possible, I will get my feet down to the earth" (J, V: 444–46; 1853.)

The theme continued to be sounded throughout the fifties—for example, in the midst of winter-weather notes in 1854: "I will be a countryman. I will not go to the city even in winter, any more than the sallows and sweet-gale by the river do" (J, VI: 86). The following year it appeared in a paragraph of some ambivalence:

Sanborn tells me that he was waked up a few nights ago in Boston, about midnight, by the sound of a flock of geese passing over the city. . . . They go honking over cities where the arts flourish, waking the inhabitants; over State houses and capitols, where legislatures sit; over harbors where fleets lie at anchor; mistaking the city, perhaps, for a swamp or the edge of a lake, about settling in it, not suspecting that greater geese than they have settled there. (J, VIII: 46; 1855.)

The details selected here add up to an attractive, even exciting composite portrait of the city, so that Thoreau's ironic comment at the end is surprising. In fact it sounds like a stock response, not deeply felt but voiced chiefly for the sake of the small joke.

The comment is indeed characteristic: Thoreau rarely had a good word to say for any city; and—although *community* was extremely important to him*—the town or village, any center of human population, often posed for him many of the same prob-

---

* See below, chapter 5.

lems.[14] Yet we should not overlook one seemingly contradictory phenomenon in the *Journal*. Under the same date (in October, 1853) which heads his long meditation on John Goodwin and the evils of trade, Thoreau devoted a paragraph to the beauty of fallen leaves on the surface of water. In the controlling simile, the leaves are compared to small boats—not a novel idea, but one which is developed with memorable insistence. Early in the paragraph the "still light, tight, and dry boats" become "dense cities of boats." After a few lines describing their "pure and delicate, though fading, tints" he returns to this simile: "then see this great fleet of scattered leaf boats, . . . scarcely moving in the sluggish current,—like the great fleets with which you mingle on entering some great mart, some New York which we are all approaching together" (*J*, V: 442–43). Worth noting here is the association of favorable references to the city (even New York!) with the communal "we" —"we all . . . together."

At a number of other points in the *Journal* Thoreau described cities he had visualized in cloud formations or in the landscape under certain atmospheric conditions—beautiful, "regal," "exciting," "historic" cities of the imagination. "Far in the eastern horizon I seem to glimpse the domes and minarets of an oriental city —and men lead a stately, civil life there, as poetical as the pastoral."[15] So he wrote in 1840, before he had experienced New York. Years later he recorded that a sunset cloud shaped like an alligator has split into "two tremendous jaws, between which glows the eternal city" (*J*, IV: 412; 1852). By this time the image was so familiar that Thoreau could be satisfied with an abbreviated reference: "the eternal city." We can be sure that for him this suggested neither a biblical heaven nor Rome, but something purely personal. Still later the oriental image reappears, in "long amber clouds, all on fire with gold . . . An Orient city," which, when looked at "with head inverted," seemed "a world of enchantment" (*J*, XI: 166, 1858). In an earlier journal we find a midday apparition: "In this bright and chaste light the world seemed like a pavilion made for holidays, . . . while on the horizon the sunshine seemed to fall on walled towns and villas, and the course of our lives was seen winding on like a country road over the plain" (*J*, I: 441). These images were incorporated into the *Week*, Chapter 2, and "our lives" doubtless refers to the life prospects of Henry and John Thoreau.

Some of this same imagery appears in another early *Journal* entry, which can be seen as a distillation of all of Thoreau's youthful moods of confidence and anticipation:

Life looks as fair at this moment as a summer's sea . . . , with its sun and grass and walled towns so bright and chaste, as fair as my own virtue which would adventure therein. Like a Persian city or hanging gardens in the distance, so washed in light. . . . All its flags are flowing, and tassels streaming and drapery flapping, like some gay pavilion. . . . It shows from afar [now, specifically, the future] as unrepulsive as the sunshine upon walls and cities, over which the passing life moves as gently as a shadow. (J, I: 224–25; 1841.)

The passage invites analysis at several points. For example, "my own virtue" seems, in spite of the preceding reference to chastity, to have extended meanings, beyond that of chastity, or morality, and to incorporate, with regard to Thoreau's sense of himself and his future, such concepts as courage and power—something like the Chaucerian *vertu*. "My future deeds bestir themselves within me and move grandly toward a consummation as ships go down the Thames," he continued in the next paragraph. Certainly there are sexual implications in "walled towns . . . chaste," and the idea of his "virtue" adventuring therein, as there are in the image of deeds stirring within him as a child stirs in the womb, and of their moving "toward a consummation." And then there is the curious word "unrepulsive"—the only discordant note. Except for that word, which surely suggests at least some misgivings about the future as well as some habitual reservations about the city, the entire passage is euphoric in tone.

My main point here, however, is that Thoreau seems to have had an ideal city in imagination (as, we shall see, he had an ideal friendship), and that he could draw upon it for urban images, but not for dealing with the reality—the sprawling, crowded, noisy, actual city. On the contrary, the imaginary ideal undoubtedly served only to exacerbate his annoyance when confronting the real, just as his ideal of friendship continually undermined his patience with real, fallible men and women.

Two

Friendship and Love: Ideal and Failure

WHATEVER else it may be taken to mean, Thoreau's statement in his letter to Emerson that "a million men are of no
importance compared with one man" suggests at least a temperamental preference. It suggests, as do certain other passages cited
above, that his discomfort when confronted by humanity en masse
was somewhat balanced by a reverence for the individual personality, and some degree of ease with individuals. Note again the remark to his mother, that the sight in New York of "so many people" made him think they must be "of less firm fibre than the few
he had known." Other letters of this period exhibit great affection
for "the few." Thoreau wrote lovingly and humorously to his family, often commending acquaintances both in New York and
Concord. He wrote, always cordially, to Emerson, dwelling on his
nostalgia for Concord and a number of its citizens. He wrote
thank-you notes of warmth and charm to friends who had made
him gifts. And, as everybody knows, he wrote intense letters to
Emerson's wife, one of them revealing so exalted a devotion as
even now to make its reader feel intrusive.[1]

Of course many of these letters reveal touches of hostility in
his dealings with individuals, as we saw in the reference to his
"disappointment" on meeting those of whom he had "heard well."
Having once again acknowledged his homesickness to the Emersons, in a paragraph of affectionate references to other Concordians (including Nathaniel Hawthorne, Lucy Brown, Elizabeth
Hoar, and Channing), he added: "But know, my friends, that I a
good deal hate you all in my most private thoughts—as the sub-
stratum of the little love I bear you. Though you are a rare band,

and do not make half use enough of one another." [2] Harding and Bode theorize that Lidian Emerson must have written a somewhat prim and chilling reply to Thoreau's ardent letter of June 20, which would help to account for the perversity of these remarks from him on July 8.[3] While that seems very likely, this paragraph also illustrates a fairly common phenomenon in both the letters and journals—a tendency to recoil after an expression of affection or sympathy. Nevertheless, there is a marked contrast in the letters between his indictments of the mass—"the herd"—and his generally favorable attitude toward individuals in his sphere.

This chapter will focus on the most passionate and complex of Thoreau's attitudes toward "the few": his feelings about love and friendship, his yearning for one-to-one relationships of an intimacy and intensity probably impossible to attain.

In addition to the evidence from the *Correspondence* and the *Journal*, the quality of Thoreau's positive responses to other individuals during the early years is well illustrated in the *Week*. One thinks first of the strong affection expressed there for his brother John; one thinks of the references to Concord worthies (and to that certain "maiden"—Ellen Sewall) in the first two chapters; of the mathematics-studying keeper at the Merrimack locks ("a serene and liberal-minded man"); of the "brawny New Hampshireman," the young stonemason near Bedford, and the wistful farmer boy; of the admiration expressed for the "woman of restless and intelligent mind" (probably Margaret Fuller), and the tributes to figures of the past—including, John Eliot, Hannah Dustan, and Chaucer (who is praised especially for his "humanity"). One thinks, above all, of the long essay on Friendship.

As Perry Miller and others have pointed out, many of the Transcendentalists talked and theorized about Friendship almost obsessively. None did so more earnestly than Thoreau in this period of his life. At many points, that "essay" (or twenty-nine-page digression) in the *Week* quite literally glorifies these interpersonal relationships:

There are passages of affection in our intercourse with mortal men and women, such as no prophecy had taught us to expect, which transcend our earthly life, and anticipate Heaven for us.

It is not the highest sympathy merely, but a pure and lofty society, a fragmentary and godlike intercourse of ancient date.... It requires immaculate and godlike qualities full-grown....

Think of the importance of Friendship in the education of men. . . . It will make a man honest; it will make him a hero; it will make him a saint.[4]

"It" is defined and redefined in terms so hyperbolic and so repetitious that the casual reader, emerging dazed (and yawning), might have overlooked the negative, even despairing, elements threaded through the essay. But the more alert reader feels no surprise to find that a relationship so ideally conceived is said to be "evanescent in every man's experience," or that "our actual Friends are but distant relations of those to whom we are pledged." And the reader already conversant with the *Journal* will pause, hearing echoes, when he reads that

in our daily intercourse with men, our nobler faculties are dormant and suffered to rust. None will pay us the compliment to expect nobleness from us. . . . We ask our neighbor to suffer himself to be dealt with truly, sincerely, nobly; but . . . he says practically, I will be content if you treat me as . . . deceitful, mean, dishonest, and selfish. For the most part, we are contented so to deal and to be dealt with, and we do not think that for the mass of men there is any truer and nobler relation possible.[5]

The pages on Friendship in the *Week*, in all their idealism and yearning as well as in their severity and perversity, echo, or are echoed by, hundreds of passages in the *Journal*. A paragraph of 1838, on the necessity of remaining aloof from "society," ends thus: "But after all, such a morsel of society as this will not satisfy a man. . . . So we go about indefatigably [like the fishermen's wives who sing out to the sea at evening], chanting our stanza of the lay, and awaiting the response of a kindred soul out of the distance" (*J*, I: 40). In 1839 the poem "Sympathy," which appeared later in the *Week*, was preceded in the *Journal* by the reflection that "Some persons carry about them the air and conviction of virtue, though they themselves are unconscious of it. . . . Such it is impossible not to love . . ." (*J*, I: 80). Surely the negative construction, "impossible not to love," tells us something about Thoreau's diffidence, his wariness, in this area of feeling. A neighboring entry consists of one sentence: "There is no remedy for love but to love more" (*J*, I: 88). Impressed by the end of this declaration, one might overlook its negative element—the implication that love requires a "remedy."

It has been assumed that this last statement refers to the young Thoreau's frustrated passion for Ellen Sewall (an idea accepted by Canby, Harding, and others, and sardonically questioned by Perry Miller). Thoreau's contemporaries in fact insisted that the poem "Sympathy" ("Lately, alas, I knew a gentle boy"), in which a quite strong attraction is evident, was a disguised tribute to Ellen. It is now believed that the poem, and its *Journal* context, of course, referred to her brother Edmund. Miller remarks that "biographers have belatedly *admitted* [my italics]" that the poem "was in truth written to a boy," and adds that "only within recent years have studies [*sic*] had the courage to call attention to the androgynous character of Thoreau's monomaniac discussions of friendship." [6] This poem will not strike every reader as warranting such excitement. The statement about scholars "admitting" that it was "in truth written to a boy" seems laughably overwrought, as does the rest of the paragraph ("courage," "monomaniac"), whether or not Miller is correct in assuming some sexual ambivalence in Thoreau. In the context of this study that question is interesting, but not central.

What the poem and this cluster of *Journal* statements certainly reveal is that Thoreau, at the age of twenty-two, was in the grip of one or several strong emotional attachments.* The fact that he appears, in a number of such passages, to have been resisting these attachments surely attests to the strength of the emotions at least as much as to his "perversity." "We will warm us at each other's fire," he declared in 1840, "Friendship is a glowing furnace in which all impurities are consumed." Even here there is a touch of negation: into a confident, ardent statement somehow crept the idea of "impurities." (One thinks with sadness of his angry definition of "good fellowship," twelve years later, as "the virtue of pigs in a litter, which lie close together to keep warm" [*J*, IV: 397].) In 1840 he might have been suggesting that whatever could be considered "impure" in sexual desire and the sexual act (about which, many *Journal* passages reveal, he felt some anxiety) is transfigured in the passionate fires of true love. Or he may have been thinking that character defects are consumed in the mutual warmth of a

---

* Letters and *Journal* entries during the next two years suggest that, aside from the attachment to Ellen Sewall, his feeling for Lucy Brown, Lidian Emerson's older sister, was at times quite intense. And see below, p. 24n., for a note on his probable attraction to still another, younger woman.

trusting relationship. Probably he meant both these things, perhaps more.

The *Journal* for 1841 includes many positive thoughts on friendship. And at that year's end appeared a significant announcement: "I want to go soon and live away by the pond. . . . It will be success if I shall have left myself behind. But my friends ask what I will do when I get there. Will it not be employment enough to watch the progress of the seasons?" (*J*, I: 299; Dec. 24, 1841). The wish—not to be realized for another three and a half years—was then first stated explicitly, and in terms particularly relevant to this study. The impulse that led Thoreau to Walden is identified here, not as misanthropic withdrawal from society, but as a need to transcend the self under the beneficent influence of Nature. Its expression is the more striking for being coupled with the simple, unqualified reference to "my friends." This passage was written during Thoreau's first long residence in the Emersons' house, and it is possible that part of what he felt a need to leave behind was his growing attachment to Lidian.

The preoccupation with friendship surfaces continually in *Journal* entries for the next few years; often they involve a direct address to an unnamed "friend," as here: "My friend, thou art not of some other race and family of men; thou art flesh of my flesh, bone of my bone. . . . Is it of no significance that I have so long partaken of the same loaf with thee, have breathed the same air summer and winter . . . and thou hast never had a thought of different fibre from my own?" (*J*, I: 468). Slightly altered, this entry reappears in the Friendship essay of the *Week*. In the *Journal*, it may have been addressed to John Thoreau; in the *Week* it is universalized—"My friend, thou . . ." becoming "The Friend"—and it follows immediately after the frequently quoted paragraph which begins, "Ignorance and bungling with love are better than wisdom and skill without. There may be courtesy, there may be even temper, and wit, and talent, and sparkling conversation, there may be good will even,—and yet the humanest and divinest faculties pine for exercise. Our life without love is like coke and ashes." [7] This passage is "literary," to be sure; doubtless the balance of the first sentence, and the cadences of the second (with their echoes of St. Paul's great "charity" speech) were consciously savored. But most readers will feel it to be sincere—it has the sound of an ardent young man in love with the idea of love, excited by many personal encounters, and eager for experience.

These passages reveal what may be called Thoreau's positive view of love and friendship. It is a complex, at times even an obsessive view, but it is positive in this sense: these passages evidence his belief that such experiences are real, that they represent major goals for human beings, and, moreover, that they are experiences available to him, which he has enjoyed and will again enjoy.

2

But, playing against this, another theme is increasingly heard in the *Journal*, a much less positive theme-with-variations on the subject of relationships, whose chief components are longing, doubt, frustration, and anger.

Early in 1842, for example, Thoreau entered a complaint which evidently had to do with a woman: "It is not easy to find one brave enough to play the game of love quite alone with you, but they must get some third person, or [the] world, to countenance them. They thrust others between" (*J*, I: 329).* And an entry of the same month includes this curious paragraph: "My friend is cold and reserved because his love for me is waxing and not waning. These are the early processes. The particles are just beginning to shoot in crystals. If the mountains came to me, I should no longer go to the mountains. So soon as that consummation takes place which I wish, it will be past. Shall I not have a friend in reserve? Heaven is to come. I hope this is not it" (*J*, I: 339). My guess is that the reference here was to Emerson, although it could have been to his wife, disguised under the masculine pronoun. In 1842 Thoreau was still living in the Emersons' household, and there are indications, both in the *Journal*, and in letters that his feeling for Lidian—to be manifested the next year in two passionate letters from New York—was now growing stronger. But, in the

---

* Canby assumed that this and similar entries in this period referred to Lidian Emerson; but Walter Harding has suggested that the woman implicated in this passage was Mary Russell, from Plymouth, a sometime governess and frequent visitor in the Emerson household, to whom Thoreau was said to have addressed the fervent poem "To the Maiden in the East" (*The Days of Henry Thoreau* [New York: Alfred A. Knopf, 1965], pp. 107–10). Whether or not this was so, the latter relationship did not develop in intensity. But Mary Russell. later married to Thoreau's friend Marston Watson, was several times hostess to Thoreau at their Plymouth farm, and remained a cordial acquaintance throughout his life.

scope of this study, it doesn't greatly matter whether Lidian, her husband, or some other friend was the subject of this paragraph. The point is that it exhibits Thoreau's very complex reaction to some fluctuation in an obviously intense relationship—whether of "love," at least on his side, or of "friendship," any difference of response in this case would, I believe, have been more of degree than of kind. The (real or fancied) coldness is at first, with a brave show of confidence, taken as proof of the friend's growing love— an assertion which rests on no evidence, however, but is merely illustrated—by an image of ice forming! The rest of the paragraph may simply be the result of Thoreau's realization that the statement is merely wishful. After suggesting that his friend's coldness was assumed in order to attract him ("If the mountains came to me, I should no longer go to the mountains"), he implies that the relationship is capable of some further development (one does wonder at that word "consummation"!), which will, however, be insufficient—at least, or because, impermanent. Finally he seems to reject this particular relationship, while looking forward to another and better.

But this paraphrase perhaps oversimplifies, for the mountain image suggests not only the friend's possible attempt to attract him, but also the idea that, were the friend less reserved and more loving, Thoreau would, after all, be repelled. The passage can therefore be interpreted in at least two ways. In one, Thoreau dreads the coldness of his friend, tries to rationalize it as being an indication of growing love, assumed in order to attract him; rationalizes further that he would not be attracted by an opposite display, of warmth, and asserts (unconvincingly) that the relationship can never satisfy him. Alternatively, he is actually convinced that this coldness is a symptom of his friend's increasing love for him; he understands it as a deliberate gambit to rekindle his interest, and he is actually repelled both by the gambit and by the friend's supposed motivation—increasing love. The latter reading suggests a deep-seated fear of intimacy and of commitment to other persons, an impulse which seems evident in a few other *Journal* passages. But I incline to the first reading for this passage, partly because it is succeeded by several paragraphs celebrating the excellence of friendship, partly because of the strong feeling of loss conveyed in its last short sentences—"Heaven is to come. I hope this is not it." It is a passage whose tone is hard to define.

In another entry of this period (1842–47) Thoreau debated the question of a friend's attitude toward him with heavy sophistry: "My friend can only be in any measure my foe, because he is fundamentally my friend; for everything is after all more nearly what it should rightfully be, than that which it is simply by failing to be the other" (J, I: 469). And early in 1850 three short paragraphs recorded a proud withdrawal—or a strategic retreat:

Woe to him who wants a companion, for he is unfit to be the companion even of himself.

We inspire friendship in men when we have contracted friendship with the gods.

When we cease to sympathize with and to be personally related to men, and begin to be universally related, then we are capable of inspiring others with the sentiment of love for us. (II, 33.)

Later in the year we find this characteristic expression of a feeling which is voiced repeatedly in the *Journal*: "I have certain friends whom I visit occasionally, but I commonly part from them early with a certain bittersweet sentiment. That which we love is so mixed and entangled with that we hate in one another that we are more grieved and disappointed, aye, and estranged from one another by meeting than by absence" (J, II: 109).

The kinds of grievances that prompted such a statement are made more explicit elsewhere, for example in February of 1851:

Fatal is the discovery that our friend is fallible, that he has prejudices. . . . Alas! Alas! when my friend begins to deal in confessions, breaks silence, makes a theme of friendship (which then is always something past), and descends to merely human relations! . . . I thought that friendship, that love was still possible between [us]. I thought that we had not withdrawn very far asunder. But now that my friend rashly, thoughtlessly, profanely speaks, *recognizes* the distance between us, that distance seems infinitely increased. (J, II: 161–62.)

We are caught up now in some kind of drama—perhaps for Thoreau it had the dimensions of tragedy—which goes on throughout this and the following year. Still, we're constrained to wonder at the complaint that a friend is "fallible," "descends to merely human relations!"—and to ask as well, who more than Henry Thoreau "makes a theme of friendship"?

In July of 1851 the yearning took on a note of helplessness: "Here I am thirty-four years old, and yet my life is almost wholly unexpanded. . . . There is such an interval between my ideal and the actual in many instances that I may say I am unborn. There is the instinct for society, but no society." This paragraph contains a shorter version of one of *Walden's* most often quoted sentences: "Let a man step to the music which he hears, however measured." [8] And here, in the process of asserting his own uniquness, Thoreau voiced his yearning for life on a plane which is neither that of ordinary human society nor yet that of absorption in physical Nature—a plane which we must, for want of a better term, call "mystical": "May not my life in nature, in proportion as it is supernatural, be only the spring and infantile portion of my spirit's life? . . . May I not sacrifice a hasty and petty completeness here to entireness there? If my curve is large, why bend it to a smaller circle? My spirit's unfolding observes not the pace of nature. The society which I was made for is not here." Nevertheless, the "instinct for society" at the passage's beginning is clearly an instinct for human society, and this need is echoed, desperately, at the passage's conclusion: "*I* did not *make* this demand for a more thorough sympathy. This is not my idiosyncracy or disease. He that made the demand will answer the demand" (J, II: 316–17).

Let us consider the identity of the other characters involved in this "drama" of 1851–52. Of whom was Thoreau making his desperate demands for sympathy? The most probable answer is—of both the Emersons. His attachment to Lidian, so ardent in 1843 (as we have seen), continued to grow during his second long stay in her house, in 1847–48. His letters to Emerson, then in England, abound in references to her which are affectionate, at times intimate, in tone. "Lidian and I make very good housekeepers. She is a very dear sister to me," he wrote a month after Emerson's departure. In this letter he also remarked that young Eddy had asked, " 'Mr. Thoreau, will you be my father?' ", and he added (one wonders with how much conscious significance) "So you must come back soon, or you will be superseded." Then, too, there were "pilgrims" to entertain: "Lidian and I have a standing quarrel as to what is a suitable state of preparedness for a traveling Professor's visits . . . but further than this we are not at war." When she was ill his concern was manifest in a long, detailed paragraph, and when she was absent he doubted "that my news will be worth sending alone." [9] In other letters of this period, as well as in 1843, he especially praised Lidian's "wisdom" and "steadiness." It is safe to assume, then, that a *Journal* passage of April, 1851, which describes a mature but circumscribed love, must have had to do with Lidian:

Love is a mutual confidence whose foundations no one knows. The one I love surpasses all the laws of nature in sureness. Love is capable of any wisdom.

... By our very mutual attraction, and our attraction to all other spheres, kept properly asunder.

... Does not the history of chivalry and knight errantry suggest or point to another relation to woman than leads to marriage, yet an elevating and all-absorbing one, perchance transcending marriage?

I am sure that the design of my maker when he has brought me nearest to woman was not the propagation, but rather the maturation, of the species. Man is capable of a love of woman quite transcending marriage.

A short paragraph follows, commenting on the fact that newspaper notices from young women seeking employment claimed to be respectable, while young men always claimed to be "smart," "from which I infer that the public opinion of New York does not require young men to be respectable in the same sense in which it requires young women to be so. May it consist with the health of some bodies to be impure?" (J, II: 184–85). The reader may be pardoned who crudely inquires, "*male* bodies?" For in view of the context it cannot be doubted that "impure" here signifies 'having sexual experience': we should remember that the term was commonly used with this connotation in these Victorian years, often more matter-of-factly than censoriously. In any case, the drift of the whole passage suggests that Thoreau's phrase "transcending marriage" cannot be taken to mean that he had, in 1851, tranquilly renounced all interest in passionate, sexual love. And at the beginning he was certainly expressing immediate feelings—specifically, I suggest, his still intense yearning toward Lidian Emerson.

But we have already noted his helpless complaint in July of 1851, about the "interval between my ideal and the actual"; and by the fall of that year he had apparently come to feel this relationship was ending, that he must try to relinquish both the real friendship with Lidian and the secret fantasies as well: "The obstacles which the heart meets with are like granite blocks which one alone cannot move. She who was as the morning light to me is now neither the morning star nor the evening star. We meet but to find each other further asunder, and the oftener we meet the more rapid our divergence" (*J*, III: 82). This begins an entry for October 27. That of the previous day is devoted entirely to recounting a dream from which Thoreau "woke this morning to infinite regret." The dream had begun with his riding a horse, then sailing, "in a small vessel such as the Northmen used." Finally he had found himself walking in a meadow,

[with] Mr. Alcott, and we fell to quoting . . . grand and pleasing couplets which we had read in times past. . . . I only know that those which I quoted expressed regret. . . . And then again the instant that I awoke, methought I was a musical instrument, . . . My body was the organ and channel of melody, as a flute is of the music that is breathed through it. . . . I awoke, therefore, to an infinite regret,—to find myself, not the thoroughfare of glorious and world-stirring inspiration, but a scuttle full of dirt, . . . Such I knew I had been and might be again, and my regret arose from the consciousness how little like a musical instrument my body was now. (*J*, III: 80–82.)

Here again we encounter suggestive juxtapositions. It seems likely that Thoreau's sense of revulsion from his own body, and the images of uncleanliness used for it, were prompted by sexual associations with the dream's movement and poetry, by sexual fantasies, and their physical manifestations, which he could not suppress during this period, but of which he was increasingly ashamed. In any case, the paragraph describing his divergence from someone ("She who was as the morning light to me": surely, in 1851, this could only be Lidian Emerson) immediately follows the report of the dream and his "infinite regret." Then, following the reference to their divergence, come these enigmatic sentences: "The night is oracular. What have been the intimations of the night? I ask. How have you passed the night? Good night!" and then a one-sentence paragraph: "My friend will be bold to conjecture; he will guess bravely at the significance of my words." The context offers no direct clue as to the identity of this "friend." But—in view of other references to him during this crucial year as simply, ironically, "my friend"—we can hardly doubt that this friend is Emerson. And so, though of course these "words" may refer to something recently spoken, the reader might be "bold to conjecture" that they were, in fact, those suffering words just written about Emerson's wife—words which Emerson was finally to read after Thoreau's death.

Then, too, there was the painful complication that, while Thoreau was conscious of a withdrawing on Lidian's part and was struggling to overcome his feeling for her, his deeply valued friendship with Emerson was also failing. Many of the brooding passages of 1851–52 must have evolved from his sense that what had perhaps been his closest realization of transcendental Friendship was in a process of disintegration. In December of 1851 an incident involving a particular individual (probably Emerson) evoked this kind of self-scrutiny, and only a guarded hopefulness:

I do not lay myself open to my friends!?... Last night I treated my dearest friend ill.... Instantly I blamed myself, and sought an atonement, but the friend avoided me, and, with kinder feelings even than before, I was obliged to depart. And now this morning I feel that it is too late to speak of the trifle.... Yet I am resolved to know that one centrally, through thick and thin, and though we should be cold to one another, though we should never speak to one another, I will know that inward and essential love may exist even under a superficial cold, and that the law of attraction speaks louder than words. (J, III: 167–68.)

Can we believe in the reported wish, the immediate effort to apologize? Was it even harder for Thoreau, than for most people, to say "I was wrong; I am sorry"? Two months after this an injunction to self-reliance was carried to absurdity: "I hate that my motive for visiting a friend should be that I want society; that it should lie in my poverty and weakness, and not in his and my riches and strength. His friendship should make me strong enough to do without him" (J, III: 304).

But surely the "drama" takes on tragic dimensions in a statement dated just two months later. Writing of his earlier observations beside a clear brook, Thoreau broke off to say that

the sound of a piano below [made him feel] as if the winter in me were at length beginning to thaw, for my spring has been even more backward than nature's. For a month past life has been a thing incredible to me. None but the kind gods can make me sane. If only they will let their south winds blow on me! I ask to be melted. You can only ask of the metals that they be tender to the fire that *melts* them. To naught else can they be tender. (J, III: 398; April 11, 1852.)*

---

* The final three sentences constitute the last item in the series of quotations from Thoreau's *Journal* which Emerson included in his "Biographical Sketch."

In that unforgettable image Thoreau seems to have acknowledged, regretted, and accepted, all at once, his own "hardness," at the same time that he voiced his unquenchable yearning for love. One month afterward he returned to an analysis and indictment of others (here chiefly of Emerson, one suspects): "The best men that I know are not serene, a world in themselves. They dwell in form. They flatter and study effect, only more finely than the rest. The world to me appears uninhabited. . . . I cannot associate with those who do not understand me" (J, IV: 46–47). And three months later Thoreau repeated these charges, but in a context of agonized self-examination. Here at last he asked himself about the demands he habitually made, in a crucial three-page outburst which must be quoted at length. It begins on the yearning note which by now is so familiar:

How far we can be apart and yet attract each other! There is one who almost wholly misunderstands me, and whom I too probably misunderstand, toward whom, nevertheless, I am distinctly drawn. I have the utmost human goodwill toward that one, and yet I know not what mistrust keeps us asunder. . . . They invite me to see them, and do not show themselves. Who *are* they, pray? I pine and starve near them. . . . How happens it that I find myself making such an enormous demand on men, and so constantly disappointed? Are my friends aware how disappointed I am? Is it all my fault? Have I no heart? Am I incapable of expansion and generosity? I shall accuse myself of everything else sooner.

Though the self-justifying answer is quickly supplied, the question at least has been asked. "They" who "do not show themselves," near whom he "starves," must surely be Emerson and his wife. The passage plunges on with renewed accusation. Thoreau had earlier been complaining of elaborate Concord dinner parties, whose hearty table fare could not make up for the thinness of the human nourishment afforded: "Think what crumbs we offer each other,— and think to make up the deficiency with our *roast meats*!"* Here he returns to this theme: "Do they think me eccentric because I refuse this chicken's meat, this babe's food? Would not men have something to communicate if they were sincere? Is not my silent

---

* This kind of complaint is echoed in *Walden*: "I sat at a table where were rich food and wine in abundance, and obsequious attendance, but sincerity and truth were not; and I went away hungry from the inhospitable board. The hospitality was as cold as the ices" (pp. 330–31).

expectation an invitation, an offer, an opportunity offered? My friend has complained of me, cursed me even, but it did not affect me; I did not know the persons he talked about. I have been disappointed from first to last in my friends. . . ." In the sentences which follow, a passing remark offers some clue to Thoreau's problems with friendship: "Intercourse with men! How little it amounts to! How rarely we love them! . . . It is remarkable if a man gives us a civil answer about the road. And how far from love still are even pretty intimate friends! How little it is that we can trust each other!" (*J*, IV: 313–15; August, 1852). We shall never be able to determine precisely the quality and the degree of "love" which Thoreau desired, and which he found lacking in "even pretty intimate" friendships. But when we read, among all these exclamations, the simple statement that "it is remarkable if a man gives us a civil answer about the road," we suddenly sense a defensiveness in Thoreau, even in his most casual encounters, a watchfulness for affront and rudeness. This may remind us of a remark from 1841, that "I almost shrink from the arduousness of meeting men erectly day by day" (*J*, I: 174); or of this entry—surely one of the most enigmatic in the *Journal*—whose import is nevertheless clear enough:

Let your mood determine the form of salutation, and approach the creature with a natural nonchalance, as though he were anything but what he is, and you were anything but what you are,—as though he were he, and you were you; in short, as though he were so insignificant that it did not signify, and so important that it did not import. Depend upon it, the timber is well seasoned and tough, and will bear rough usage. . . . I am no piece of china-ware that cannot be jostled against my neighbor without danger of rupture from the collision. (*J*, I: 179; 1841.)*

---

* The latter part of this passage, beginning "Depend upon it," was worked into the *Week*'s Friendship section, near the end, where Thoreau addressed "My most serene and irresponsible neighbors." In the hostile *Journal* context it is defiant; in the *Week* it merely serves to proclaim his sturdiness and his usefulness, in the course of that elaborate invitation to his "neighbors" to "scale . . . the mountains" which separate them, to "strike boldly at head or heart or any vital part," and to "use me, then, for I am useful in my way (p. 304). In contemplating this last sentence, we must, as with every sentence Thoreau ever wrote, take care to give due weight to every element. From another writer, "useful in my way" might simply be polite self-deprecation, even a mere tag-phrase to end the sentence with a pleasant cadence. From Thoreau, as the following context makes clear, it means precisely what it says —"useful in *my* way."

And finally, a "civil answer" being the issue, we cannot help recalling the rhetorical question asked earlier in the 1852 passage under examination: "Is not my silent expectation an invitation, an offer, an opportunity offered?" For of course that silence might have seemed uncivil as readily as expectant.

There follows a final long paragraph in which Thoreau compares himself to the cuttlefish, which darkens the water around it for concealment. Perry Miller cites this simile in a discussion of his "callousness," and of his friends' efforts to refute charges such as that made by Robert Louis Stevenson that Thoreau was "dry, priggish and selfish"—or, as Miller put it, "a congenital misanthrope." [10] But Miller says nothing of the context of the remark, in which it is made clear that Thoreau considered all human beings subject to this isolation and concealment, and that he viewed this *condition humaine* with profound regret: *

Like cuttlefish we conceal ourselves, we darken the atmosphere in which we move; we are not transparent. I pine for one to whom I can speak my first thoughts; thoughts which represent me truly, which are no better and no worse than I. . . . I know of no one to whom I can be transparent instinctively. I live the life of the cuttlefish; another appears, and the element in which I move is tinged and I am concealed. My first thoughts are azure; there is a bloom and a dew on them. . . . Only to a friend can I expose them. To all parties, though they be youth and maiden, if they are transparent to each other, and their thoughts can be expressed, there can be no further nakedness. I cannot be surprised by an intimacy which reveals the outside, when it has shown me the inside. The result of a full communication of our thoughts would be the immediate neglect of those coverings which a false modesty wears. (*J*, IV: 315; August, 1852.)

---

* Emerson too had noticed this correspondence, possibly had even called it to Thoreau's attention: "I spoke of friendship, but my friends and I are fishes in their [*sic*] habit. . . ." (*Journals*, [Cambridge: Harvard University Press, 1960–], X: 343). There are a number of other passages in which the seemingly gregarious and friendly Emerson deplored his sense of his own isolation, coldness, lack of "animal spirits," etc. See, for example, *Journals*, I: 134; II: 241; III: 45; V: 322, 456; VII: 27; IX: 18; XI: 447. In the last-cited entry, of October, 1851, he reported an instance of shared melancholy—"last night's talk with Henry Thoreau," in which "we stated over again, to sadness almost, the eternal loneliness . . . how insular and pathetically solitary are all the people we know." In any discussion of Thoreau's self-proclaimed isolation we should keep in mind the habit of intense introspection common to all the Transcendentalists.

The wish expressed is, again, for a greater measure of sincerity and trust in Thoreau's own relationships and in human relations generally. Clearly there is also a wish for some more satisfying intimacy; and the fact that the passage takes on sexual overtones is interesting, but not, as Miller says, "astonishing." * The idea that a perfect intimacy of the mind could render physical intimacy quite natural and innocent, or that an exposure of the body is negligible compared to the exposure of one's most intimate thoughts, is hardly unique to Thoreau.** All this is not intended to suggest, however, that the cuttlefish simile is not to be taken seriously. Taken altogether, this passage reveals a serious crisis in Thoreau's life; it appears that he had suffered such frustration in some one relationship, or in several, as to make him question his chances of ever maintaining any relationship.

The cuttlefish passage echoes a *Journal* entry for the preceding April, an examination of which may help to round out the sorrowful drama of these months:

April 4, Sunday. I have got to that pass with my friend that our words do not pass with each other for what they are worth. We speak in vain; there is none to hear. He finds fault with me that I walk alone, when I pine for want of a companion; that I commit my thoughts to a diary even on my walks, instead of seeking to share them generously with a friend; curses my practise even. Awful as it is to contemplate, I pray that, if I am the cold intellectual skeptic whom he rebukes, his curse may take effect, and wither and dry up those sources of my life,

---

* Miller disposed of the entire passage with this sentence, in which, I confess, the sequence of his thought is not clear to me: "The least suspecting reader feels uncomfortable when he finds that by ... 1852, Thoreau is accusing himself of being a cuttlefish who darkens the atmosphere in which he moves, and astonishingly is writing, 'To all parties, though they be youth and maiden, if ... their thoughts can be expressed, there can be no further nakedness.'" (*Consciousness in Concord*, p. 82).

** These sentences are consistent, however, with other pronouncements of Thoreau's on false modesty: with his wish expressed in an essay written for Harrison Blake that sexual matters might be discussed "more naturally and simply," and with his admiration of the "calmness and gentleness" with which "the Hindoo philosophers" treated these subjects (*Writings*, VI, *Letters*, ed. Franklin B. Sanborn, p. 205; and J, II: 3). One other comment on false modesty may be recalled, which offers also an extreme instance of Thoreau's intermittent misogyny (see below p. 60): "In the East, women religiously conceal that they have faces; in the West, that they have legs. In both cases they make it evident that they have but little brains" (J, III: 258).

and my journal no longer yield me pleasure nor life. (*J*, III: 389–90; 1852.)

There seems little doubt that this friend was Emerson—for this is the kind of complaint that he made against Thoreau more than once in his own journal. An entry in Thoreau's *Journal* some three months before this must also refer to Emerson: "I never realized so distinctly as at this moment that I am peacefully parting company with the best friend I ever had, by each pursuing his proper path. I perceive that it is possible that we may have a better understanding now than when we were more at one. Not expecting such essential agreement as before. Simply our paths diverge" (*J*, III: 214; January 12, 1852).

And that farewell is echoed in another entry, dated nine days later: "I feel as if I were gradually parting company with certain friends, just as I perceive familiar objects successively disappear when I am leaving my native town in the cars" (*J*, III: 250). Probably Lidian Emerson was included in this valedictory. Given the intensity of Thoreau's feeling for the familiar, and for his native town, the tone of this sentence seems quite desolate. It is closely followed by these two short paragraphs, which are surely à propos: (1) "One must not complain that his friend is cold, for heat is generated between them." (Perhaps there is a conscious ambiguity in "heat," which can suggest either the "warmth" of friendship, or hostility, as in "heat of anger."); (2) "I doubt if Emerson could trundle a wheelbarrow through the streets, because it would be out of character. One needs to have a comprehensive character." And the following day Thoreau wrote: "——— is too grand for me. He belongs to the nobility and wears their cloak and manners. . . . I am a commoner. To me there is something devilish in manners. . . . I should value E's praise more, which is always so discriminating, if there were not some alloy of patronage and hence of flattery about [it]" (*J*, III: 256).

A fuller account of the disintegration of this relationship can be found in Joel Porte's *Emerson and Thoreau, Transcendentalists in Conflict.* Porte mentions the fall of 1851 as "the time of [Thoreau's] crisis with Emerson."[11] Sherman Paul also discusses the progress of Thoreau's "disappointment in Emerson."[12] This failure came about for many reasons of course: Thoreau's resentment of Emerson's patronage; his annoyance at what he took to be Emerson's "establishment" loyalties, and Emerson's cool politeness; Emerson's annoyance, in turn, at Thoreau's negativism; and still more fundamental philosophic and temperamental disagreements.* We cannot safely conclude that all the troubled, frustrated passages cited in this chapter have to do with the Emersons, but certainly his frustration in these relationships was a central and an extremely bitter element in Thoreau's life at this time.

If the identification of Emerson in both those 1852 passages cited above (January 21 and April 4) is correct, then the calm resignation of the January entry is of course undercut by the suffering paragraph of April 4: "I have got to that pass with my friend. . . . We speak in vain." That this paragraph voices real suffering is evident in every line. The first two sentences have the controlled, tight-lipped tone of one saying "I will face the worst." At this point, responsibility for the "pass" to which the relationship has come is felt, by implication, to be mutual. The friend's charges are itemized, and then Thoreau faces the worst; obviously the possibility that such charges might be just was for him a terrible thought. Perry Miller does not refer to this passage in his discussion of Thoreau's relationships. But he would surely acknowledge as evidence of a profound emotion the fact that Thoreau's "prayer," or vow, took this form: "I pray that, if I am the cold intellectual skeptic whom he rebukes, his curse may . . . wither and dry up those sources of my life, and my journal no longer yield me pleasure nor life." For it is Miller's contention that by 1852 the *Journal* was fast becoming not only Thoreau's major creative outlet, but a kind of surrogate friend—was becoming in fact the focus of his life.[13] This hypothesis would seem to support the real friend's accusation in this passage, and, conversely, the passage tends to support the hypothesis. Yet the desperate seriousness of the sentence beginning "I pray . . ." is convincing: at that moment Thoreau was ready to sacrifice his satisfaction in his journal—in his vocation as a writer—rather than be "the cold intellectual skeptic" and fail in friendship.

However lingering it was, the crisis in Thoreau's relations with the Emersons seems to have passed by the end of 1852. But the note of desolate longing can still be heard in the journals for subsequent years. It occurs, for example, in this 1855 entry: "What if we feel a yearning to which no breast answers? I walk alone. My heart is full. Feelings impede the current of my thoughts. I

---

* See Joel Porte, *Emerson and Thoreau*, chapter 5.

knock on the earth for my friend. . . . I am tired of frivolous society, in which silence is forever the most natural and the best manners" (*J*, VII: 416–17).

And still later Thoreau wrote a sequence of passages, which probably, H. S. Canby suggests, represents "the last pangs," a "delayed climax," in his lingering "ethereal relationship" with Lidian Emerson. "And now another friendship has ended," the first passage of February 8, 1857, begins; ". . . I am perfectly sad at parting from you. I could better have the earth taken away from under my feet than the thought of you from my mind" (*J*, IX: 249–50). The sadness persisted; two weeks later he wrote that "Morning, noon, and night, I suffer a physical pain, an aching of the breast which unfits me for my tasks. It is perhaps most intense at evening. . . . If the teeth ache they can be pulled. If the heart aches, what then? Shall we pluck it out?" (*J*, IX: 276, 278, February 23). Although the feminine pronoun is not used, I believe, in view of the intensity of these statements—especially "physical pain"— that Canby is correct in assuming they refer to Lidian.[14]

If we turn to *Walden*, we find no such nakedly yearning passages as this, although there are hints of the same feeling in the first chapter's parable of loss, about the hound, the bay horse, and the turtle dove. A clearer hint appears at the end of chapter 14, ". . . Winter Visitors." Following the glowing paragraphs on Alcott (see below, pp. 53–54) and a brief nod toward Emerson, Thoreau wrote, "There too, as every where, I sometimes expected the Visitor who never comes. The Vishnu Purana says, 'The householder is to remain at eventide in his court-yard, as long as it takes to milk a cow, or longer if he pleases, to await the arrival of a guest.' I often performed this duty of hospitality, waited long enough to milk a whole herd of cows, but did not see the man approaching from the town." [15] Some readers have speculated that "the man" might be a disguised reference to "the woman," Lidian Emerson; others that—especially in view of the reference to the Vishnu Purana—Thoreau here voices his longing for a renewal of mystical experience. In the context, however, it seems most likely that this visitor who never comes is the Ideal Friend, that imagined "one"—whether male or female—to whom Thoreau could express "my *first thoughts*, . . . which represent me truly."

Three

Seven Friendships

PERRY MILLER made much, as I have noted, of the "efforts of Thoreau's friends," in the years following his death, to establish the story of the Ellen Sewall "romance"—their motives, in his theory, having been to rehabilitate Henry's reputation, counteract charges of his coldness, and even to allay their own uneasiness about that possibly "androgynous" impulse which Miller deduced from the poem "Sympathy." Yet at the same time Miller failed to comment on the simple fact of these friendships, and the significance of this (alleged) solicitousness on the part of Thoreau's friends. That a number of people did care deeply for Thoreau is evident in the Harding-Bode edition of his *Correspondence*. It contains many admiring and affectionate communications—from such diverse acquaintances as Bronson and Abby Alcott, Nathaniel and Sophia Hawthorne, Mary Emerson, Charles Sumner, Elizabeth Hoar, J. A. Frounde, Mary Mann, his cousin George Thatcher, and the energetically helpful Horace Greeley—as well as from such "disciples" as Harrison Blake, Thomas Cholmondeley, Isaiah Williams, Benjamin Wiley, Franklin B. Sanborn, and the loyal Ricketson.

And, one must add, from the loyal Emerson. The break that occurred between Thoreau and the Emersons in the early fifties was by no means a complete one. There are casual references to Emerson scattered throughout the *Journal* from 1853 through 1860 —including references to remarks he made, to walks taken with him, and to dinners and "Conversations" attended at his house.*

---

* A rapid survey of *Journal* passages in which Emerson is named, between 1853 and 1860, reveals eight whose tone can be described as friendly, five

On Emerson's side, there is ample evidence of concern and friendly communication, throughout Thoreau's life. The tribute written after his death is well known; its few criticisms only point up the profound admiration and tenderness it expresses as a whole.[1] But a private, and therefore even more convincing, piece of evidence is to be found in Emerson's *Journal*. When in 1871, in a retrospective mood, he set down a list of his most valued friends (headed simply "My Men"), "Henry Thoreau" found a place among them.[2] The letters also reveal a continuing neighborly intercourse, year to year, in the village to which both were committed. At the beginning of 1854, for instance, Emerson, then curator of the Lyceum lecture series, wrote with humorous familiarity to "Dear Henry," requesting him to receive two lecturers ("these lonely pilgrims") scheduled to appear during his own absence from the town. Thoreau was asked to "guide them to our house and help the alarmed wife to entertain them, and see that they do not lose the way to the Lyceum, nor the hour."[3] A year later, writing to a woman who had lectured in Concord, Thoreau was able to add that "Mrs. Emerson sends her love," along with messages from Mrs. Emerson which fill a short paragraph.[4] His letters to Cholmondeley from that same year contain several friendly references to Emerson, news of his latest "western" lecture tour ("mingling his thunder with that of Niagara"), and of his interest in Cholmondeley's gift to Thoreau: "[Emerson's] constant enquiry for the last fortnight has been 'Have your books come?'" This point is made again, in a second thank-you letter written the following year: "The books . . . are the admiration of all beholders. Alcott and Emerson, besides myself, have been cracking some of the nuts." And the letter ends, "I am pleased to think of you *in* that England . . . which Emerson values so much."[5]

Thus, a relationship of sorts persisted—doubtless more reserved on Thoreau's part, still moderately relaxed and warm on Emerson's. One of Thoreau's later letters to Blake includes a long account of a "Conversation" he attended at the Emersons' in 1859, and during that year and the next he and Emerson shared a con-

which are critical-satirical, and sixteen that are quite neutral in tone. The critical references are all very hostile. On the other hand, the neutral ones indicate, in every instance, Emerson's friendliness to Thoreau, and, at the least, Thoreau's acceptance of it. They have to do with observations of nature brought to his attention by Emerson, with Thoreau's having dined at the Emersons in company, and with other visits.

cern about the fate of John Brown. Finally, in the *Correspondence*, there is Emerson's letter of May, 1861, in which he listed a number of "good men" upon whom he hoped Thoreau would call as he journeyed to Minnesota in search of better health. The "good men" are charged to render "any aid and comfort they can . . . to an invalid traveler, one so dear and valued by me and all good Americans." [6]

The *Correspondence* contains very few communications between Thoreau and Ellery Channing,[7] but a comment Channing made elsewhere is appropriate to this discussion:

[Thoreau] made no useless professions, never asked one of those questions which destroy all relation; but he was on the spot at the time. . . . He meant friendship, and meant nothing else, and stood by it without the slightest abatement. . . .[8]

Their correspondence was sparse because from the late forties onward neither Thoreau nor Channing was long absent from Concord. And the *Journal* suggests that during these years they were very often together: they were, as Thoreau told Ricketson, cronies. In the same notebooks that record Thoreau's painful difficulties with the Emersons, we find many cheerful accounts of "excursions" with Channing. One early-spring entry in 1852, for example, is devoted to an all-day river voyage they took together (*J*, III: 394–97). That this account, which occupies four pages of the published *Journal*, nowhere mentions Channing by name is typical of a number of passages scattered throughout the journals from 1850 to 1860. Such entries (beginning "To Conantum," "To Fair Haven," etc., as this one begins "Down river to half a mile below Carlisle Bridge") often go on for a page or more before the reader becomes aware that the excursions were shared by a companion. Again and again, in my early acquaintance with the *Journal*, I found myself assuming that Thoreau was out on a solitary ramble, only to be confronted at some point by a plural pronoun. And I began to learn that this "we," when the companion is unspecified, seems always to mean "Channing and I." This is confirmed by a casual comparison of these passages with others which Thoreau began "To . . . with W. E. C.," or in which he included some remark of Channing's ("C. says") or a scrap of dialogue. One specific clue, in the passages whose "we" is unexplained, lies in references to private place names, descriptive and whimsical, bestowed by one or the other, or both in consultation. At least two *Journal* entries describe this habit of theirs explicitly:

as C. and I go through the town, we hear the cool peep of the robin calling to its young.... We continued on, round the head of "Cedar Swamp," and *may* say that we drank at the source of it or of Saw Mill Brook.... What shall this great wild tract over which we strolled be called?... It is a paradise for walkers in the fall.... Shall we call it the Easterbrooks Country? It would make a princely estate in Europe.... C. proposes to call [it] ... the Melvin Preserve, for it is favorite hunting-ground with George Melvin. It is a sort of Robin Hood Ground. Shall we call it the Apple Pastures? (*J*, V: 238–40; 1853.)*

In the river-voyage passage of April, 1852, one is aware, also, of the sense of unharried ease which characterized all these excursions; and the identification of Channing is clinched by a reference to his dog, who usually made a third companion: "As we ate our luncheon on the peninsula off Carlisle Shore, saw a large ring round the sun.... We lay to in the lee of an island, ... with an agreeable sense of protection.... It is warm here in the sun, and the dog is drying his wet coat after so many voyages, and is drowsily nodding" (*J*, III: 395–97).

The *Journal* contains many instances of Thoreau's appreciation of Channing's humor and inventiveness, and of their indulgence in light banter as well as serious nature study and philosophizing:

Entering Wayland, the sluggish country town, C. remarked that we might take the town if we had a couple of oyster-knives.... C. was much amused here by a bigger schoolboy whom we saw on the common, one of those who stretch themselves on the back seats and can chew up a whole newspaper into a spitball to plaster the wall with when the master's back is turned ... thought this the *event* of Wayland.
... C. kept up an incessant strain of wit, banter, about my legs, which were so springy and unweariable, declared ... that they were not cork but steel, that I ... should have sent them to the World's Fair, etc., etc.... (*J*, III: 92–93, 96; 1851.)

The sun has set. We are in Dennis's field.... Some fine clouds which have just escaped being condensed in a dew, hang on the skirts of day.... C., as usual, calls it a Mediterranean sky. (*J*, IV: 192; 1852.)

---

* See also *J*, XI: 103; 1858: "Suggesting to C. an Indian name for one of our localities, he thought it had too many syllables...."

William Wheeler has raised a new staring house beyond the Corner Bridge, and so done irreparable injury to a large section of country for walkers. . . . Channing proposes that we petition him to put his house out of sight; that we send it to him in the form of a round-robin, with his name on one side and mine on the other,—so to abate a nuisance. (*J*, V: 150; 1853.)

Called to C. from the outside of his house the other afternoon in the rain. At length he put his head out the attic window, and I inquired if he didn't want to take a walk, but he excused himself, saying that he had a cold. "But," added he, "you can take so much the longer walk. Double it." (*J*, XI: 283; 1858.)

These examples—and their number could be multiplied many times—illustrate the quality of one of Thoreau's most durable and important relationships. The passage on William Wheeler's ugly house suggests one special aspect of that relationship—a kind of complicity. It was an alliance of two, formed for the cultivation of leisure, "Natural history," and the muses, formed against ugliness, petty social conventions, and the American business mentality. This can be seen even more clearly in other brief entries: "C. says, 'After you have been to the post-office once you are damned!' But I answer that it depends somewhat. . . . If you should not get a letter there is some hope for you" (*J*, III: 456).* Once Thoreau reported an experience of Channing's at some length: he had met a "lurker" (a tramp) in the woods, "oldish and grizzled . . . a wretched looking creature, an escaped convict hiding in the woods perhaps . . . holding on to his paunch, and wheezing as if it would kill him." Thoreau notes with approval the delicacy of Channing, who tried to conceal himself, "fearing to hurt his feelings if the man should mistake him for the proprietor." The tramp obviously had come straight through the swamp; he next proceeded straight through a field of rye, "which was fully grown, not regarding it in the least," and observing Channing, gave him "a short bow," and disappeared into the woods opposite. This was the "most interesting [thing] about him, and proved him to be a lurker of the first class,—one of *our party*, as C. said. . . . He went through everything" [my italics] (*J*, V: 247–48; 1853).

---

* The post office was a favorite negative symbol for Thoreau—center of "The Mill Dam," Concord's commercial heart, and center of "herd"-like congregating for gossip and *newspaper* reading, against which his prejudice was firm and lifelong.

Of course this complicity did not insulate the relationship from all friction, nor prevent Thoreau from criticizing Channing. For example, as they returned one day from a voyage in heavy rain, Channing began to be concerned "about the condition of his money," and transferred his wallet to an innermost pocket—a reflex which Thoreau noted with irony (J, V: 494). Other instances are recorded of Channing's capriciousness and rudeness—his kicking his dog, his obvious annoyance (though he professed himself a "lurker") when two unknown young men made a short cut across his yard (J, V: 189–90). One of Thoreau's severest criticisms was expressed in an entry of 1852, in that April during which other relationships were turning sour and he had begun to question his own capacity for friendship; and when, as we have seen, he was particularly sensitive to the subject of sexual love:

I am made somewhat sad this afternoon by the coarseness and vulgarity of my companion, because he is one with whom I have made myself intimate. He inclines latterly to speak with coarse jesting of facts which should always be treated with delicacy and reverence. I lose my respect for the man who can make the mystery of sex the subject of a coarse jest, yet, when you speak earnestly and seriously on the subject, is silent. . . . I can have no really serious conversation with my companion. He seems not capable of it. (J, III: 406–7; April 12, 1852.)

There is no doubt that this companion was Channing, who was much given to jesting, and whose own marriage was, by all accounts, unsatisfactory. But Thoreau's disappointment seems to have blown over in the wind that prompted the next sailing excursion, for we find casually friendly references to Channing under the headings of April 15, 17, 18, and 19. On the eighteenth, for example, while on a rainy hike, they had stopped to watch a great flock of wild geese alight at the river's edge: "We held the dog close the while,—C., lying on his back in the rain, had him in his arms,—and thus we gradually edged round . . . the ground in this cold, wet, windy storm, keeping our feet to the tree, and the great wet calf of a dog with his eyes shut so meekly in our arms. We laughed well at our adventure."

Another entry of this period, though mildly critical, offers a judicious portrait of this mercurial friend, which at several points is reminiscent of that drawn in Thoreau's 1856 letter to Ricketson. Here he tells how Channing often tried to emulate his own meticulous note-taking in the field, only to become impatient and give it up:

> Observing me still scribbling, he will say that he confines himself to the ideal . . . he leaves the facts to me. Sometimes, too, he will say a little petulantly, "*I* am universal; I have nothing to do with the particular and definite." He is the moodiest person, perhaps, that I ever saw. As naturally whimsical as a cow is brindled, both in his tenderness and his roughness he belies himself. He can be incredibly selfish and unexpectedly generous. He is conceited, and yet there is in him far more than usual to ground conceit upon.* (*J,* III: 99; 1851.)

And still another portrait of Channing reveals Thoreau's generosity as well as his critical acumen:

> Heard C. lecture to-night. It was a bushel of nuts. Perhaps the most original lecture I ever heard. Ever so unexpected. . . . For, well as I know C., he more than any man disappoints my expectation. . . . He will be strange, unexpected, to his best acquaintance. I cannot associate the lecturer with the companion of my walks. . . . A thick succession of mountain passes and no intermediate slopes and plains. Other lectures, even the best, in which so much space is given to the elaborate development of a few ideas, seemed somewhat meagre in comparison. Yet it would be how much more glorious if talent were added to genius, if there [were] a just arrangement and development of the thoughts, and each step were not a leap, but he ran a space to take a higher leap! (*J,* III: 249; 1852.)

Did Thoreau ever feel he had found in Channing, despite the disappointments we have noted, the true Friend to whom he could speak his "first thoughts"—those unedited thoughts "with the bloom on them"–and with whom he could be unreservedly serious as well as comradely, comic, and cheerful? The *Journal* does not certify this. But it does include a number of passages which show Thoreau to have been simply happy in Channing's company—as *content,* that is (a condition distinct from his descriptions of mystical "joy"), as he ever appeared to be. At these times he seems to have felt none of that opposition between love of nature and

---

* The sentence about Channing's conceit is very like the generous judgment Thoreau later made of Walt Whitman: "He may turn out the least of a braggart of all, having a better right to be confident" (*Correspondence,* p. 445).

sympathy with humankind upon which he so insisted at other times. This contentment is evident in a passage of December, 1852, which Thoreau prefaced simply with "The pleasantest day of all" (*J*, IV: 419–23). And an entry for 1851 shows his willingness to share even one of his treasured "nocturnes": "July 11. At 7:15 p.m. with W.E.C. go forth to see the moon, the glimpses of the moon. We think she is not quite full. . . . Shall we wear thick coats? . . . Which way shall we walk? Northwest, that we may see the moon returning? . . . In Baker's orchard, the thick grass looks like a sea of mowing in this weird moonlight, a bottomless sea of grass. Our feet must be imaginative, must know the earth in imagination only, as well as our heads" (*J*, II: 297–300).

Another such experience of shared adventure and deep satisfaction was recorded the following summer. Beginning, "To Flag Hill . . . with C., with bread and butter and cheese in pocket. . . . A fine, clear day, a journey day," the account of this excursion occupies nine pages in the published *Journal*, about half of which are devoted to botanical notes—which sometimes "I" and sometimes "we" were amassing on the way. The narrative includes a ritual drink at "Willis's Spring" ("A cocoanut shell from the other side of the globe to drink at a New England spring"), a cheerful tally of the ants that ran over them as they lunched, and an encounter with a bull in an upland pasture: ". . . we gave him a wide berth, for they are not to be reasoned with." Almost a page is taken up with a half-playful discussion of the "considerable skill required to avoid the houses and too cultivated parts" in an expedition of this kind. "We crawled through the end of a swamp on our bellies, the bushes were so thick, to screen us from a house forty rods off. . . ." Evidently there was no question of trespass involved; this was simply a familiar game. The long entry rises to a triumphant note (evocative as the "cocoanut shell from the other side of the globe to drink at a New England spring"): "On our right is Acton, on our left is Stow, and forward, Boxboro. Thus King Richard sailed the Aegean and passed kingdoms on his right and left" (*J*, IV: 114–23; 1852). And the tone of contentment continues to pervade Thoreau's descriptions of time spent with Channing in later years—for example, in an entry of April, 1857: "We sit on the shore at Wheeler's fence, opposite Merriam's. At this season still we go seeking the sunniest, most sheltered and warmest place. C. says this is the warmest place he has been in this year. We are in this like snakes that lie out on banks. In sunny and sheltered nooks we are in our best estate. There our thoughts flow and we flourish most" (J, IX: 343).

This was a relationship which endured to the end. In Thoreau's last illness Channing was almost constantly in attendance—"has looked after me very faithfully," Thoreau wrote to Ricketson, "says he has made a study of my case, knows me better than I know myself, &c., &c." [9] In 1860, a year before the illness became acute, the two had gone camping together on Mount Monadnock. This was Thoreau's last long expedition on foot, and his account of it occupies forty-four pages in the Journal's volume 14. A letter carries a more concentrated and vivid account:

Well, we went up in the rain—wet through, and found ourselves in a cloud there at mid pm.... So I proceeded at once ... to build a substantial house, which C. declared the handsomest he ever saw. (He had never camped out before, and was, no doubt, prejudiced in its favor.) ... We had the mt. all to ourselves that pm and night. The Genius of the mts. saw us starting from Concord and it said,—There come two of our folks. Let us get ready for them—Get up a serious storm, that will send a packing these holiday guests.... Let us receive them with true mt. hospitality—kill the fatted cloud....

... After several nights' experience C. came to the conclusion that he was "lying out doors," and inquired what was the largest beast that might nibble his legs.... I had asked him to go and spend a week there. We spent 5 nights, being gone 6 days, for C. suggested that 6 working days made a week, and I saw that he was ready to de-camp. However, he found his account in it, as well as I.[10]

2

The letter quoted above was written to Harrison Blake of Worcester, with whom Thoreau also made several excursions, with whom he corresponded at length from 1848 until his death, and who qualifies, if anyone does, for the designation "disciple." Although the two had a number of meetings, in Concord and in Worcester (often together with Theo Brown, another friend of Blake's), there are relatively few references to Blake in the Journal. But letters to "Mr. Blake"—since Blake preserved them "religiously" —occupy more space in Thoreau's published correspondence than do those to any other person. It is interesting that Thoreau consistently addressed him thus, "Mr. Blake," while, with equal con-

sistency, addressing other correspondents as "Dear Friend" (once,
"Dear Waldo"), "Friend Ricketson," "My dear Cholmondeley,"
"Friend Greeley," and so on.

Blake was an earnest and somewhat literal person. Although
the Monadnock letter reveals a good measure of Thoreauvian high
spirits and humor, as do a few others to Blake, many of Thoreau's
letters to him have more the tone of an essay or lecture than of
the usual familiar letter. From the beginning Blake had the habit
of asking Thoreau for words of wisdom on a variety of subjects;
and Thoreau's replies tend to be correspondingly formal, and self-
conscious. Thus Blake, contemplating matrimony, requested Thoreau's thoughts on Love and Marriage, "Chastity and Sensuality,"
thereby drawing from him the long treatise I have cited elsewhere—so clearly an essay that the editors of the *Correspondence*
printed only its brief accompanying note. Other letters to Blake
contain significant statements of Thoreau's most characteristic attitudes, on topics as divergent as the mystery of "identity," the virtues of poverty and independence, the value of "exaggeration,"
and the emptiness of America's goals—"Progress" and expansion.

It must be added that these statements are sometimes marred
by a ponderousness, a posturing, which in all of Thoreau's correspondence is uniquely evident in his letters to Blake.[11] Frequently,
he insisted on assuming the role of misanthrope: "I very rarely
indeed, if ever, 'feel any itching to be what is called useful to my
fellowmen.' " "All that men have said or are is a very faint rumor,
and it is not worth the while to remember or refer to that." "I find
it, as ever, very unprofitable to have much to do with men. . . .
I have seen more men than usual, lately; and . . . I am surprised
to find what vulgar fellows they are." [12] These remarks to Blake
between 1850–54 echo passages in the *Journal,* as we have seen;
but, except for his early outbursts to his family and to Emerson
about New York City, Thoreau never made such statements in
letters to any other person.

In other passages written to Blake we see an over-elaboration
of slight ideas, as well as a kind of coyness uncharacteristic of
Thoreau. For example:

As for missing friends, . . . how can he be said to miss his friend, whom
the fruits still nourish and the elements sustain?

Your words make me think of a man of my acquaintance whom I occasionally meet, whom you appear to have met, one Myself, as he is

called. Yet why not call him *Yourself?* If you have met with him and know him it is all I have done. . . .

Methinks I will write to you. Methinks you will be glad to hear. We will stand on solid foundations to one another,—I a column . . . on this shore, you on that. . . . We will not mutually fall over that we may meet, but will grandly and eternally guard the straits.[13]

The last two quotations illustrate the complexity of this relationship. That it was at times intense is evident as much from the self-conscious mannerisms of Thoreau's expression in such passages as from what he actually was saying. Perry Miller remarked that when Blake "devoted himself in the 1850's to becoming friend to Henry Thoreau . . . he might as well have taken a marriage vow," and elsewhere he implies that the Blake-Thoreau relationship exhibited some of that "unconscious homoerotic orientation" which he discussed in yet another connection (the Friendship essay in the *Week!*)[14] A passage in another letter would, I think, best support such an assertion. It is a relatively short letter, beginning, as usual, "Mr. Blake," and expressing Thoreau's regret that he had been away from Concord when Blake had recently come to call. But "perhaps you come nearer tò me," he continued, "for not finding me at home"—their relationship is one that transcends time and space.

I hear what you say about personal relations with joy. It is as if you were to say, I value the best and finest part of you, and not the worst. I can even endure your very near and real approach, and prefer it to a shake of the hand.

"Consider this a business letter," Thoreau concluded, rather surprisingly, "which you know *counts* nothing in the game we play. Remember me particularly to Brown." In two intervening paragraphs he had matter-of-factly informed Blake of "a very long new and faithful letter from Cholmondeley," expressed a wish that Blake might meet Ricketson ("the frankest man I know"), remarked that Ricketson and Alcott now "get along very well together," and that "Channing has returned to Concord."[15] But, all in all—judging from such intimate phrases as "the game we play," and "your very near and real approach," together with a few other passages—I would say that a certain amount of unconscious erotic attraction probably did exist for a time between Thoreau and Blake. If so, my guess is that it began to dwindle, at least on Thoreau's part, not long after this letter was written. Such an attraction—if its existence could be proved—would simply furnish further evidence of Thoreau's perennial longing for intimacy, for a genuine human sympathy. "Love is a thirst that is never slaked" he wrote in 1856 (J, VIII: 231).

In any case, the last two letters cited above provide examples of extreme fluctuations in Thoreau's feelings, of his both acknowledging intimacy and retreating—the hand put forth and withdrawn. The elaborate metaphor of the two columns (amateur Freudians may make what they can of the image) on opposite shores may be the result of some embarrassment Thoreau felt at having begged for Blake's company about two months before. He then had written two very warm letters urging Blake and Brown to join him at Cape Cod. Now he appears to be backing off. The guardian columns will communicate (and there is possibly a suggestion of social usefulness in the idea of their guarding the straits); but—he makes quite a point of it—they are to remain separate.

Actually, the two July letters in which Thoreau invited Blake to join him (and Channing) at Truro are among the most attractive in the *Correspondence*. This was in 1855; Thoreau had been ill, and, still weak, was seeking recovery in the Cape Cod sun and salt air. In these letters he is wryly humorous about his afflictions, appreciative of the lighthouse keeper with whom he was staying, and simply cordial to Blake. A few other letters to him have this easy, unselfconscious tone; in general they belong to the later fifties, suggesting that the relationship did settle somewhat during that decade. Several letters describe persons whom Thoreau admired and enjoyed, and commend them to Blake's interest—Walt Whitman, Mary Emerson, Ricketson, Cholmondeley, and Joe Polis, the Indian guide.[16] And one of the liveliest tells of some hours spent at the Worcester railroad station in the middle of the night, when "you and B. [Brown] were . . . no where, and good for nothing—not even for society,—not for horse-races,—nor the taking back of a Putnam's magazine." Thoreau details certain small station dramas ("a cat caught a mouse . . . and gave it to kitten to play with," a tender moment between an Irish mother and son), "which, I will venture to say were not put into the Transcript," after which the long letter climaxes on a strikingly euphoric note: "Blake! Blake! Are you awake? Are you aware what an ever-glorious morning this is?" Thoreau now declares that he could be "content . . . to be a cedar-post," gathering lichens, though he "should not care" if he "sprouted into a living tree, put forth leaves and flowers, and have fruit."

I am grateful for what I am and have. My thanksgiving is perpetual. It is surprising how contented one can be with nothing definite—only a sense of existence.... I am ready to try this for the next thousand years, and exhaust it.... O how I laugh when I think of my vague indefinite riches. No run on my bank can drain it—for my wealth is not possession but enjoyment.[17]

The journey which kept him waiting in Worcester between trains in late November, 1856, had included a stay in Eagleswood, New Jersey, as surveyor-lecturer to "a small Quakerish community," as well as visits, with Alcott, to Horace Greeley and to Whitman in New York. This letter invites the conclusion that, after all, a little travel and socializing suited Thoreau rather well.

But we are constantly reminded that the Blake-Thoreau relationship was essentially one of disciple and master; and even so friendly and playful a letter as this carries two sharp admonitions. Having asserted that (the sleeping) Blake and Brown were "nowhere and good for nothing," Thoreau added, "It is true I might have recalled you to life, but it would have been a cruel act, considering the kind of life you would have come back to." And, in a subsequent paragraph, "I would fain . . . report to you some of my life, such as it is, and recall you to your life, which is not always lived by you, even by daylight." There are such scolding passages in many letters to him, aside from the "lectures" which Blake himself regularly invited. In one of the latter, where the issue was "how to live a simple life," and teach others to do so, the master wrote irritably that it is impossible to teach, ". . . and so all our lives be *simplified* merely, like an algebraic formula." [18] And when Blake begged his thoughts on "doing and being, and the vanity, real or apparent, of much doing," Thoreau took a witty and eloquent stand for doing. It all must have seemed bewildering to the disciple, in view of the enthusiasm for "only a sense of existence" which the author of *Walden* so often expressed. Having described the towering structure of twigs and mud that the river muskrats raise, Thoreau concluded that

we must heap up a great pile of doing, for a small diameter of being. It may seem trivial, this piling up of weeds, but so the race of muskrats is preserved. . . . There are so many layers of mere white lime in every shell to that thin inner one so beautifully tinted. Let not the shell-fish think to build his house of that alone; . . . With him too it is a Song of the Shirt, "Work,-work,-work!" And the work is not merely a police in the gross sense, but in the higher sense a discipline.[19]

In another letter Thoreau urged this disciple to do *something*: "You need some absorbing pursuit. It does not much matter what." [20]

On the basis of all these letters, can we conclude that Blake was, more than any other person, *the* "one" to whom Thoreau could speak his "first thoughts"? I am inclined to think that Thoreau for a brief while thought so, or for a longer while wished to think so, but that Blake did not consistently "measure up" by any means.*

Curiously enough, it seems that the man who came closest to that distinction was Bronson Alcott, although he was probably never aware of it. Viewed in his time primarily as a disciple of Emerson, and the author of a few books now deemed all but unreadable, the sanguine and voluble Alcott nevertheless commanded, as did few others, the continuing respect and affection of Henry Thoreau. A *Journal* description from the mid-forties suggests one basic reason for this: Alcott was, in Thoreau's view, a true "free-thinker," less inhibited by inherited assumptions and conventions than anyone he knew. He "seeks to realize an entire life; a catholic observer; habitually takes the farthest star and nebula into his scheme." The appraisal is not uncritical; Thoreau acknowledges that his friend has "sight beyond talents," ** and "undue share, for a philosopher, of the weaknesses of humanity." He also makes a point of Alcott's unshakable optimism (an atti-

---

* I base this judgment in part on the signs of Thoreau's exasperation in several letters, on his uncharacteristically strained didacticism in many others, and also on the very small space Blake occupies in the journals. But we must recognize that Blake's letters (of which only one earnest example survives: see *Correspondence*, p. 213) had at least the value of challenging Thoreau to formulate, or to restate, some of his most basic and cherished ideas.

** Thoreau had been assessing the proportion of "talent to genius" in several writers. Carlyle was found to have talent "quite equal to his genius"; Wordsworth, "with very feeble talent, has not so great and admirable as unquestionable and persevering genius"; and this entry includes one of Thoreau's most generous estimates of Emerson.

tude which, in other men, could appear offensive to Thoreau):
"[Alcott] will be the last man to be disappointed as the ages revolve.... [He has] greater faith and expectation than any man
I know." But weaknesses and differences are brushed aside, in view
of that "breadth" which Thoreau so valued. The paragraph concludes with a sentence whose juxtapositions are uniquely Thoreauvian: Alcott's is "the most hospitable intellect, embracing high
and low. For children how much that means, for the insane and
vagabond, for the poet and scholar!" (*J*, I: 432).[21]

At several other points in the *Journal* Thoreau praised that
quality of Alcott's thinking, most notably in a long entry of May,
1853:

I have devoted most of my day to Mr. Alcott. He is broad and genial,
but indefinite; some would say feeble, forever feeling about vainly in
his speech and touching nothing. But this is a very negative account of
him, for he thus suggests far more than the sharp and definite practical
mind.... He has no creed. He is not pledged to any institution. The
sanest man I ever knew, the fewest crotchets, after all, has he.[22]

It is this entry which reveals most clearly Thoreau's belief that
Alcott was the Friend to whom he could speak spontaneously and
intimately: "In his society almost alone I can express at my leisure,
with more or less success, my vaguest but most cherished fancy
or thought. There are never any obstacles in the way of our meeting" (*J*, V: 130). But in so characterizing Alcott it is important
to add that this relationship seems seldom to have had the emotional intensity that has been noted in several others—for example,
in Thoreau's relationships with Blake, with the Emersons, or even
with Channing; and Alcott occupies much less space in the *Journal*
than do Emerson and Channing. The little character sketch of the
mid-forties again supplies a possible explanation. There, in commenting that Alcott possessed "sight beyond talents," Thoreau
also noted "more intellect, less of the affections." * In the long
passage of 1853, however—and only there—we do find that the
feeling in Thoreau's account of his day with Alcott became very
intense. Having called him "The sanest man I ever knew," he proceeded to describe their conversation in two striking metaphors:

---

* In Thoreau's time, the word "affections" could denote either one's capacity
for tenderness or one's emotional nature generally. In this early journal
entry Emerson was graded as having "affections and intellect equally developed" (*J*, I: 432).

It has occurred to me, while I am thinking with pleasure of our day's intercourse, "Why should I not think aloud to you?" Having each some shingles of thought well dried, we walk and whittle them, trying our knives. . . . We wade so gently, or we pull together so smoothly, that the fishes of thought are not scared from the stream, but come and go grandly, like yonder clouds that float peacefully through the western sky.

So far, though the thought is rather elaborately set forth, the tone is calm; but a somewhat purple passage follows, suggesting that Thoreau's emotions went a little out of control:

When we walk it seems as if the heavens . . . and the earth had met together, and righteousness and peace had kissed each other. I have an ally against the arch-enemy. A blue-robed man dwells under the blue concave. The blue sky is a distant reflection of the azure serenity that looks out from under a human brow. We walk together like the most innocent children. . . . (*J*, V: 130, 131.)

Much of this passage (together with a few phrases from the earlier character sketch) appears in *Walden*, but there purged of the excesses which here seem slightly embarrassing.[23] "Serenity" is not "azure," for example, and the conceit of righteousness and peace kissing each other is missing, as is "I have an ally against the arch-enemy." (But what is the meaning of that striking *Journal* statement? In its context "the arch-enemy" can suggest a number of things: loneliness, the rigid conventionality of society, and even death itself.) Finally the *Journal* passage returns to a criticism of "most [men] with whom I endeavor to talk," who, in contrast to Alcott, "soon fetch up against some institution or particular way of viewing things, theirs not being a universal view" (*J*, V: 131).

There is only one instance recorded of Thoreau's having seriously disapproved of and criticized Alcott. This had occurred a year before, when he learned that his friend had succumbed to an obsessive interest in his ancestors—Alcott, "the spiritual philosopher, . . . he whom only the genealogy of humanity, the descent of man from God, should concern," had been exploring Connecticut cemeteries and town records in an effort to trace the history of his family in America—much to Thoreau's disgust (*J*, V: 292–94; 1852). But obviously his disgust was prompted by—and proportionate to—the great esteem he felt for Alcott. And that Thoreau, in turn, valued Alcott's praise is clear from a later *Journal* entry: "Alcott spent the day with me yesterday. He spent the day before with Emerson. He observed that he had got his wine and now he had come after his venison. Such was the compliment he paid me" (J, V: 365).

This friendship lasted throughout Thoreau's life. We know that he and Alcott continued walking and philosophizing together, that together they visited Ricketson in New Bedford and sought out Whitman in New York, and that in 1856 Thoreau visited the Alcotts in New Hampshire, news of which he reported to Cholmondeley thus: "I have just taken a run up-country . . . where I saw Alcott, King of men." * [24]

3

Cholmondeley and Ricketson. Although they were very different, and differed as much from Thoreau as they did from one another, both were devoted to him, and his letters to each of them express real affection. His relationship with these two friends seems to have been more placid, less fraught with tension and conflict than were his relationships with the Emersons, Channing, and Blake, or even Alcott.

Both these friendships were formed in the mid-fifties. Daniel Ricketson, the impulsive provincial squire, wrote an admiring letter to the author of *Walden* soon after the book appeared in 1854. Thoreau's reply, while not lengthy, was cordial; but Ricketson confided in his diary that he thought it "hastily written and hardly satisfactory, evidently well-meant, though overcautious." [25] This gap between Ricketson's expectations and Thoreau's ability to meet them would be apparent from time to time throughout the eight years of their friendship. Yet it was a friendship that developed rapidly—Thoreau visited the Ricketsons only two and a half months after this first exchange of letters—and one that endured:

---

* See below, p. 57 for a reference to Thoreau's approving account of a later success of Alcott's. The *Correspondence* includes a note written during an earlier period, when the Alcotts had lived in Concord, in which "My dear friend Mr. Thoreau" is warmly invited "to our home this day to celebrate the marriage of our dear Anna and John," from (Mrs.) "Abby Alcott" (p. 580; May, 1850). Anna Alcott Pratt's diary reveals that Thoreau did attend that wedding. And from Channing, via Sanborn, we have a moving account of Alcott's last visit and his parting kiss given to Thoreau on the day before his death (see Walter Harding. *The Days of Henry Thoreau* [New York: Alfred A. Knopf, 1965], pp. 431, 465).

the last five letters printed in the *Correspondence* are from "Yours faithfully, D. Ricketson," dated from March to May 4, 1862. There were a number of other visits—both to New Bedford and Concord—and some of Thoreau's most relaxed and gayest letters were written to this ardent follower. Voluminous answers flowed from Ricketson's "Shanty," a retreat he had made for himself at some distance from his house. His letters reveal a character rather naive, eager, affectionate, and frank—as Thoreau himself remarked to Blake, "the frankest man I know." [26] We have noted the affection and concern in Thoreau's commendation of Channing to Ricketson. There are similarly warm references to Ricketson in several letters to Blake and others, and these references, along with the letters addressed to "Friend Ricketson" himself, convince us that Thoreau did take him seriously, valuing his peculiar qualities to the same degree that he enjoyed his company.

An exchange of letters in 1857 reveals the extent of this enjoyment. Early in this spring Thoreau had invited himself to New Bedford, and it was during that visit that he distinguished himself at dancing and ballad-singing with Ricketson, Alcott, and Ricketsons's lively children.[27] In May, Thoreau wrote Ricketson (who was talking of moving to Concord!) about a house just then available, and invited him and his wife to stay with the Thoreaus while they considered it. This letter concludes with witty messages for the whole Ricketson family, and a reference to Thoreau's favorite ballad, "Tom Bowling." [28] A *Journal* entry of 1857 contains an appreciative description of Ricketson's "Shanty," its architecture, furnishings, curiosities, books, and the quotations tacked on the walls,—all of which, as Thoreau remarked, added up to an attractive composite portrait of the man (J, IX: 322–25).

On one occasion Thoreau expressed a mild annoyance when Ricketson postponed a visit to Concord because of Channing's absence.[29] But at other times he felt obliged to decline Ricketson's pressing invitations, and was obviously unable to keep up the rate of correspondence that his friend expected. The late fall of 1860 brought a small crisis. Ricketson sent a letter complaining bitterly of Thoreau's neglect—"your almost sepulchral silence towards me." To this Thoreau, whose health was already failing, replied at length and patiently. Ricketson must "infer from [my silence] what you might from the silence of a dense pine wood." There has been no feeling of coldness on his part, he insists; he has been unwontedly busy, although he acknowledges that at all times Ricketson is "far more attentive to 'the common courtesies of life'" than he. "You must not regard me as a regular diet, but at most only as acorns," he warns. The letter concludes, as do almost all of his letters to Ricketson, "Please remember me to your family"; and here he adds, "I have a very pleasant recollection of your fireside, and I trust I shall revisit it—also of your shanty and the surrounding regions. Yours truly, Henry D. Thoreau."[30] This seems to have satisfied Ricketson, who wrote in February, announcing the sighting of the first bluebird. Having mentioned Thoreau's "welcome letter," he remarked simply that "We must 'bear and forbear' with each other," and once again invited Thoreau to visit him.[31] Thoreau, now seriously ill, replied in March, in a letter remarkable for both its cheerfulness and the warm regard it reveals for Ricketson and others. Beginning playfully, "The bluebirds were here the 26 of Feb. at least, which is one day earlier than your date," he touched briefly on his illness, but added, "I thank you for your invitation to come to New Bedford, and will bear it in mind. . . ." The letter continues with the reference, cited above, to Channing's faithful nursing, followed by news of a visit from Blake and Brown, with whom "I had a solid talk . . . for a day and a half," then the report of a letter from Cholmondeley, and a long and enthusiastic account of Alcott's great success as new superintendent of the Concord schools. Thoreau's satisfaction in communicating all this is strikingly evident; and this is one of the letters which can bear out his remark to Blake, in 1859, that "I seem to myself a most befriended man."[32]

Thomas Cholmondeley is best known to students of Thoreau's life as the man who presented him with a splendid gift—forty-four volumes of Indian and other Oriental writings. Of this event Thoreau wrote to Ricketson in some detail, ending, "I am familiar with many of them and know how to prize them. I send you information of this as I might of the birth of a child."[33] The young Englishman had visited Concord in 1854, first seeking out Emerson, but ultimately spending much time with Thoreau. He paid Thoreau another visit in 1859, and in the intervening years they corresponded fairly frequently, with a hiatus in 1855–56, when Cholmondeley went off to the Crimean war—a decision frankly, though gently, deplored by Thoreau.[34]

Cholmondeley's letters are in the best sense "familiar." His admiration and affection are obvious; but, unlike Ricketson and Blake, he appears never to have been in awe of Thoreau, and

never to have tailored his news or his attitudes to suit this particular correspondent. After Thoreau had made a sardonic comment about someone's addiction to tobacco, Ricketson wrote a
rather abject apology for having "offended" him with his ubiqui-
tous pipe. Cholmondeley, on the other hand (and it is refreshing
to come upon this in the atmosphere of the *Correspondence*),
once discoursed to Thoreau for half a page about the salutary
effects of alcoholic beverages, as well as the pleasures of girl-
watching. He is going, he says, to hear an American temperance
lecturer, but "I go forearmed against him—being convinced in my
mind that a good man is all the better for a bottle of Port under
his belt every day of his life. . . . London is cram-full. Not a bed!
Not a corner! After all the finest sight is to see such numbers of
beautiful girls riding about and riding well. There are certainly
no women in the world like ours." Next he informs Thoreau that
he is losing his teeth, because, he says, of hot drinks, coffee, tea,
chocolate; he should have stuck to good brown "ale for breakfast
and claret or Port or ale again for dinner." He closes with: "Farewell Thoreau. Success and the bounty of the gods attend you."
The letter is full of Cholmondeley's abounding love of life. He is
both worldly and unworldly, delighting in the "newness" of Whitman's poetry (which Thoreau had sent him), and slightly shocked
by its frank sexuality; enchanted by "the fairness of the oak trees"
as well as by the ladies in the park.[35] It is worth noting that
Thoreau took the trouble to report this letter's arrival to Blake—
whereas to Ricketson's apologies he replied impatiently, "What do
you mean by that ado about smoking and my 'purer tastes'?"[36]

In another letter Cholmondeley had ventured, as no other
friend ever quite dared, to question at length Thoreau's own mode
of life, admitting that "You are not living altogether as I could
wish," and warning against too much solitude.[37] There are no indications that Thoreau agreed with this, or even reflected seriously
upon it. But we know it was not resented, for he mentioned the
letter to both Blake and Ricketson, in almost the same words: "I
have a very long new and faithful letter from Cholmondeley, which
I wish to show you."[38]

Four

Other Relationships; Thoreau As Neighbor, Son,

Brother; As Story-Teller and Myth-Maker

I HAVE reviewed these key relationships—with Cholmondeley, Ricketson, Blake, Alcott, the Emersons, and Channing—in some detail, not only in order to counterbalance Miller's portrait of Thoreau, but also to establish a basis for the further explorations of this study. Considered together, these relationships support the assertion that Thoreau was, after all, "a most befriended" and befriending man—that however severe his *Journal* denunciations of "Men," and however despairing at times his reflections on Friendship, he did in fact experience a continuing rapport with a number of complex and interesting individuals.

It is equally important to remember other relationships in Thoreau's life, most of them simpler, less absorbing, than those discussed above, which were nonetheless stimulating and supportive over long periods of time. One of the more significant involved Emerson's aunt, Mary Moody Emerson. Thoreau described her to Blake as "the youngest person in Concord, though about eighty,— and the most apprehensive of a genuine thought; earnest to know of your inner life; most stimulating society and exceedingly witty withal. She says they called her old when she was young and she has never grown any older. I wish you could see her." [1]

Mary Emerson was a devout Christian, and the *Journal* records several instances in which she scolded her friend Henry for his heresies; but, interestingly enough, Thoreau made no serious complaint of her "commitment to institutions," as he did of many others'. And her occasional capriciousness was a delight to him, as is clear from another *Journal* anecdote. On the way to a Lyceum lecture, Miss Mary grumbled unceasingly that "she did not want to go, she did not think it was worth while to be running after such amusements, etc., etc." When finally asked, "What do you go for, then?" she snappishly replied, "None of your business" (*J*, III: 204). There is *Journal* evidence that Thoreau read from the manuscript of *Walden* to this friend (*J*, III: 179); and there is evidence in the *Correspondence* of her fondness for him. One surviving note requested "my young friend" to "visit me tomorrow early as he can"; in another she begged "Dear Henry" to write to her while she was away from Concord.[2]

In one *Journal* entry where Thoreau praised Mary Emerson's receptiveness and wit, the context is sharply critical of "any other woman" (*J*, III: 114; 1851). And, indeed, there are other instances in the *Journal* of an explicit misogyny—that is, whether or not Thoreau intended to include women with men in at least some of the misanthropic utterances cited earlier, they were upon occasion singled out for special censure. Women are said to be "weaker" than men in reason as in physique; and they are charged with "conformity" (*J*, II: 116; 1850). Thoreau several times complained that he could not endure evening parties, where he was bored (and, obviously, awkward) in "the society of young women." "I derive no pleasure," he wrote after one of those occasions, "from talking with a young woman half an hour simply because she has regular features" (*J*, III: 116; 1851). An encounter with a feminist lecturer left him equally disappointed, however. He was impressed by the lecture—"on womanhood"—and went to see the lecturer afterward, but

she was a woman in the too common sense after all. You had to fire small charges. . . . You had to substitute courtesy for sense and argument. It requires nothing less than a chivalric feeling to sustain a conversation with a lady. I carried her lecture for her in my pocket wrapped in her handkerchief; my pocket exhales cologne to this moment. The championess of women's rights still asks you to be a ladies' man. I can't fire a salute, even, for fear some of the guns may be shotted. (*J*, III: 168; 1851.)

Although Thoreau's tone here is half-humorous, his insistent use of the shotgun imagery suggests a real hostility.*

---

* See the *Correspondence* (p. 373; letter to Mrs. Elizabeth O. Smith, Feb. 19, 1855), however, for a sympathetic letter written by Thoreau to this lady. At the letter's end Thoreau added one of his superbly concise transcendental admonitions, of the kind he especially liked to give to "reformers": "As for

Yet the same ambivalence which is evident in his statements about humanity pervaded his attitudes toward women in particular. "The practise of giving the feminine gender—to all ideal excellence personified, is a mark of refinement, observable in the mythologies even of the most barbarous nations," he wrote in 1840; "Man is masculine, but his manliness (virtus) feminine. It is the inclination of brute force to moral power." [3] And—in addition to early attractions to Ellen Sewall, Mary Russell, and Lucy Brown, and his long preoccupation with Lidian Emerson—there are indications in both the *Journal* and letters of Thoreau's approval of and ease with a number of other females in his sphere. Young Ellen and Edith Emerson were continuing favorites.* Elizabeth Hoar is always mentioned with respect, as was her mother—"a strong-willed, managing woman" (*J*, X: 223),[4] and there are references to boating and picnicking excursions with unnamed "ladies." The *Correspondence* includes cordial communications to and from Mary Brown, a nature-lover in Vermont, as well as from Sophia Hawthorne, Abby Alcott, and Mrs. Horace Mann. In a late *Journal* entry we find an enthusiastic description of a Kate Brady, whom Thoreau had met at the Ricketsons'. She was a schoolteacher, with "a strong head and a love for good reading," and, he added, "I never heard a girl or woman express so strong a love for nature." Miss Brady had talked of returning to her old family homestead, living alone if necessary, and said that "she knows all about farming and keeping sheep and spinning and weaving, though it would puzzle her to shingle the old house." Thoreau's utterly characteristic comment was, "I would by no means discourage, nor yet particularly encourage her, for I would have her so strong as to succeed in spite of all ordinary discouragements" (*J*, IX: 335–36; 1857).[5]

---

the good time that is coming, let us not forget that there is a good time *going* too, and see that we dwell on that eternal ridge between the two which neither comes nor goes." For an account of Thoreau's much more positive response to another leading feminist, Caroline Dall, see Walter Harding, *The Days of Henry Thoreau* (New York: Alfred A. Knopf, 1965), p. 412.

* A poem, "To Edith," written while Thoreau lived at the Emersons' in 1841, when Edith was between one and two, was cherished by Emerson and so found its way into the published *Poems* (*Collected Poems of Henry Thoreau*, ed. Carl Bode [Baltimore: Johns Hopkins Press, 1965], p. 397). And the *Correspondence* includes a letter of 1849 from Thoreau to Ellen, then aged ten, which, in its tact, affection and anticipation of her interests, might serve as a model for addressing children (*Correspondence*, pp. 245–46; July 31, 1849).

Apart from Lidian Emerson, the women who figured most pervasively in Thoreau's life were those in his family—above all, his strong-willed and assertive mother. Although something of their closeness is suggested in the letter I have cited above, and in others, there is surprisingly little documentation of this crucial relationship in either the *Correspondence* or the *Journal*. Richard Lebeaux, drawing partly on commentary from Thoreau's contemporaries, as well as on Eriksonian theory, has recently subjected the relationship to a persuasive psychological analysis, which stresses a word already familiar in this study—ambivalence:

I would contend that the young Thoreau came to be extremely ambivalent about his mother and their relationship. On the one hand, he loved her and greatly needed her maternal support and presence—especially without an "influential" father to balance out his dependencies and provide him with an identity model. She—and to a lesser extent, his sisters—supplied a maternal presence that he needed and sought his entire life. He became highly dependent upon mother and home and never was able fully to break away, either in terms of separation by physical distance or by establishing a sexual relationship and household with another woman. In fact, women—by association with and transference from the mother—became lifelong objects of ambivalence for Henry.

Lebeaux goes on to argue that "Thoreau not only depended upon his mother for acceptance, approval, and love; he also came to regard her as threatening, possessive, emasculating, limiting." [6]

While the rarity of *Journal* references to Cynthia Thoreau may tend to support Lebeaux's theory of ambivalence, the passages that do mention her all seem relaxed and mildly appreciative in tone. They have to do with her reminiscences, her moderate interest in Thoreau's nature studies (we know that she shared, much more strongly, his antislavery position), with her enterprising nature, with various motherly services rendered, and other casually revealing details of their common daily life.* One of Thoreau's responses to that everyday family scene is expressed in a *Journal* sentence of 1841: "I go and feel my pulse in all the recesses of the house and see if I am of force to carry a homely life and comfort into them" (*J*, I: 224). Both *Journal* and letters contain affectionate and respectful references to Thoreau's less "influential" father (follow-

---

* See, for instance, *J*, V: 444; VIII: 93, 94; IX: 381.

ing his death in 1859 a letter to Ricketson emphasized his integrity and quiet sociability) [7]; and the comradeship and affection that Thoreau experienced with his only brother John have become almost legendary. Two biographers have seen John's sudden death in 1842 as the central trauma in Henry's life.* [8] At the least, it was an event which left the family circle lopsidedly female, for, along with his mother and two sisters, there were usually one or two aunts staying in the house.

With the elder sister, Helen, Thoreau seems to have had a close and fairly intellectual relationship, comparable to that which he enjoyed with John. Early letters to her are serious and affectionate, dwelling in detail on her education, but in one case—in a letter written in Latin—bidding her to be less earnest, more "carefree," and to prepare for boating expeditions with him in the spring.[9] It was to Helen that Thoreau sent, from Staten Island, the poem he had written after John's death.[10] The *Poems* also include an elegy in her memory,[11] and one wonders whether Helen was the subject of a highly emotional passage in the *Journal*, which is dated a few months after her death in 1849. Beginning "My dear, my dewy sister, let thy rain descend on me," the passage rushes on for half a page of rhapsodic invocation: "I not only love thee, but I love the best of thee; that is to love thee rarely. I do not love thee every day. Commonly I love those who are less than thou. I love thee only on great days. Thy dewy words feed me like the manna of the morning." F. B. Sanborn interpreted this passage as "the sincere ascription of a New England hunter . . . to the 'Queen of Night, the Huntress Diana' [and therefore, the moon]. . . . In such a lofty mystical strain did this Concord Endymion declare his passion for Nature. . . ." [12] This interpretation was based on the one instance in which the name Diana is invoked, at the passage's climax—precisely the point at which later readers have thought of Lidian Emerson: "Thou dost not have to woo me. I do not have

---

* That Thoreau suffered a sympathetic attack of tetanus after John's death is widely known, as is the poem he wrote in his brother's memory. Of course, the entire *Week*, which bears an epigraph verse addressed to him ("Be thou my Muse, my Brother"), can be considered a memorial to John. Briefer memorials are found here and there in the later journals—for example, in that of 1850: "I have heard my brother playing on his flute at evening half a mile off through the houses of the village, every note with perfect distinctness. It seemed a more beautiful communication with me than the sending up of a rocket would have been" (J, II: 12).

to woo thee. O my sister! O Diana, thy tracks are on the eastern hills. . . . My eyes are the hounds that pursue thee." * Yet there are indications that this Diana may after all have been his actual sister, the departed Helen: "I am as much thy sister as thy brother. Thou are as much my brother as my sister. It is a portion of thee and a portion of me which are of kin. . . . Ah, my friend, what if I do not answer thee? I hear thee. Thou canst speak; I cannot. I hear and forget to answer. I am occupied with hearing. I awoke and thought of thee; thou wast present in my mind. How camest thou there? Was I not present to thee likewise?" (J, II: 78). I, for one, have difficulty in assuming that these sentences were addressed to the moon, or to "Nature." At any rate, whatever else we may conjecture about it, this passage is clearly not the work of a cold, scientifically-oriented man, nor of a wholly self-centered man (nor yet of a literary opportunist). Like so many others, it voices a deep yearning; it begs for some kind of relatedness.

Thoreau's letters to Sophia, the second sister, are generally more matter-of-fact than those written to Helen; their tone is at times playful, at times somewhat patronizing.[13] Yet the journals of the middle and later years reveal the importance, in his day-to-day life, of this one remaining sibling, who cared for him at the end, and tried to defend his fame thereafter. Often a boating and walking companion, she was also a source of village news and gossip, which Henry was not always above receiving, and recording. And she was a listener, eager to share the smaller interests and excitements of the day. One of the Journal's longest and most attractive animal stories involves Sophia, who, on a rowing excursion, helped Thoreau rescue "a little dot of a kitten" (J, V: 180–83; 1853). On another boating trip, she shared one of his memorable midsummer-night vigils, in which he contemplated his small universe by moonlight. And here again (as in the narration of a similar outing with Channing), Thoreau displayed no impatience at having a companion, but rather a distinct contentment,

---

* The Journal editors have indicated that four and two-thirds pages are missing from the manuscript journal just before the beginning of this passage. And see Henry Seidel Canby (Thoreau [Boston: Houghton Mifflin Co., 1939], pp. 160–62) for a discussion of a loose manuscript in the Huntington Library, dated by Sanborn as of 1848–50, which is strikingly similar to this. Although the Huntington manuscript was titled "A Sister," apparently by Thoreau, Canby concluded (with some reason, I should say, judging from the passages quoted) that it had to do with Lidian Emerson.

together with a heightened responsiveness to the poetry of the familiar village scene: "To Nawshawtuct at moonrise, with Sophia . . . you are pretty sure to hear some human music, vocal or instrumental, far or near. . . . Now we row through a thin low mist. . . . And the [river's] apparent depth where stars are reflected frightens Sophia. These Yankee houses and gardens seen rising beyond this oily moon-lit water, on whose surface the circling insects are like sparks of fire, are like Italian dwellings on the shores of Italian lakes" (J, V: 319–22; 1853). Sophia brought home specimens of flowers, leaves, butterflies, as well as news* [14]; and it was Sophia who was called outdoors to see a "rare and beautiful bird" (J, V: 247; 1853), or to the window when a load of great New Hampshire pine trunks went "shooting through the town" on a train car (J, V: 298–99; 1853).

Certain letters to Sophia and to Thoreau's mother contain dutiful messages to "the aunts"; one brief Journal entry, tolerant if not affectionate in tone, captured them for posterity: "My Aunt Maria asked me to read the life of Dr. Chalmers, which however I did not promise to do. Yesterday, Sunday, she was heard through the partition shouting to my Aunt Jane, who is deaf. 'Think of it! He stood half an hour to-day to hear the frogs croak, and he wouldn't read the life of Chalmers' " (J, V: 58; 1853). An uncle, Charles Dunbar, was also frequently resident in the Thoreau household. The Journal contains many references to his youthful exploits, of which this is a fair example: "E. Hosmer says that a man told him that he had seen my Uncle Charles take a twelve-foot ladder, set it up straight, and then run up and down the other side, kicking it from behind him as he went down. E. H. told of seeing him often at the tavern toss his hat to the ceiling, twirling it over, and catch it on his head every time" (J, XII: 38; 1859). And Thoreau set down two brief but vivid sketches of Charles Dunbar in old age. One, in a letter to his mother, portrayed his

* Her unwitting transportation of some "specimens" occasioned one of those dryly comic reflections which surprise and delight one in the later journals: "Grasshoppers have been very abundant. . . . Sophia walked through the Depot Field a fortnight ago, and when she got home picked fifty or sixty [of them] from her skirts,–for she wore hoops and crinoline. Would not this be a good way to clear a field of them,–to send a bevy of fashionably dressed ladies across a field and leave them to clean their skirts when they get home? It would supplant anything at the patent office, and the motive power is cheap" (J, XII: 332; 1859).

uncle drowsing after dinner in his chair, waking, reminiscing, and exclaiming in comically disconnected fashion (". . . Some [are] wise and some otherwise—Heighho!") He was then "sound asleep again." [15] The other, from a journal of 1853, deserves full quotation:

After talking with Uncle Charles the other night about the worthies of this country, Webster and the rest, as usual, considering who were geniuses and who not, I showed him up to bed, and when I had got into bed myself, I heard his chamber door opened, after eleven o'clock, and he called out, in an earnest, stentorian voice, loud enough to wake the whole house, "Henry! was John Quincy Adams a genius?" "No, I think not," was my reply. "Well, I didn't think he was," answered he. (*J*, IV: 440.)

Clearly Uncle Charles was what is popularly known as a character—so, to some extent, was Mary Emerson—and we sense that Thoreau saw and enjoyed them as such, though this did not diminish his affection or respect. Concord in those days abounded in "characters"—Thoreau himself was clearly a character to his fellow townsmen—and the journals are filled with portraits and anecdotes of other, less illustrious ones. Sam Staples, for instance, town jailer, farmer, and sometime politician, who once had the strange duty of locking up Henry Thoreau; Perez Blood, a farmer and amateur astronomer, whose telescope drew many curious visitors (including Thoreau), but, as it also contributed to a certain haughtiness, did not increase his popularity; and the Hosmers: Edmund ("the most intelligent farmer in Concord," who was never too busy to talk with Thoreau), and Joseph ("[Saw] old Mr. Joe Hosmer, chopping wood. . . . He is full of meat. Had a crack with him.") [16] And there was also Israel Rice:

Rice was very ready to go with us to his boat, which we borrowed, as soon as he had driven his cow into the barn. . . . He was very obliging, persisted, without regard to our suggestions that we could help ourselves, in going with us to his boat, showed us after a larger boat and made no remark on the miserableness of it. Thanks and compliments fell off him like water off a rock. If the king of the French should send him a medal, . . . it would fail of its intended effect. (*J*, III: 379–80; 1852.)

Still another farmer, George Minott, was an important personage in Thoreau's life. He occupies more space in the journals than Emerson—indeed, of human subjects, he is second only to Channing. If Hosmer was "the most intelligent," Minott was "perhaps the most poetical farmer—who most realizes to me the poetry of the farmer's life—that I know. He does nothing with haste and drudgery, but as if he loved it." In this *Journal* portrait, Thoreau dwelt on Minott's simplicity of life, his leisureliness, his closeness to nature, his self-sufficiency and lack of interest in financial speculation—on those Thoreauvian virtues, in other words, that are exalted in *Walden* and "Life Without Principle." But Minott's appeal for Thoreau went far beyond his usefulness as an exemplar, and this portrait includes several individuating details: his passion for hunting (of which in others Thoreau often disapproved), the fact that "he loves to walk in a swamp in windy weather and hear the wind groan through the pines," and the special quality of his speech. "Though he never reads a book,—since he has finished the 'Naval Monument,' " the portrait concludes, "he speaks the best of English" (*J*, III: 41–43; 1851).

Minott was one of Thoreau's chief authorities on "natural history," wise in the ways of farming and hunting, of animals, birds, and insects, of forest trees as well as crops, and of Indian lore. He was also an authority on the town of Concord; and his anecdotes about the Mill Dam, the Great Snow, the old grist mill, a slave's escape, and Thoreau's Uncle Charles, were zestfully recorded. So was his criticism of another "authority": Minott said that a certain Shattuck's account in his "History of Concord" "is not right by a jugful, that he does not come within half a mile of the truth, not as he has heard tell" (*J*, XI: 110; 1858).

The judgment that Minott "speaks the best of English" meant that his speech, though not "educated," was clear, precise and vivid. Thoreau adds that he often looked up Minott's expressions— "good old English words, and I am always sure to find them in the dictionary, though I never heard them before in my life." Often he would slip into Minott's style of speech: "[Minott] saw [in a September gale] an elm . . . break off ten feet from the ground . . . and the barn bent and gave so that he thought it was time to be moving. He saw stones 'as big as that stove, blown right out of the wall.' " "Minott told me again the reason why the bushes were coming in so fast in the river meadows. Now that the mower takes nothing stronger [to drink] than molasses and water, he darsn't meddle with anything bigger than a pipe-stem." [17] Note the "again"—he "told me again." Thoreau's appreciation of both Minott's matter and his manner are expressed elsewhere in the simple declaration that "I willingly listen to the stories he has told me half a dozen times already" (J, VIII: 194; 1856).

This old farmer's own acknowledgment that he was "in some respects . . . still a boy" (J, III: 67) was, of course, a matter for congratulation in Thoreau's eyes. Another thoroughgoing tribute appears in his remark that "Minott is a very pleasing figure in nature. He improves every scenery,—he and his comrades, Harry Hooper, John Wyman, Oliver Williams, etc. If he gets into a pond-hole he disturbs it no more than a water-spirit for me" (J, X: 168; 1857). Three years before, Thoreau had recorded this exchange without comment: "Channing, talking with Minott the other day about his health, said, 'I suppose you'd like to die now.' 'No,' said Minott, 'I've toughed it through the winter, and I want to stay and hear the bluebirds once more'" (J, VI: 152; 1854). As it turned out, he survived, with his uncanny ear for bird calls, to hear the bluebirds announcing six more springs. In July, 1860, "confined to his room with dropsy," he remarked to Thoreau that it was a cold summer. "He knew it was cold; the whip-poor-will told him so. It sung once and then stopped" (J, XIII: 410). The feeling that is apparent in both these passages—and apparent without any insistence or sentimentalizing—is more explicit in the draft of a letter which Thoreau (now seriously ill himself) wrote to Ricketson in March, 1861, shortly after Minott's death. "Minott had been on his last legs for some time,—at last off his legs, expecting weekly to take his departure,—a burden to himself and friends,—yet dry and natural as ever." The people who had been caring for him—the eighty-year-old sister who shared the house, another sister, and an elderly housekeeper—all had died during February within the space of three weeks: "All departed as gently as the sun goes down, leaving George alone."

I called to see him [Thoreau went on] the other day,—the 27th of February . . . ,—and as I was climbing the sunny slope to his strangely deserted house, I heard the first bluebirds upon the elm that hangs over it. They had come as usual, though some who used to hear them were gone. Even Minott had not heard them, though the door was open,—for he was thinking of other things. Perhaps there will be a time when the bluebirds themselves will not return any more.

I hear that George, a few days after this, called out to his niece, who had come to take care of him, and was in the next room, to know if she did not feel lonely? "Yes, I do," said she, "So do I," added he. He said he was like an old oak, all shattered and decaying.

Soon after this the draft breaks off. The editor noted that "either this topic was too painful for Thoreau to finish the letter, or perchance he thought it not likely to interest his friend; for he threw aside this draft for three days, and then, with the same beginning, wrote a very different letter." [18]

2

Staples, the Hosmers, the Rices, and Minott were all reasonably solid citizens. But there were others, several steps below them on the social scale (in the eyes of respectable Concord), who exerted a fascination upon Thoreau that was in some ways even stronger. Readers of *Walden* are not likely to forget the French-Canadian woodchopper ("a true Homeric or Paphlagonian man"), whose physical strength and unqualified enjoyment of life are celebrated at length in chapter 6. Indeed, in his simplicity and "wildness," Alek Therien* represents an important facet of Thoreau's own nature. The difference—an enormous one—is that in Therien these qualities were "pure"—he was incapable of reflecting on them, and, in fact, was depicted by Thoreau as a man almost without self-consciousness. Of course his unquestioning acceptance of his Roman Catholic heritage caused Thoreau some pain (and some effort "to suggest a substitute within him for the priest without"). But this was mitigated by his appreciation of Homer (read aloud by Thoreau), by his honesty and gaiety, and, above all, by his casual acceptance of Thoreau's own presence in the woods.[19] It was a mutual acceptance, ungrudging on both sides.

Other solitary and shabby figures—even less "respectable" than Therien—come and go throughout the *Journal's* fourteen volumes, such figures as one-eyed John Goodwin, Sudbury Haines, Bill Wheeler, and George Melvin. Haines and Goodwin were odd-job men and fishermen by profession, gatherers of driftwood, and —when those enterprises failed—poachers and pilferers in other men's wood lots. It was the sight of Goodwin getting his winter wood that stirred Thoreau to the outburst on the evils of trade and the artificiality of society cited in an earlier chapter. (See above, p. 15.) It may have been Goodwin—"the one-eyed Ajax"— who appears, with his birch pole and his dog, in the first chapter

---

* The woodchopper is so identified in the *Journal*, where he is described in a number of entries written both before and after the publication of *Walden*. See for example *J*, I: 365–67; 1845; VI: 23–24; 1853.

of the *Week*—"the last of our townsmen whom we saw,"—as Henry and John Thoreau rowed downriver toward the Merrimack.[20] Years after this, at one of their many meetings, Thoreau and Goodwin amused themselves at guessing each other's ages; and Goodwin "thought that Emerson was a very young-looking man for his age, 'But,' said he, 'he has not been out o' nights as much as you have.'" Elsewhere, a single-sentence paragraph summed up this Concord character: "Goodwin cannot be a very bad man, he is so cheery" (*J*, XI: 289, 351; 1858).

Bill Wheeler appears only once in the *Journal*, and this only after his death, in a concentrated three-page "memorial." Wheeler was a ne'er-do-well and drunkard, whose story may remind *Walden* readers of the fate of Hugh Quoil. At some remote time, lying drunk in a snow bank, he had frozen his feet, and was thereafter to be seen, "once in five years, progressing into the town on his stubs, holding the middle of the road as if he drove an invisible herd before him. . . . He seemed to belong to a different caste from other men, and reminded me of both the Indian Pariah and martyr." Once Thoreau had found him asleep in an isolated hut, and had then reflected upon the probable quality of his existence—"how low he lived, perhaps from a deep principle. . . . simplifying life, returning to nature, having turned his back on towns. . . ." "I was not to be deceived," he added, "by a few stupid words, of course, and apparent besottedness. It was his position and career that I contemplated." Now, hearing of his death (he had been found in the woods, "over back of the hill,—so far decomposed that his coffin was carried to his body"), Thoreau again questioned "what view he took of life." It was possible that "he may have died a Brahmin's death, dwelling at the roots of trees at last, and been absorbed into the spirit of Brahm"; but, "I have since been assured that he suffered from disappointed love. . . . than which can there be any nobler suffering, any fairer death, for a a human creature?—that that made him to drink, froze his feet, and did all the rest for him. Why have not the world the benefit of his long trial?" (*J*, III: 195–98). (This was written in 1852, by which time Thoreau had had, as we have seen, some first-hand experience of "disappointed love.") These pages on Bill Wheeler provide a fascinating example of the tonal fluctuations Thoreau's prose could undergo when his emotions were roused. Here pity, mixed with some condescension, gives way to an intense, almost reverent, myth-making impulse. The controlling past tense—this is, after all, an obituary—is curiously interspersed with the present: "Must he not see things with an impartial eye? . . . he indulges . . .", "he is. . . ." Above all, there are extreme differences in the roles which Thoreau assigned to Wheeler: those of contemptible reprobate, pitiable weakling, courageous exemplar of a way of life, archetypal, druidical hero, and, finally, simple suffering man—whose sufferings, for love, are explicitly sanctified by Thoreau.

George Melvin—"the muskrat man"—has been mentioned earlier in this study: Thoreau and Channing thought of calling one of their favorite "wild" places "The Melvin Preserve," for Melvin was primarily a hunter, just as Goodwin was primarily a fisherman. It is interesting to observe Thoreau's almost complete acceptance of these men's activities, although he himself had given up hunting, rarely fished, and in *Walden* discussed both hunting and fishing as symptoms of arrested development.[21] But Goodwin, Sudbury Haines, Melvin, and, to some degree, Minott, fished and hunted for their livelihood—a far cry, in Thoreau's view, from the "gentleman's" killing of animals for sport. If Melvin took muskrats and mink for their pelts and sold the fur, at least he was a true supplier, vastly superior to the middlemen fur-dealers who bought from him; and he also had a daily experience of Nature. Thoreau's tendency to mythologize such characters as Melvin, and his effort to reconcile Melvin's practice with his own concern for wildlife, are well illustrated in a passage of 1859:

The musquash-hunter (last night), with his increased supply of powder and shot and boat turned up somewhere on the bank . . . dreaming of his exploits to-day in shooting . . . even he, dark, dull, and battered flint as he is, is an inspired man to his extent now, perhaps the most inspired by this freshet of any, and the Musketaquid Meadows cannot spare him. There are poets of all kinds and degrees, little known to each other. The Lake School is not the only or the principal one. They love various things. Some love beauty, and some love rum. Some go to Rome, and some go a-fishing, and are sent to the house of correction once a month. . . . I meet these gods of the river and woods with sparkling faces (like Apollo's) late from the house of correction, it may be carrying whatever mystic and forbidden bottles or other vessels concealed, while the dull regular priests are steering their parish rafts in a prose mood. . . . If you read the Rig Veda, oldest of books, as it were, describing a very primitive people and condition of things, you hear in their

prayers of a still older, more primitive and aboriginal race in their midst
and round about, warring on them and seizing their flocks and herds,
infesting their pastures. Thus it is in another sense in all communities,
and hence the prisons and police.

I hear these guns going to-day, and I must confess they are to me
a springlike and exhilarating sound, like the cock-crowing, though each
one may report the death of a musquash. . . .

As a mother loves to see her child imbibe nourishment and expand,
so God loves to see his children thrive on the nourishment he has fur-
nished them. . . . These aboriginal men cannot be repressed, but under
some guise or other they survive and reappear continually. (J, XI:
423–25; 1859.)

This passage—a beautiful example of the myth-making process in
Thoreau—is also one of his most radical celebrations of the Wild.
As the reference to "the Lake School" hints, it goes far beyond a
Wordsworthian, civilized sensitivity to outward Nature ("beauty"),
to acknowledge, and to some degree glorify, the deepest instinctual
and primitive impulses in man's nature. Here Thoreau also recognizes that these impulses can be dangerously chaotic and disruptive
of social order—hence his references to established society ("the
dull regular priests . . . all communities . . . the prisons and police"),
while not sympathetic, are perceptibly less hostile than those in
certain other passages—and yet this recognition gives rise to a
still more basic commitment to wildness. That this is a crucial
passage in Thoreau's canon of the Wild is further attested by the
passage's stylistic and tonal complexities. Some of it seems reasonably calm and considered—for example, the analysis of primitive societies and the admission that he finds the sound of the
guns is "springlike and exhilarating," despite his usual aversion
to hunting. These lines serve mainly as anchors, however, in a
context of impetuous free association, whose style is rhythmically
varied and rich in imagery.

But the actual George Melvin is completely submerged in the
passage just cited. He is more readily discerned in another, written
three years earlier, in which, nevertheless, Thoreau again views
him partly as symbol, as a personification of wildness:

Saw Melvin's lank bluish-white black-spotted hound, and Melvin with
his gun near, going home at eve. He follows hunting, praise be to him,
as regularly in our tame fields as the farmers follow farming. Persistent Genius! . . . I trust the Lord will provide us with another Melvin

when he is gone. How good of him to follow his own bent, and not continue at the Sabbath-school all his days! ... I thank my stars for Melvin. I think of him with gratitude when I am going to sleep, grateful that he exists,—that Melvin who is such a trial to his mother. ... Awkward, gawky, loose-hung, dragging his legs after him. He is my contemporary and neighbor. He is one tribe, I am another, and we are not at war. (*J*, IX: 148; 1856.)

Here too we find a stream-of-consciousness stylistic freedom, and a mounting intensity. There is something else as well—though at first (because this passage celebrates wildness) one may fail to notice it: a hint of *community* feeling threads the passage. One is aware of it in "our tame fields," "I trust the Lord will provide us with another Melvin when he is gone," "He is ... my neighbor."

Since Melvin, like Minott, also provided Thoreau with nature-information and specimens, the *Journal* affords us many more mundane glimpses of him, and one sustained anecdote (abounding in community lore) which surely comes nearer than anything else to capturing the "real," historical George Melvin. At the end of a journal entry for May 30, 1853, Thoreau noted that Melvin had given some pink azalea blossoms to his neighbor George Brooks. The long entry for the next day (*J*, V: 203–8) begins with a reflection on "some incidents in my life [that] have seemed far more allegorical than actual," such as the finding of this "rare and beautiful flower." This seems a clear indication that he had the flower then in hand, and had himself plucked it. Therefore the declaration which follows, that "I am going in search of the *Azalea nudiflora*," alerts us to Thoreau's interest in the drama of the search—finding the specimen was even more interesting than the specimen itself—and his desire to relive the experience in his *Journal*.

This "detective story" begins with Sophia's bringing home a blossom of pink azalea from Mrs. Brooks's—the rare *Azalea nudiflora!* Thoreau betakes himself to Mrs. Brooks, to learn that she had gotten it from her son George. Thoreau goes at once to George's office on the Mill Dam. Here the passage includes a little village vignette: Brooks and a few other cronies had been sitting around in "Mr. Gourgas's office ... Saturday evening," when Melvin had brought in an armful of azalea and given each one a sprig—but Brooks "doesn't know where he got it." Thoreau departs. There is a slight diversion: somebody tells him that Captain Jarvis has a sprig, and Thoreau goes to Jarvis; he had received his from Melvin too, but did not learn the source. Next "a young man working at Stedman Buttrick's" tells Thoreau that its source is "a secret." There is "only one bush in the town" (i.e., in the entire township of Concord), and only Stedman Buttrick and Melvin know its location. The young man guesses at it; Thoreau is doubtful. And so he sets out to find Melvin.

The element of suspense already present in the story is now deliberately cultivated—will Melvin be found, "so early in the afternoon," at his house some distance from the village? Yes, Thoreau sees first the spotted hound-dog that never strays from its master. Melvin, tracked into his lair, is found to have been drinking; he tells a confused story of some fish caught that morning. Asked about the flower, he stalls for time, struggles to his feet, and shouts over to his neighbor, "Razor" Farmer, "to know if he could tell me where that flower grew." But Thoreau is not to be put off; "This was to prolong the time and make the most of his secret.... I saw that I should get it out of him." And now he recalls having met Melvin "some weeks before" on the riverbank near the place suggested by Buttrick's young employee, where they had some talk of flowers.... "Well, I told him he had better tell me where it was; I was a botanist and ought to know.... I told him he'd better tell me and have the glory of it, for I should surely find it if he didn't; I'd got a clue to it, and shouldn't give it up. ... I could smell it a good way, you know. He thought I could smell it half a mile, and he wondered that I hadn't stumbled on it...." Now Melvin, sobering and chuckling, tells Thoreau that he had met Channing, one recent day, wandering near the bush—and *he* hadn't found it.

By this time "Razor" Farmer has strolled over to the wall for a chat. The talk turns to a remarkable spring of water on his property. And now Thoreau, confident of victory or shrewdly biding his time, is willing to be leisurely. They all go to see Razor Farmer's spring, about which various opinions are aired. And then, only then, "we went ...—Melvin and I and his dog,—and crossed the river in his boat, and he conducted me to where the *Azalea nudiflora* grew ...—and showed me how near Channing came. ('You won't tell him what I said; will you?' said he.)" Thoreau offers to pay Melvin for his trouble, but "he wouldn't take anything. He had just as lief I'd know as not."

Even then, the goal achieved, Thoreau was apparently reluctant to end his narrative, or to drop the characterization of Melvin that he had so deftly, though casually, been constructing. Their return along the riverbank, at the saga's end, is detailed in a leisurely way; Melvin shows Thoreau some interesting driftwood. And still others of his opinions and habits are recorded: "Melvin says the gray squirrel nests are made of leaves, the red squirrel of pine stuff. Jarvis tells me that Stedman Buttrick once hired Melvin to work for him on condition that he should not take his gun into the field, but he had known him to do so when Buttrick was away and earn two or three dollars with his game beside his day's work, but of course the last was neglected" (*J*, V: 203–8; May 31, 1853). Even this does not seem extraneous, since the personae all figured in the azalea search, and since Melvin (we are now able to judge) appears so much "in character." The six-page entry has both subject focus and narrative shape; one remembers it as a unified whole.

3

At least once in *Walden*, and more than once in the *Journal*, Thoreau expressed disdain for the popular fiction of his day. Yet some readers have felt that he could have become a novelist.[22] Aside from the azalea story, a number of other passages reveal this kind of talent—such passages as the Monadnock narrative, the story of Channing and the "lurker," the character studies of Rice and Minott, and the brief anecdotes involving Mary Emerson, Uncle Charles, and "the aunts." These entries exhibit an ease in handling dialogue, a perception of details which reveal character, and an economical narrative skill which any aspiring writer of fiction might envy. But Thoreau himself was entirely convinced that *facts* ("Never underestimate the power of a fact. . . .") were infinitely more interesting than any fiction. And the journals are rich in miniature stories, as well as character sketches, drawn from the human life that went on around him.

One of these, a terse two-thirds of a page in length, relates a slapstick series of neighborhood mishaps which occurred in March—mudtime—of 1856. It seems that Mrs. Brooks's hired girl fell down the cellar stairs, and as she lay there, "apparently lifeless," Mrs. Brooks called out the front door for help. A passing lady, hurrying across the street to summon the blacksmith, "fell flat in a puddle of melted snow, and came back to Mrs. Brooks's, bruised and dripping." George Bigelow, next appealed to, "ran nimbly about . . . and fell flat in another puddle," but somehow "raised the blacksmith." Another passerby, James Burke, "rushing in to render aid, fell off one side of the cellar stairs in the dark," after which "the girl . . . came to and went raving, then had a fit." Thoreau's poker-faced comment was, "Haste makes waste. It never rains but it pours. I have this from those who have heard Mrs. Brooks's story, seen the girl, the stairs, and the puddles." This *jeu d'esprit* is even blessed with a punning title: "What Befell at Mrs. Brooks's" (*J*, VIII: 212; 1856).

The account of another village comedy occupies six pages (*J*, VIII: 451–57; 1856), this time with Thoreau himself as protagonist. He was setting out for a summer afternoon on the river, he begins, only to find that his father's pig had just escaped. Even in the first complaining paragraph he warmed to the humor of the situation—and cavalierly threw in a quotation from Emerson! "I felt chagrined . . . but I could not ignore the fact nor shirk the duty that lay so near. . . . Do the duty that lies nearest to thee. . . . Father looked at me, and I ceased to look at the river." Soon the story takes on a mock-heroic quality which is casually sustained throughout. Thoreau finds the pig's tracks, but

Of what avail to know where he has been, even where he is? . . . he cannot be tempted by a swill-pail. . . . At most, probably we shall only have the satisfaction of glimpsing the nimble beast at a distance, from time to time, as he trots swiftly through the green meadows and corn-fields. But, now I speak, what is that I see pacing deliberately up the middle of the street forty rods off? It is *he*. As if to tantalize, to tempt us to waste our afternoon without further hesitation, he thus offers himself. . . . He hears me coming afar off, he foresees danger, and, with swinish cunning and speed, he scampers out. . . . We lose him; we beat the bushes in vain; he may be far away. But hark! I hear a grunt. Nevertheless for half an hour I do not see him who grunted.

The mock-heroic narrative is accompanied by mock-philosophical reflections, which include a glancing reference to "Lycidas." Having remarked that the pig "invariably turned his piggish head toward me, dodged from side to side, and finally ran up the narrow street or down the main one," Thoreau added: "But really he is no more obstinate than I. I cannot but respect his tactics and his independence. He will be he, and I may be I. He is not unreasonable because he thwarts me, but only the more reasonable. He has a strong will. He stands upon his idea. . . . Once more he glides down the narrow street, . . . and disappears through an open-work fence eastward. He has gone to fresh gardens and pastures new."

Except for the pig and Thoreau, there are no sharply defined character sketches here. But there are many glimpses of other villagers, and the story conveys a sustained impression of that important but seldom-remarked-upon phenomenon which can be called Thoreau's "sense of community." At one point, "my neighbor in the street tries to head [the pig]; he jumps to this side the road, then to that, before him; but the third time the pig was there first and went by. 'Whose is it?' he shouts. 'It's ours.' " A reader thoroughly familiar with the *Journal* will not wonder at the neighbor's question; for, despite his satirical darts at the idea of "usefulness" and philanthropy, it would have been not at all surprising for Henry Thoreau to spend his summer afternoon trying to catch someone else's lost pig. Now the pig has darted into another yard: ". . . see what work he has made in his flower-garden! He must be fond of bulbs. Our neighbor picks up one tall flower with its bulb attached, holds it out at arm's length. He is excited about the pig; it is a subject he is interested in."

Community feeling continues to pervade the narrative: "Each neighbor whose garden I traverse tells me some anecdote of losing pigs, or the attempt to drive them, by which I am not encouraged. . . . Other neighbors stand in the doorways but half sympathizing, only observing, 'Ugly thing to catch.' 'You have a job on your hands.' . . . One suggests a dog to track him. Father is meanwhile selling him to the blacksmith, who also is trying to get sight of him."

At last, Thoreau writes,

I see a carriage-manufactory door open. "Let him go in there. . . . For once the pig and I are of one mind; he bolts in, and the door is closed. Now for a rope. . . . He is resting quietly on his belly in the further corner, thinking unutterable things.

Now the course recommences within narrower limits. Bump, bump, bump he goes, against wheels and shafts. We get no hold yet. He is all ear and eye. Small boys are sent under the carriages to drive him out. He froths at the mouth and deters them. At length he is stuck for an instant between the spokes of a wheel, and I am securely attached to his hind leg.

After further comic maneuvering, some of it in a sudden thunder-shower, the pig was finally restored to its pen. And, "so," Thoreau grumbled, "I get home at dark, wet through and supperless, covered with mud and wheel-grease, without any rare flowers." Surely the force of that complaint is undercut by both the length and the zestful humor of this entry. And before ending the entry, he wrote one more paragraph, which might bear some relation to that sense of community which the pig episode had awakened: "To the eyes of men there is something tragic in death. We hear of the death of any member of the human family with something more than regret,—not without a slight shudder and feeling of commiseration. The churchyard is a *grave* place" (*J*, VIII: 451–57; 1856).

No one can claim to know Thoreau without having reflected on such passages as these. As comedies, "What Befell at Mrs. Brooks's" and the pig story are unsurpassed—for narrative drive, unity, and sheer drollery—by anything else in the journals, but they are by no means unique. Two other examples that come to mind are the *Journal* description of a drunken Dutch sailor Thoreau encountered on Long Island, and the long passage in *Cape Cod* dealing with Thoreau's Wellfleet host. The latter is familiar enough to require only a reference here, with the reminder that it too is loosely narrative in form, and involves sustained sequences of dialogue, that it achieves a memorable, rounded portrait of the loquacious old oysterman, and is liberally laced with comedy.[23] Note also that much of this comedy is made at Thoreau's own expense, as is the case in the pig story.

The character of the drunken Dutchman appears twice in the *Journal*. Its editors regarded these two passages as "an example of Thoreau's practise work," and of course the second passage may in part have had that function. But, as I have remarked before, Thoreau's having taken up a subject a second time (after an interval, in this case, of two months) can also suggest his emotional preoccupation with that subject. After reading on pages 49 and 50 (*J*, II; 1850) that the Dutchman's wit "reminded me of Shakespeare," and he was "one of the few remarkable men whom I have met," we should not be surprised to find him introduced again on page 78, nor so quick to infer that both passages constitute merely a literary exercise. The fascination exerted upon Thoreau by this Dutch sailor was akin to that he had felt when contemplating the woodchopper Therien, Bill Wheeler, and *Wal-*

den's Hugh Quoil. On the one hand, it was the fascination of a character of extreme simplicity, possessed of a native wit, and totally at *ease* in the world (as was Therien); it was also a fascination with an extreme of debauchery—drunkenness carried to the point of "illumination," of "divinity," as another *Journal* entry suggested of Bill Wheeler.

We know that Thoreau usually deplored drunkenness, or even a moderate use of alcohol, that he advocated abstinence and simplicity of diet in an almost mystical way, believing, as did Emily Dickinson—"inebriate of air"—that one could be more truly intoxicated by the marvels of nature and of day-to-day experience.* But it is important to recognize that he did not deplore "intoxication" itself. Indeed, a kind of intoxication—euphoria, ecstasy—was valued by Thoreau above all things.** And so, the states of advanced alcoholism could interest him, even arouse a kind of sympathy. Moreover, the *Journal* contains at least three instances of his having been fascinated by other "intoxicating" experiences. Undergoing dental surgery in 1851, he was given ether. "The value of the experiment," he wrote afterward, "is that it does give you experience of an interval as between one life and another,— a greater space than you ever travelled. You are a sane mind without organs,—groping for organs,—which if it did not soon recover its old senses would get new ones. You expand like a seed in the ground. You exist in your roots, like a tree in the winter.† If you have an inclination to travel, take the ether; you go beyond the furthest star." The terms of the description resemble those often employed to describe a drug-induced "trip." The measure of Thoreau's fascination with the experience may perhaps be gauged by his quick recoil from it, in the next sober paragraph: "It is not necessary for them to take ether, who in their sane and waking hours are ever translated by a thought; . . . nor listen to

---

* See *Walden*, Chapter 11, "Higher Laws," and especially p. 217.

** "Oh if I could be intoxicated on air and water! on hope and memory! and always see the maples standing red in the midst of the waters on the meadow!" (J, II: 72; 1850). Sometimes this thought was linked to his misanthropic impulses: his response to a wood thrush's song, in 1853, was a wish to be "drunk, drunk, drunk,—dead drunk to this world with it forever" (J, VI: 39).

† Note the similarity (both of content, and of cadence) between these two short sentences and Thoreau's reflections upon his similarly "mystical" reveries beside the pond in *Walden*: "I grew in those seasons like corn in the night" ("I realized what the Orientals mean by contemplation.") (pp. 111–12.)

the spiritual knockings, who attend to the intimations of reason and conscience" (*J*, II: 194; 1851). This is clearly self-admonition; yet the fascination remained, to be echoed five years later: "When I took the ether my consciousness amounted to this: I put my finger on myself in order to keep the place, otherwise I should never have returned to this world" (*J*, VIII: 142; 1856). Note that, in both passages, the experience was described as a balancing not between life and death, but between one "world," or one life, and another; that is, it was felt, however fleetingly, as a *mystical* experience (as were the experiences reported by Aldous Huxley and others after experimenting with psychedelic drugs). The date of Thoreau's dental surgery was not specified; the first passage (dated May 12, 1851) simply says "the other day." It seems probable, therefore, that a *Journal* passage of May 6, which deals with his reading in Hindu literature, had some bearing on his response to "taking the ether":

The Harivansa describes a "substance called *Poroucha*, a spiritual substance known also under the name of Mahat, spirit united to the five elements, soul of being, now enclosing itself in a body like ours, now returning to the eternal body; it is mysterious wisdom, the perpetual sacrifice made by the virtue of the *Yoga*. . . .

"The Mouni who desires his final emancipation will have care evening and morning to subdue his senses, to fix his mind on the divine essence, and to transport himself by the force of his soul to the eternal abode of Vichnou." (*J*, II: 190–91; 1851.)

The interest evidenced here was in a true mystical experience, in which the lonely spirit transcends the distractions of this world in order to commune with a Universal Spirit. At another point, however, Thoreau's response to his reading about the Orient was of a different character. Again, a kind of intoxication is described, but the emphasis this time is on a perfection of life *in this* world, upon sociability and communication with others:

Arabia, Persia, Hindostan. . . . Those Eastern nations have perfected the luxury of idleness. Mount Sabér, according to the French traveller and naturalist Botta, is celebrated for producing the Kát tree. "The soft tops of the twigs and tender leaves are eaten, . . . and produce an agreeable soothing excitement, restoring from fatigue, banishing sleep, and disposing to the enjoyment of conversation." What could be more dignified than to browse the tree-tops with the camelopard? . . . It is not hard to discover an instinct for the opium and betel and tobacco chewers. (*J*, I: 343, 1842.)

Such passages as these suggest facets of Thoreau's temperament that have not often been discussed,* nor even widely recognized. Certainly they help us to a fuller understanding of the fascination and the degree of sympathy which he was able to feel in the company of the Dutch sailor. Actually his tone in that passage is complex, and his attitude ambivalent. At first he registered a predictably censorious reaction to the drunkenness of the sailor and his companion: "I was less disgusted by their filthiness and vulgarity, because I was compelled to look on them as animals, as swine in their sty. For the whole voyage they lay flat on their backs on the bottom of the boat, in the bilge-water and wet with each bailing, half insensible, and wallowing in their vomit." But gradually the fascination took over, along with a measure of tolerance: "But ever and anon, when aroused by the rude kicks or curses of the skipper, the Dutchman, who never lost his wit nor equanimity, though snoring and rolling in the vomit produced by his debauch, blurted forth some happy repartee like an illuminated swine. It was the earthiest, slimiest wit I ever heard." The boat had been aground, awaiting the tide at Patchogue. At one point, when Thoreau was removing his shoes in order to wade to it, the Dutchman insisted on carrying him out piggyback. When they were finally afloat, late at night, and

groping up the narrow creek ... the two inebriates roused themselves betimes.... And the Dutchman gave wise directions to the steerer, which were not heeded.... At last he suddenly stepped on to another boat which was moored to the shore, with a divine ease and sureness, saying, "Well, good-night, take care of yourselves, I can't be with you any longer." He was one of the few remarkable men whom I have met. I have been impressed by one or two men in their cups. There was really a divinity stirred within them, so that in their case I have reverenced the drunken, as savages the insane, man. (*J*, II: 49–50; 1850.)

Here the phenomenon of drunkenness is apparently the chief source of interest. The Dutchman is called "stupid" twice in this

---

* William Braden touched upon Thoreau's mystical bent, along with his knowledge of Oriental literature, in *The Private Sea: LSD and the Search for God* ([Chicago: Quadrangle Press, 1967], pp. 92–95), although he did not cite any of these instances of Thoreau's own fleeting interest in drug- and alcohol-intoxication.

passage—"an indescribably mynheerish stupidity," and even "so stupid that he could never be intoxicated." Despite this, and the fact that he is elsewhere credited with real, native "wits," the implication is that his "extra dram" conferred additional wit upon him, and also that, freeing him from ordinary restraints and vacillations, it gave him something of a god-like poise and spontaneity.

But Thoreau was also impressed by his face (which is described more vividly in the second passage, as having eyes of "a singular bullfrog or trilobite expression . . . in the broad platter of his cheeks" [J, II: 79]), and by his "Dutchness." "The countenance was one of a million. It was unmistakable Dutch. In the midst of a million faces of other races it could not be mistaken. It told of Amsterdam" (J, II: 49–50). And, because this wandering Dutchman was strong, friendly, and impressively knowledgeable about the sea, Thoreau was led to sympathize even more directly: "I kept racking my brains to conceive how he could have been born in America, how lonely he must feel, what he did for fellowship" (J, II: 50). A sense of "fellowship" in fact, pervades this passage, in spite of the revulsion intermittently felt by Thoreau— the fellowship of shared effort in pushing off the boat, and of shared suspense as it "groped" its way along in the dark, as well as the fellowship engendered by the Dutchman's witty sallies and his benevolent goodnight.

Thoreau's writings offer many more examples of non-narrative character sketches. Some of them are of people he knew well (like Concord's old Cyrus Hubbard), some of people he briefly met (such as a Captain Hewit of Plymouth). Still others are of people only fleetingly observed, yet vividly, shrewdly captured in a look, word, or gesture—people as diverse as the locker-keeper in the *Week*, the old Irishwoman at the shanty near Walden woods, and an intelligent runaway slave.[24]

Of course, Thoreau's attitude in these sketches is often ambivalent, as in the case of the Dutch sailor. He saw Cyrus Hubbard, "the old pale-faced farmer out again on his sled now for the five-thousandth time," and at first felt him to be "a man of a certain New England probity and worth . . . like a natural product, like the sweetness of a nut, like the toughness of hickory." But then a shift occurred: his speech is said to be "clean, cold, moderate as the snow," and his impression is, after all, a "faint" one. (J, IX: 144–45; 1856). The shift operates in reverse—i.e., from an adverse to a more appreciative appraisal—in the case of Captain

Hewit, "a fair specimen of a retired Yankee sea-captain," a type "not so remarkable for anything as the quality of hardness," which is evident in the "rigidity of their jaws and necks." Yet, after analyzing this physical and mental rigidity at length—although Hewit is so old and infirm that his hand trembles, he is still "hopelessly hard"—Thoreau continues: "But there is another view of him. He is somebody. He has an opinion to express, if you will wait to hear him. A certain manliness and refreshing resistance is in him" (J, II: 361–62).*

Such passages are typical of many others in their ambivalence, in their tonal shifts—now warm, now cool—within a single paragraph. Their striking quality, aside from that ambivalence, and the interest in human personality that they reveal, is the fullness and clarity of the portraiture, achieved by the combining of only a few details.

4

There was one class of human beings about whom (except in its urban manifestations!) Thoreau was never critical, never ambivalent. For all children he felt the liveliest sympathy. This attitude was of course consistent with his glorification of Nature, and the associated denigration of institutions and of society generally. Indeed, the idea that children are "unfallen men," that they epitomize innocence and spontaneity, was a central assumption of Transcendentalism, as it was of Wordsworthian Romanticism.** But Thoreau's response to children was clearly as much personal as theoretical. They invariably aroused both his interest and his tenderness. Readers of *Walden* will recall his remark that children

---

* Sensing a measure of real empathy here, one remembers a detail from Emerson's "Biographical Sketch" of Thoreau: "There was somewhat military in his nature, not to be subdued, always manly and able, but rarely tender, as if he did not feel himself except in opposition. . . . It cost him nothing to say No" (Intro. in Thoreau, *Week*, pp. xii–xiii).

** Thoreau quoted Wordsworth, and especially the Immortality Ode, on many occasions. Another aspect of his own reverence for children has to do with the nostalgia he felt for the mystical-ecstatic experiences of his own youth. Both the experiences and the nostalgia seem to have paralleled Wordsworth's rather closely. "In youth, before I lost any of my senses, I can remember that I was all alive. . . . This earth was the most glorious musical instrument, and I was audience to its strains. To have such sweet impressions made on us, such ecstasies begotten of breezes!" (J, II: 306–7; 1851).

were always less surprised by, and more sympathetic to, the idea of his solitary retreat than were adults—because "children, who play life, discern its true law and relations more clearly than men. . . ." [25] And the *Journal* contains many meditations on the innocence and freshness of children, the acuteness of their senses, the accuracy of their observations, and their sympathy for animal life and all Nature. [26]

In these *Journal* passages we are once again impressed by Thoreau's own accuracy of observation, and his capacity for enjoyment—when we read, for example, his notes on the delight of all children in noise, pure *sound*, including cacophonies deeply offensive to their elders (*J*, IV: 85; 1852). This former schoolmaster always viewed with pleasure a party of truants stealing off to go swimming or berry-picking in the late spring.* He remarked on the pleasure of farm boys, driving the cattle to hill pastures in May, and their delighted reunion with the calves and yearlings in the fall. (" ' She knows me, father; she knows me.' ") A paragraph on "evening sounds" includes "some children calling their kitten home by some endearing name"; and another *Journal* entry characterizes the life of a particular cat ("sweet Sylvia") as an enviable one—comprising both "wildness . . . and domestic affection," the joy of adventuring in the woods and then of being "caressed by children and cherished with a saucer of milk." [27] A reference to "our first snow," one November, concludes, "The children greet it with a shout when they come out at recess." And a December thaw brings out "the boys in the streets playing with the sluices," and "the boys . . . under the hill to pitch coppers." [28]

---

* In a *Journal* entry of August, 1853, Thoreau remarked matter-of-factly that. on a berry-picking party, "a boy" had spilled his berries, and "I saw that Nature was making use of him to disperse her berries." But the *Journal's* editors were able to provide a gloss on this incident which offers a striking illustration of Thoreau's way with children: "I recall [wrote another member of the berrying party] . . . when little Edward Emerson, carrying a basket of fine huckleberries, had a fall and spilt them all. Great was his distress, and our offers of berries could not console him. . . . But Thoreau came, put his arm around the troubled child, and explained to him that if the crop of huckleberries was to continue it was necessary that some should be scattered. Nature had provided that little boys should now and then stumble and sow the berries. We shall have a grand lot of bushes and berries in this spot, and we shall owe them to you. Edward began to smile." (*J*, V: 358–359). The anecdote is quoted from Moncure Daniel Conway, *Autobiography* V. 1, p. 148 (Boston; 1904.) See page 61 above for references to Thoreau's affection for Edward Emerson's sisters Edith and Ellen.

I have remarked on the admirable absence of sentimentality in the anecdotes about George Minott in his last illness. Perhaps the nearest Thoreau ever came to this literary pitfall was in a *Journal* passage and a poem that deal with a specific Concord child, Johnny Riordan, the son of an immigrant Irish laborer. Yet even here Thoreau cannot be charged with sentimentalizing. For the feeling expressed is clearly genuine; the problem is rather that it was so painful a feeling as to be difficult for him to deal with artistically, with the result that these passages seem at times a little overwrought, in somewhat the same way as did the passage on "my dewy sister." Nevertheless, we sense Thoreau's resolute struggle to deal with it:

They showed me Johnny Riordan to-day, with one thickness of ragged cloth over his little shirt for all this cold weather, with shoes with large holes in the toes, into which the snow got, as he said, without an outer garment, to walk a mile to school every day over the bleakest of causeways,—the clothes with countless patches, which hailed from, claimed descent from, were originally identical with, pantaloons of mine, which set as if his mother had fitted them to a tea-kettle first. This little mass of humanity, this tender gobbet for the fates, cast into a cold world with a torn lichen leaf wrapped about him,—Oh, I should rather hear that America's first-born were all slain than that his little fingers and toes should feel cold while I am warm. . . . Let the mature rich wear the rags and insufficient clothing; let the infant poor wear the purple and fine linen. . . . Our charitable institutions are an insult to humanity. A charity which dispenses the crumbs that fall from its overloaded tables, which are left over after its feasts! (J, III: 242; 1852.)

Another long passage on this child, found among some loose manuscript sheets, was included by the *Journal* editors in a footnote to this one. It begins in almost identical fashion—"They showed me little Johnny Riordan the other day,"—and incorporates a few other phrases found in the 1852 passage along with earlier material and a draft of a poem. Here too Thoreau revealed his distress at the thought that part of the child's scant apparel was made from his own castoff trousers: "clothes, with countless patches, which had for vehicle—O shame! shame!—pantaloons that had been mine" (J, III: 242–43). And here too is evidence that when Thoreau worked over experiences and ideas in two or more versions he was not merely "practising." To me it looks more like a wrestling with thoughts which evoked painful emotions, an effort to subdue these emotions to manageable proportions, and to obtain relief. That he may have entertained the idea of "using" some of this material in a lecture or essay is also quite possible, particularly in view of his assaults on the complacency of the rich and the inadequacy of their (—but no, he says "our") charities.

Despite the implication of the repeated introductory, "They showed me Johnny Riordan," it is fairly certain that Thoreau had noticed this child at least two years earlier, for a version of the Johnny Riordan poem was written into a journal entry in November, 1850:

I am the little Irish boy
That lives in the shanty.
I am four years old to-day
And shall soon be one and twenty.

I shall grow up / And be a great man,
And shovel all day / As hard as I can.

. . . . .

For supper
I have some potato / And sometimes some bread,
And then, if it's cold, / I go right to bed.

. . . . .

Every day I go to school / Along the railroad.
It was so cold it made me cry / The day that it snowed.

And if my feet ache / I do not mind the cold,
For I am a little Irish boy, / And I'm four years old.

The apparent contradiction in the last two stanzas is rendered more understandable by the 1850 context of this poem, which shows Thoreau to have been struggling against, or trying to rationalize, the same compassionate distress that became so explicit in 1852: "The thought of its greater independence and its closeness to nature diminishes the pain I feel when I see a more interesting child than usual destined to be brought up in a shanty. . . . Have I not faith that its tenderness will in some way be cherished and protected. . . ?" (J, II: 116–18; 1850). In 1851 he composed a kind of apotheosis for Johnny, some of which also appears in the version of the unbound sheets:

I have seen, in the form, in the expression of face, of a child three [sic] years old, the tried magnanimity and grave nobility of ancient and departed worthies. Just saw a little Irish boy, come from the distant shanty in the woods over the bleak railroad to school this morning, take his last step from his last snow-drift on to the schoolhouse door-step, floundering still; ... Has not the world waited for such a generation? ... Little Johnny Riordan, who faces cold and routs it like a Persian army. ... While the charitable waddle about cased in furs, he, lively as a cricket, passes them on his way to school. (*J*, III: 149–50; 1851.)

But the efforts to rationalize his distress, and to "mythologize" the child, did not suffice; characteristically, Thoreau determined to *do* something ("What is my softness *good for*?"). A month after the pitying and angry outburst of 1852, he recorded that he had "carried a new cloak to Johnny Riordan. I found that the shanty was warmed by the simple social relations of the Irish. On Sunday they come from the town and stand in the doorway and so keep out the cold. One is not cold among his brothers and sisters. ... It is musical news to hear that Johnny does not love to be kept at home from school in deep snows" (*J*, III: 289; 1852).

Five

Communitas

THE phrase "They showed me little Johnny Riordan" indicates that other Concordians had noticed the boy and commended him to Thoreau's attention. And the fact that he recorded this phrase twice, together with his approval of "the simple social relations of the Irish," reveals again that quality so strikingly evident in the pig story—Thoreau's sense of community. It is present even in his indictment of token charities, since the indictment included Thoreau himself as a target—"*our* charitable institutions."

Despite his lifelong prejudice against cities, this sense of community is often apparent in the *Journal*, and was clearly a sustaining element in Thoreau's life, on both the personal and the intellectual-artistic levels. Indeed, such a feeling was not at all inconsistent with his anti-urban pronouncements. Sherman Paul refers to Thoreau's "hatred" of the city, but this is by way of emphasizing his basic human sympathies: Paul argues that what most distressed him was the city's "lamentable depersonalization." [1] Similarly, it was an image of Concord village as a convention-ridden center of church-going, dinner-"exchanging," gossip-mongering, and financial speculation that repelled Thoreau. It is essentially this image which prevails in *Walden's* chapter 8, "The Village," where the main emphases are on the incident of Thoreau's being jailed ("Wherever a man goes men will pursue and paw him with their dirty institutions. . . ."), and on the phenomenon of gossip, "which is incessantly going on there, circulating either from mouth to mouth, or from newspaper to newspaper. . . ." [2]

But Thoreau was attracted and comforted by another image of the village—that of a true *community*, small enough to be fully comprehended, made up of self-reliant, idiosyncratic individuals, whose self-reliance would be nurtured by familiar association and mutual respect. His feeling for such a community issued in such activities as his service to the Lyceum, his lectures, his showing botanical and geological specimens, and his procuring a Christmas tree for the town hall. It issued in such writings as the passage in *Walden* urging a cultural renaissance and adult education,* in "Civil Disobedience" and "Life Without Principle"—in short, in all his efforts to educate and to persuade the people within his own small sphere, and, beyond that, those who would read the sentences he fashioned. It issued, also, in those sometimes passionate declarations of faith in the human race which occur throughout the *Journal*, and which we shall examine in a later chapter. Underlying all of these efforts and utterances was Thoreau's appreciative awareness of a community esprit—an awareness arising from a network of village relationships, and revealed in innumerable offhand remarks in the journals.

The Melvin-azalea story, which is pervaded by the village ambiance, also illustrates the operation of a specialized subcommunity created by Thoreau's presence in Concord—a community of nature-students. "This is my year of observation," he had written in 1852, "and I fancy that my friends are also more devoted to outward observation, as if it were an epidemic" (*J*, IV; 174). The *Journal* shows that by 1853, when the azalea search occurred, a large cross-section of Concord's citizens had been enlisted in the service of Thoreau's wide-ranging researches. In this service George Minott and Channing loomed especially large and Emerson had long played an honorable part, but the journals of the late fifties show that the company of observers and reporters was constantly being augmented.

These were the years during which Thoreau became increasingly occupied with detailed nature study, impelled by a vision of some grand, unifying work in which "fact" should indisputably "flower into truth." The journal volumes that reflect this growing preoccupation—in page after page of zoological, botanical, geological and meteorological notations, accompanied by classification

---

* "It is time that villages were universities.... To act collectively is according to the spirit of our institutions.... New England can hire all the wise men in the world to come and teach her ... and not be provincial at all" (pp. 108–10).

lists and diagrams—have discouraged many a reader; and even some serious students of Thoreau have implied that these are volumes largely given over to field notes. But this is far from true, as *Journal* references from the latter fifties in this study have already shown. And the passages of natural-history notes themselves are often given a community coloring, a human interest, by Thoreau's habit of recording the names of his informants. Only rarely did he write, "Someone told me," or "I heard. . . ." Almost always the report is specifically credited: "RWE told me," "Channing saw," "Minott heard," "Rice says," "Bigelow showed me"; "Miss Caroline Pratt saw the white bobolink yesterday where Channing saw it the day before, in the midst of a large flock" (*J*, X: 111; 1858). Often references to the observations of others occur in dense clusters: a bird just sighted is identified as "George Minott's 'huckleberry bird' "; this is followed by "Old Mr. Francis Wheeler's" valued opinion on the current April flood—he thought it must be a record one, and "Noah Wheeler never saw it so high as lately"; then, "F. Wheeler, Jr., saw dandelions in bloom the 20th of April; Garfield's folks use them as greens" (*J*, III: 481; 1852). Some of the observations are second- or third-hand: "Minott said that Abel Heywood told him he had been down to the Great Meadows . . . to look at the grass, and that there wasn't agoing to be much of a crop" (*J*, IV: 202). Minott's rendering of "Old Sam Nutting's" story of a bear and a moose is recounted in detail (*J*, V: 16); and "Mrs. Ripley told me this afternoon that Russell had decided that that green . . . dust on the under side of stones in walls was a decaying state of *Lepraria chlorina*, a lichen. . . ." Here Thoreau paused to reflect upon the usefulness of his fellow observers: "Science suggests the value of mutual intelligence. I have long known this dust, but as I did not know the name of it, i.e., what others called [it], and therefore could not conveniently speak of it, it has suggested less to me and I have made less use of it. I now first feel that I had got hold of it" (*J*, IV: 467).

It is obvious that Abel Heywood's verdict on the meadow grass is transcribed at least partly for the flavor of his speech. This blending of a sober scientific interest with appreciation (like a novelist's) of human idiosyncrasy is beautifully illustrated in the *Journal* account of a blacksnake laying her eggs, originally related to Thoreau by Jacob Farmer, an "authority" he cited frequently. "He found the snake lying with her head and tail both at once in the hole" (a diagram illustrates the slant of the hole); there were fourteen eggs in all, "not connected . . . soft shelled" (another diagram), and the hole "bore a general resemblance to a turtle's hole." Now comes a sudden shift in focus, and probably the most laconic of all Thoreau's renderings of Concord folklore: "Was close by where his uncle (?) tried to dig through to the other side of the world. Dug more or less for three years. Used to dig nights, as long as one candle lasted. Left a stone just between him and the other side, not to be removed till he was ready to marry Washington's sister. The foxes now occupy his hole" (*J*, XIII: 375–76). The telegraphic style suggests that Thoreau may have had to bear with Farmer's rehashing of an old and well-known story; nevertheless it found a place in the capacious *Journal*—in its next-to-last volume, of 1860.

Often neighbors came to Thoreau with questions, some of which had a practical motive, while others suggested a purely scientific curiosity. For example, "Mr. Pratt asked me to what animal a spine and broken skull found in the wall of James Adams's shop belonged." Skull measurements and a tooth identification led Thoreau to suspect it was a muskrat, "which probably got into the building at a time of high water," but Pratt was skeptical. A microscope examination assured Thoreau: "I told Pratt it was a muskrat and gave him my proofs; but he could not distinguish the three molars even with a glass, . . . for he had thought them one tooth, when, taking out his pincers, he pulled one out and was convinced, much to his and to my satisfaction and our confidence in science!" (*J*, V: 325–26; 1853).

Thoreau's local reputation as an encyclopedia of natural facts is attested to in another late *Journal* entry: "When I came downstairs this morning, it raining hard and steadily, I found an Irishman sitting with his coat on his arm in the kitchen, waiting to see me. He wanted to inquire what I thought the weather would be today!" (*J*, XI: 94; 1858).

The well-known 1853 passage on the giant parasol fungus, fascinating for many other reasons, shows Thoreau playing a community role. He had found and brought home a huge white mushroom shortly after dawn—holding it carefully erect while paddling his boat with one hand! He then sat down and wrote a two-page description of it, for the most part scientific in tone, but expanding in the direction of myth, suggesting the lure of the primitive as well: "Such growths ally our age to former periods such as geology reveals. . . . It suggests a vegetative force which may almost make man tremble for his dominion. It carries me back to the era of the formation of the coal-measures—the age of the saurus and pleiosaurus. . . . It made you think of parasols of Chinese mandarins." By nightfall, though carefully placed in the cool cellar, the fungus had collapsed and "dissolved"—to become for Thoreau a witness of some distinctly unwholesome principle in Nature, indeed an emblem of "evil," both natural and societal.* But in the interval his attitude was still one of interest and his impulse was to share; the toadstool functioned as a vehicle for community contacts:

I have just been out (7:30 A.M.) to show my fungus. The milkman and the butcher followed me to inquire what it was, and children and young ladies addressed me in the street who never spoke to me before. It is so fragile I was obliged to walk at a funereal pace for fear of jarring it. . . . They wish me to send it to the first of a series of exhibitions of flowers and fruits to be held at the court-house this afternoon, which I promise to do if it is presentable then. Perhaps it might be placed in the court-house cellar and the company be invited at last to walk down and examine it.

One cannot help speculating about connections in this long *Journal* entry, between, for example, the early remark that "It suggests a vegetative force which may almost make man tremble for his dominion," and the bitter paragraph three pages later in which the rotting fungus becomes an emblem of human error. Perhaps this bitterness reflects an anxiety Thoreau felt about a possible threat to "man's dominion." At any rate, we learn farther along that although the fungus was not "presentable" by afternoon, and remained in Thoreau's cellar, he did attend the court-house flower show. And the paragraph on the exhibition is concluded thus: "This unexpected display of flowers culled from the gardens of the village suggests how many virtues also are cultivated by the villagers, more than meet the eye" (J, V: 270–76; 1853).

---

* "It defiled all it touched. . . . the mould which is the flower of humid darkness and ignorance. The Pyramids of Egypt are a vast mildew or toadstools which have met with no light of day sufficient to waste them away. Slavery is such a mould, and superstition. . . . The humblest, puniest weed that can endure the sun is thus superior to the largest fungus, as is the peasant's cabin to those foul temples. . . . The priest is the fungus of the graveyard, the mildew of the tomb. In the animal world there are toads and lizards."

2

Just as his growing "scientific" reputation gave him added stature in the eyes of the community, so, no doubt, the participation of many villagers in his nature observations in turn contributed to Thoreau's own fund of community feeling. In 1857 he recorded with amusement how

at the post-office, Abel Brooks, who is pretty deaf, sidling up to me, observed in a loud voice which all could hear, "Let me see, your society is pretty large, ain't it?" "Oh yes, large enough," said I, not knowing what he meant. "There's Stewart belongs to it, and Collier, he's one of them, and Emerson, ... and Channing, I believe he goes there." "You mean the *walkers,* don't you?" "Ye-es, I call you the Society. All go to the woods, don't you?" "Do you miss any of your wood?" I asked. "No, I hain't worried any yet. I believe you're a pretty clever set, as good as the average."

Thoreau added that he had told this anecdote to Frank Sanborn, and there is an unmistakable note of satisfaction in his report of Sanborn's comment: "He said that, when he first came to town and boarded at Holbrook's, he asked H. how many religious societies there were in town. H. said that there were three,—the Unitarian, the Orthodox, and the Walden Pond Society. I asked Sanborn with which Holbrook classed himself. He said he believed that he put himself with the last" (*J,* IX: 331–32).

One facet of Thoreau's community feeling grew out of his overall feeling for Nature—a great, enveloping love for the country which was part of Concord township, for that particular portion of the planet Earth, and all the animal and vegetable life upon it. "I cannot but regard it as a kindness in those who have the steering of me," he wrote in 1853, "that, by the want of pecuniary wealth, I have been nailed down to this my native region so long and steadily, and made to study and love this spot of earth more and more" (*J,* V: 496–97). But another facet was his interest in the town's human history. Some of this he learned from books, more he pieced together from the stories of Hosmer and Minott, and he was familiar with most of the historic buildings in the area. This antiquarian interest was early displayed in *A Week,* of course, but the *Journal* suggests that it deepened as Thoreau grew older. In 1857 he devoted three entries to "the old Lee House," which he first visited in January. When the house burned in February, he went again and again to see the ruins, and especially to examine the faint inscriptions on the chimney, and this experience inspired him to reread Shattuck's *History of Concord* (*J*, IX: 203, 255–59, 261–64). One day later, as if to forestall its possible destruction, he went to look over "the Old Hunt House"; his observations on its dimensions, materials and workmanship are interspersed with the reminiscences of Abel Hunt and E. Hosmer (*J*, IX: 265–66). In 1859, he wrote that "I go to get one more sight of the old house which Hosmer is pulling down. . . ." Both the phrase "one more sight" and the present tense alert us to the feeling involved here. A paragraph of description and of speculation about the age of this house ends, "if this [1703] was the date of the chimney, it would appear that the old part belonged to the Winthrops, and it may go back to near the settlement of the town" (*J*, XII: 36–38).

Often Thoreau's community feeling is perceived in a very small detail—sometimes solely in his use of the first-person plural pronoun. Melvin was praised for following his own wild bent "in our tame fields," as I have pointed out, and Thoreau trusted that "the Lord will provide us with another Melvin when he is gone." Similarly, a meteorological note shades off into a village vignette: "It has been oppressively warm to-day, so that we were prepared for a thunder-storm at evening. . . . heavy, wet-looking clouds are seen in the northern horizon, perhaps over the Merrimack Valley, and we say it is going down the river, and we shall not get a drop. . . . People stand at their doors in the warm evening, listening to the muttering of distant thunder" (*J*, V: 161). And we find the following remark tucked into a wholly unrelated context: "Our new citizen Sam Wheeler has a brave new weathercock all gilt on his new barn" (*J*, V: 95).

The point has been made that Thoreau's feeling for "my native town" included both the populous village and the wilder surrounding countryside within its legal boundaries. In a few instances we find him considering, not only his own relationship to these entities—village and "earth"—but also their relationship to each other:

I should like to ask the assessors what is the value of that blue mountain range in the northwest horizon of Concord, and see if they would laugh or seriously set about calculating it. How poor, comparatively, should we be without it! . . . The privilege of beholding it, as an ornament, a suggestion, a provocation, a heaven on earth. If I were one of the fathers of the town I would not sell this right which we now enjoy for all the merely material wealth and prosperity conceivable. If need were, we would rather all go down together. (*J*, IV: 263–64.)

The word "rather" is ambiguous; did Thoreau mean "we would all prefer not to live without sight of the mountains," or did he mean "If I were one of the town fathers I would decree that all should perish rather than live without sight of the mountains?" In either case, a sense of communal solidarity is expressed. The identification of mountains with the idea of community recurs a week later:

Wachusett from Fair Haven Hill . . . In many moods it is cheering to look across hence to that blue rim of the earth, and be reminded of the invisible towns and communities . . . which lie in the further and deeper hollows between me and those hills. Towns of sturdy uplandish fame, where some of the morning and primeval vigor still lingers, I trust. Ashburnham, Rindge, Jaffrey, etc.,—it is cheering to think that it is with such communities that we survive or perish. . . . The melancholy man who had come forth to commit suicide on this hill might be saved by being thus reminded how many brave and contented lives are lived between him and the horizon. Those hills extend our plot of earth. (*J*, IV: 273–74.)

This passage is not unique in its close association of natural grandeur (especially of "mountain," and of "earth"—both mystical sources of creative power for Thoreau) with a tender regard for the human life around him. Note that in both these passages Thoreau was treating the community as a corporate *institution*—in speaking of the assessors, for instance, of the town's assets (however intangible), and again in the puzzling phrase "that we survive or perish." When he wrote that phrase, in 1852, he may have been conscious of the growing sectional struggle, of oncoming war and the possible dissolution of the American Union, or of questions of economic survival. Whatever the implication, it was "cheering" to think that it is "with such communities that *we* [some few hundreds of individuals who made up the corporate community of Concord] survive or perish."

Another, more cheerful reference to a neighboring township appears in one of those poetic "nocturnes" which occur with regularity (at least one in each summer) in the *Journal:* "I hear the nine o'clock bell ringing in Bedford. . . . Pleasantly sounds the voice of one village to another." We have seen how some of these night wanderings called forth Thoreau's latent misanthropy, a tendency to contrast the tranquil moonlit beauty of Nature with the mundane and disorderly daytime lives of men. In this passage he recorded a temptation to "lie out here on this pinnacle rock all night," observing the changing patterns of the stars. "But, if I should do so," he added, "I should not wonder if the town were raised to hunt me up." One senses no resentment in that thought; there is rather a touch of satisfaction, which echoes his pleasure in the idea of village "voices" calling to each other.* (*J*, II: 381; 1851).

During another of his "nocturnes," an awareness of the specific community to which he belonged led Thoreau's thoughts to the formation of communities in the American wilderness. He paused on a hillside bordering the town to identify various sounds, and enjoy the odor of a burning meadow being readied for the plough: "I love the smell of that burning as a man may love his pipe. It reminds me of a new country offering sites for the hearths of men. It is cheering as the scent of the peat fire of the first settler" (*J*, V: 278; 1853). His sensitivity to sound occasioned another such passage, which ends with a striking metaphor:

I hear now, at five o'clock, from this hill, a farmer's horn calling his hands in from the field to an early tea.... This is one of the most suggestive and pleasing of the country sounds produced by man. I hear a sound which I know to be produced by human breath ... and I see in my mind the hired man and master dropping the implements of their labor in the field and wending their way with a sober satisfaction toward the house.... It is a significant hum in a distant part of the hive. (*J*, V: 212–13.)

These passages offer something of a revelation—that Thoreau, the champion of wildness, who so rejoiced in the few uninhabited tracts still existing in Concord, and who valued the West precisely for its "primeval" quality, could also write so eloquently of "new country offering sites for the hearths of men," and, contemplating a mountain panorama, could find his highest satisfaction in the thought of "the sturdy villages" hidden in the valleys. Many

---

* Both the idea of neighborliness between towns and Thoreau's affection for his own town are suggested in his remark about a fisherman with whom he talked during a surveying stint in Haverhill, that "he called it Little Concord where I lived." (*J*, V: 113; 1853.)

of his readers, while fully aware of his individualistic, primitivistic bent, have been less alert to the riches of human portraiture and community feeling scattered throughout the *Journal* and other works.[3] Striking though the contrasts are, however, they do not add up to a baffling contradiction which scholars must struggle to "resolve." The need for solitude and wildness, and the need for community—these are impulses which coexist, in some measure, in all of us. The extent to which they coexist in Thoreau simply evidences the complexity of his thought and feeling—a complexity which is one source of his stature as a writer.

In a *Journal* entry of 1856, in which Thoreau glanced back over his life in Concord, these seemingly contradictory impulses are held in a kind of equilibrium, in which, amusingly, the fulfillment of his need for solitude and wildness is seen as being to some degree dependent upon the good will of his fellow townspeople:

How I love the simple, reserved countrymen, my neighbors, who mind their own business and let me alone, who never waylaid nor shot at me, to my knowledge, when I crossed their fields, though each one had a gun in his house. For nearly twoscore years I have known, at a distance, these long-suffering men, some of whom I never spoke to, who never spoke to me, and now feel a certain tenderness for them, as if this long probation were but the prelude to an eternal friendship. (*J*, IX: 151.)

Here the scale is somewhat tipped, of course. The first impulsive "love" (conditioned upon his being left alone—not being shot at!) becomes "a certain tenderness," though at least the possible first stage of real friendship.

In another passage Thoreau balanced these contrasting needs explicitly, determined that community must outweigh solitude, and yet saluted the idea of community in a (redundant) wilderness metaphor!

I sometimes think that I may go forth and walk hard and earnestly, and live a more substantial life and get a glorious experience. . . . live more, expend more atmospheres, etc., etc. But then swiftly the thought comes to me, Go not so far out of your way for a truer life; keep strictly onward in that path alone which your genius points out. Do the things which lie nearest to you, but which are difficult to do. Live a purer, a more thoughtful and laborious life, more true to your friends and neighbors, more noble and magnanimous, and that will be better than a wild walk. To live in relations of truth and sincerity with men is to dwell in frontier country. What a wild and unfrequented wilderness that would be! (*J*, III: 184–85.)

This passage was entered in January of that meridian year, 1852, during which (if the biographical consensus is correct) Thoreau was still suffering his gradual alienation from the Emersons. Yet here, again, is an echo of that Emersonian injunction about doing "the duty that lies nearest thee," and the paragraph identifies those "things which lie nearest" with a commitment to community, to sincere human relations, and increased magnanimity. Although these are the things "which are *difficult* to do," they belong to "that path alone which your [i.e., "my"] genius points out." The sentence of self-admonition, beginning "live a . . . more thoughtful life, . . . more true to your friends and neighbors," is quite hopeful in tone. And the hopefulness builds to the assertion (still capable of surprising us) that "that *will be better* [my italics] than a wild walk." On a first reading, the striking final sentences also seem hopeful; but actually they echo the "difficulty" previously asserted. The frontier image suggests that "truth and sincerity" in human relations are rarely achieved, perhaps seldom attempted. And that suggestion is borne out by the adjective "unfrequented" and the conditional "would " in the last sentence: "What a wild and unfrequented wilderness that would be!"

Six

Thoreau's Humanism

Iɴ the preceding chapters I have tried to show that Thoreau's misanthropic statements—numerous and often bitter though they are—are balanced by expressions of interest in and of yearning toward many individual human beings, and by his obviously strong sense of belonging to a community. At a more abstract level, there are passages of his writing which exhibit a philosophical humanism[1] quite as wholehearted as the misanthropy found elsewhere—passages which voice an admiration and reverence for mankind unsurpassed anywhere else in literature.

Of these, the *Journal* is again the richest repository. The same early notebooks which contain those biting comparisons of men to ants, cattle, and pigs in a litter, also contain glowing reflections upon human dignity, courage, and resourcefulness. "In their unconscious daily life all are braver than they know," a typical one begins; "Man slumbers and wakes in his twilight with the confidence of noonday; he is not palsied nor struck dumb by the inexplicable riddle of the universe" (*J*, I: 97–98; 1839). At one point, surprisingly, "routine" is praised: "Mankind is as busy as the flowers in summer. . . . Routine is a ground to stand on, . . . we cannot draw on our boots without bracing ourselves against it. It is the fence over which neighbors lean when they talk" (*J*, I: 173; 1841). Elsewhere, even "fretfulness and despondency" were found to be tolerable—in their "total disinterestedness"!—and moved Thoreau to "congratulate myself on the richness of human nature."[2] "Nothing is so attractive and unceasingly curious as character," he continued in a later entry of that year; ". . . I hear no good news ever but some trait of a noble character. . . . I am mean in contrast, but again am thrilled and elevated that I can see my own mean-ness, and . . . that my own aspiration is realized in that other" (*J*, I: 290; 1841). The unity and interdependency of humankind are stressed in other entries: "I have not succeeded if I have an antago-nist who fails. It must be humanity's success." (*J*, I: 342; 1842). "Man has a million eyes, and the race knows infinitely more than the individual. Consent to be wise through your race" (*J*, II: 69; 1850).

These early reflections culminate in a long meditation of 1851 —a prime instance of Thoreauvian extravagance, which announces his discovery of mankind as if the earlier statements had never been made: "I think we are not commonly aware that man is our contemporary,—that in this strange, outlandish world, so barren, so prosaic, fit not to live in but merely to pass through, that even here so divine a creature as man does actually live. Man, the crowning fact, the god we know. . . . It is only within a year that it has occurred to me that there is such a being actually existing on the globe." These sentences begin a passage (*J*, II: 207–8) which is probably the most extreme expression of Thoreau's humanistic feeling in the entire *Journal*. In length and assertiveness it equals the passage from 1852 that I have called his "most sustained effort to formulate a philosophical statement of his misanthropy" (—the passage beginning "It appears to me that to one standing on the heights of philosophy mankind and the works of man will have shrunk out of sight altogether.") With the 1852 passage in mind, one experiences a series of small shocks in reading this one. They begin in the first sentence, with the characterization of "this world" as "strange . . . barren, prosaic" *except* for the presence of human-ity. Thoreau often uses the word "world" specifically for society and the man-made environment, which are discredited (exactly as in Wordsworth's "The world is too much with us"), in contrast to the serenity and mystery of "earth"—non-human Nature. But here it is clear that "world" encompasses everything that is not-human; and "earth" is commended in the next sentence merely for being the planet which "supports so rare an inhabitant" as Man. Indeed, farther on in the passage, the claims of Nature are recognized, only to be seen as outweighed by the claims of humanity:

The revelations of nature are infinitely glorious and cheering, hinting to us of a remote future, of possibilities untold; but startlingly near to us some day we find a fellow-man. . . . From nature we turn astonished to this *near* but supernatural fact. I think that the existence of man in nature is the divinest and most startling of all facts. It is a fact which few have realized.

This statement apparently reflects some specific and striking experience, and some literally new ponderings of "man's nature and destiny." "Now that I perceive that it is so" (that "such a being" exists), the passage continues, "many questions assume a new aspect."

We have not only the idea and vision of the divine ourselves, but we have brothers, it seems, who have this idea also.... I think that the standing miracle to man is man. Beyond the paling yonder, come rain or shine, hope or doubt, there dwells a man, an actual being who can sympathize with our sublimest thoughts.

It seems probable that this recognition of idealism in others, and of the very real possibility of sympathy, formed the original basis of this entry. Toward the end of it, Thoreau included a little fable, which confers on the entire passage a new dimension:

The frog had eyed the heavens from his marsh, until his mind was filled with visions, and he saw more than belongs to this fenny earth. He mistrusted that he was become a dreamer and visionary. Leaping across the swamp to his fellow, what was his joy and consolation to find that he too had seen the same sights in the heavens, he too had dreamed the same dreams! (*J*, II: 207–8.)

Here we find evidence, once again, of the mysticism which is perhaps the central element in Thoreau's thought. In the fable, he seems at first to be repudiating this mystical experience: the thought that he may be a "dreamer and visionary" breeds "mistrust," and (because we are aware of the power that word had for him) we sense his impulse of loyalty to "earth." Indeed, we half expect the fable to be rounded out in that way—with the finding of a "fellow" to confirm his contentment with "what belongs to this fenny earth." But it is not so. Instead, the frog finds a kindred being to share the mystical vision, and the fable underscores the phrase, "sympathize with our sublimest thoughts." This relates, of course, to the Friendship passages examined in chapter 2, particularly to those in which Thoreau articulated his yearning for— and sometimes his despair of finding that "one" to whom his "first thoughts" could be freely expressed. But this passage has a far wider scope than any of those. While it does suggest that he had recently experienced some rare and memorable rapport, it does not dwell on Friendship as such, nor upon The Friend. It celebrates the strengths and the aspirations of humanity—ultimately, the very existence of humanity. Perhaps most striking in the passage is Thoreau's repeated use of the word "fact"—for him another very positive and powerful word:* "The existence of man in nature is the divinest and most startling of all facts ... a fact which few have realized"; man is "this *near* but supernatural fact"; "Man is the crowning fact, the god we know."

The date of this entry (1851) marks it as a product of the mature Thoreau's thinking (he was then thirty-three), at least equal in significance to any of the violently misanthropic passages I have quoted from the journals of this period. Again featuring the word "fact," a remarkable entry dated later in 1851 also challenges some of those passages—in quite specific terms:

It is a very remarkable and significant fact that, though no man is quite well or healthy, yet every one believes practically that health is the rule and disease the exception. . . . But it may be some encouragement to men to know that in this respect they stand on the same platform, that disease is, in fact, the *rule* of our terrestrial life and the prophecy of a *celestial* life. . . . They gave us life on exactly these conditions, and methinks we shall live it with more heart when we perceive clearly that these are the terms on which we have it. . . . Man begins by quarreling with the animal in him, and the result is immediate disease. In proportion as the spirit is the more ambitious and persevering, the more obstacles it will meet with. It is as a seer that man asserts his disease to be exceptional. (*J*, II: 449–50.)

Elsewhere, Thoreau minimized or repudiated bodily weakness and disease, and once, as we know, when he did admit himself vulnerable to them, he made a scapegoat of them, seeing them as the source of a spurious and shameful "sympathy" with mankind. But

---

* "The fact will one day flower out into a truth" (*J*, I: 18; 1837). "Facts fall from the poetic observer as ripe seeds" (*J*, IV: 116; 1852). "I went to the woods because I wished to ... front only the essential facts of life...." "In sane moments we regard only the facts, the case that is." "If you stand right fronting and face to face to a fact, you will see the sun glimmer on both its surfaces ... , and feel its sweet edge dividing you through the heart and marrow, and so you will happily conclude your mortal career" (*Walden*, pp. 20, 327, 98).

here, accepted, they become the occasion for an affirmation of human solidarity. Moreover, "man" in general is here again credited with feeling the same spiritual "ambitions" that Thoreau himself has felt.

In a later entry a familiar phrase, one which was intimately identified with Thoreau's misanthropic impulses—"the mass of men"—takes on connotations of sympathy: "Perhaps the value of any statement may be measured by its susceptibility to be expressed in popular language. . . . A man may be permitted to state a very meagre truth to a fellow-student, using technical terms, but when he stands up before the mass of men, he must have some distinct and important truth to communicate; and the most important it will always be the most easy to communicate. . . ." (J, III: 327-28; 1852). The technical-scientific vocabulary is fit only for "meagre truth" because it is *undemocratic.* Two years later Thoreau expressed his reservations about science even more forcefully, in a passionately humanistic context:

There is no such thing as pure *objective* observation. Your observation, to be interesting, i.e., to be significant, must be *subjective.* The sum of what the writer . . . has to report is simply some human experience, whether he be poet or philosopher or man of science. . . . I look over the report of the doings of a scientific association and am surprised that there is so little life to be reported. . . . All that a man has to say or do that can possibly concern mankind, is in some shape or other to tell the story of his love,—to sing; and, if he is fortunate and keeps alive, he will be forever in love. This alone is to be alive to the extremities. It is a pity that this divine creature should ever suffer from cold feet. . . . (J, VI: 237; 1854.)

Such expressions of dissatisfaction with objective science became ever more numerous in the later journals, as Thoreau found himself increasingly preoccupied with detailed nature study; one remembers his outburst in 1853 against the questionnaire sent to him by the Association for the Advancement of Science.* There and elsewhere his dissatisfaction took the form of his championing a mystical view of Nature with an emphasis on subjectivity, as

---

* ". . . inasmuch as they do not believe in a science which deals with the higher law . . . I was obliged to speak to their condition and describe to them that poor part of me which alone they can understand. The fact is I am a mystic, a transcendentalist, and a natural philosopher to boot" (J, V: 4; 1853).

against the dispassionately analytical. But the climactic sentence of this 1854 passage appears even to dismiss Nature itself—all of Nature that is not human. It asserts that "If it is possible to conceive of an event outside of humanity, it is not of the slightest significance, though it were the explosion of a planet" (*J*, VI: 237).

A still more explicit dismissal of Nature occurs in another entry of the same month, whose first two sentences can shock even the reader long accustomed to Thoreau's contradictions. "We soon get through with Nature," he wrote. "She excites an expectation which she cannot satisfy." In this passage the emphasis again falls on his own desire for some transcendent insight (a "more celestial song ... music that was not of the earth"), yet at several points his "we" seems much more definite than the mere editorial substitute for "I"; it suggests that Thoreau, at that moment, felt both his "expectation" and his disappointment to have been shared by other human beings: "We soon get through with Nature. ... The merest child which has rambled into a copsewood dreams of a wilderness so wild and strange and inexhaustible as Nature can never show him. ... We *condescend* [Thoreau's italics] to climb the crags of earth. It is our weary legs alone that praise them" (*J*, VI: 293–94; 1854).

No other passage in Thoreau's work expresses quite this degree of disillusionment with Nature,* and even the most casual

---

* One is reminded, however, of another negative response (not simply disillusionment, but dismay) recorded back in 1845—this one, interestingly enough, following his visit to the uttermost "wilderness ... wild and strange" which Thoreau had yet confronted. When he reached the summit of Maine's Mount Ktaadn, he felt himself dwarfed by "vast, Titanic, inhuman Nature," which "has got him at disadvantage, caught him alone, and pilfers him of some of his divine faculty" (*Writings, III: Maine Woods*, p. 71). Walter Harding comments that "this was not the ... kindly Nature he knew on the banks of Walden Pond and he did not like it" (*The Days of Henry Thoreau* [New York: Alfred A. Knopf, 1965], p. 210); and Frederick Garber has devoted most of a chapter to a discussion of this important, troubling experience, in which he often emphasizes the need Thoreau evidenced to "domesticate" that wilderness, somehow to see it as hospitable, or at least meaningful, to human beings (*Thoreau's Redemptive Imagination*, pp. 79–128). Whenever I read Thoreau's description of Mount Ktaadn, I am reminded of Aldous Huxley's essay "Wordsworth in the Tropics," which makes the point that experience of the jungle would surely have forced upon Wordsworth a somewhat different attitude toward Nature, and a different idea of his relation to it, from that which he developed in the kindlier English Lake District (*Do What You Will* [New York: Doubleday-Doran, 1929], pp. 123–39).

reader could call to mind dozens of statements, from the *Journal* and from *Walden*, which flatly contradict it. Many of those statements reveal an intimate connection between Thoreau's responses to Nature and the mystical ecstasies of his youth. Many others, as we have seen, posit an irresolvable conflict between the love of Nature and sympathy with mankind. This passage therefore represents a significant rearrangement of Thoreau's values—with Nature, seen as *inadequate*, on the one side, and mankind, capable of a super-natural experience, on the other.

Both this passage and the surprising statement that no event "outside of humanity . . . is . . . of the slightest significance" were set down within a mere three weeks' time, which suggests that some crucial review of Thoreau's loyalties and values may have been taking place. But if so, it had been foreshadowed in the notebooks of the years just preceding this. "I would fain travel by a footpath round the world," he had written in 1851; "Pray what other path would you have. . . ? This is the track of man alone. . . . One walks in a wheel track with less emotion; he is at a greater distance from man; but this footpath was, perchance, worn by the bare feet of human beings, and he cannot but think with interest of them" (*J*, II: 455–56). Shortly after that, hearing "the sound of singers on the river, young men and women . . . returning from their row," he was moved to assert that "Man's voice, thus uttered, fits well the spaces. It fills nature. And, after all, the singing of men is something far grander than any natural sound" (*J*, II: 474; 1851). Later in that entry, the appearance of a dramatic and rarely visible natural phenomenon prompted an immediate association with humanity: "I see the northern lights over my shoulder, to remind me of the Esquimaux and that they are still my contemporaries on this globe, that they too are taking their walks on another part of the planet. . . ." (*J*, II: 475). Even the cutting of trees, always a painful thing for Thoreau, could be tolerated in view of human needs. The sound of "Barrett's sawmill running by night" seemed to him to "ring . . . from the nerves of the tortured log. Tearing its entrails." Yet at first it had struck him as "taming timber, in a rude Orphean fashion preparing it for dwellings of men and musical instruments, perchance" (*J*, IV: 23; 1852). And in 1853 he found himself "somewhat oppressed and saddened by the sameness and apparent poverty of the heavens. . . . A few good anecdotes is our science, with a few imposing statements respecting distance and size, and little or nothing about the stars as they concern man. . . . Man's eye [the inner eye which needs no telescope] is the true star-finder. . . . If the elements are not human, . . . my life runs shallow" (*J*, IV: 469–72).

Such statements are not rare. On the contrary, these companion themes—that Nature exists for mankind, and that mankind is more *interesting* than Nature—persist in the middle and later volumes of the *Journal*:

What is Nature unless there is an eventful human life passing within her? Many joys and many sorrows are the lights and shadows in which she shows most beautiful. (*J*, V: 472; 1853.)

It is for man the seasons and all their fruits exist. The winter was made to concentrate and harden and mature the kernel of his brain, to give tone and firmness and consistency to his thought. (*J*, VI: 85; 1854.)

"Look," Thoreau exclaimed at one point in the long account of an October outing in 1857—"Look into that hollow all aglow where the trees are clothed in their vestures of most dazzling tints. Does it not suggest a thousand gipsies beneath, rows of booths, and that man's spirits should rise as high, that the routine of his life should be interrupted by an analogous festivity and rejoicing?" (*J*, X: 72). Here, in an instance of transcendentalist "correspondence"-seeking, Thoreau was viewing Nature as a teacher of mankind. And in 1860 he declared simply that "a fact stated barely is dry. It must be the vehicle of some humanity in order to interest us." (*J*, XIII: 160.)

For a final illustration of the ways in which Thoreau could subordinate Nature to the interests of humanity, consider this reference to John Brown: "I have been so absorbed of late in Captain Brown's fate as to be surprised whenever I detected the old routine running still, . . . It appeared strange to me that the little dipper should be still diving in the river as of yore. . . . Any affecting human event may blind our eyes to natural objects" (*J*, XII: 447–48; Nov. 17, 1859).

Obviously, when all of these passages are set side by side with the misanthropic utterances discussed in the first chapter, we are faced with startling contradictions. Compared to these contradictions, the apparent conflict between Thoreau's desires for wilderness and for community seems minor, and can be understood as merely a specific reflection of the basic conflict—forever unresolved in Thoreau—between an exclusive allegiance to humankind on the one hand, or to some non-human conception, whether "earth" or "heaven," on the other.

Seen in the context of the passages quoted above, an earlier-cited entry of the fifties represents still another variation in his hierarchic arrangement of values: "I love Nature partly *because* she is not man, but a retreat from him. . . . He makes me wish for another world. She makes me content with this" (J, IV: 445; 1853). In one typical formulation, Nature, which can stimulate mystical ecstasies for Thoreau, is exalted at Man's expense, while in another Nature is valued simply for her "gifts," both material and inspirational, to all mankind. In this passage Thoreau explicitly states that, whereas his dissatisfaction with humankind has fostered his desire for "another world," the contemplation of Nature alone ("real" physical Nature, but viewed apart from mankind) renders *this world* perfectly satisfying. And in still other passages, as we have recently seen, he depicts mankind, including himself, seeking some transcendent experience and disappointed by Nature.

Finding ourselves bewildered by all these contradictions, we may have to take refuge—at least provisionally—in a pendulum theory: given such extreme statements as those reviewed in chapter 1, we might well predict a pendulum-like swing to the opposite extreme. When a man of Thoreau's emotional intensity damns humanity on one page, he might be expected to revert to an admiring or a compassionate attitude on the next. When such a man seeks "sympathy" and a kind of personal transfiguration in the contemplation of a sunset or the sound of a wind harp—when he records an impulse to embrace a shrub-oak tree, to kiss the "sward" on an island in spring, or to "fall in love with the crescent moon"—it would seem, not surprising, but inevitable that he should—sooner or later—recoil in disappointment, and write "We soon get through with Nature," thinking with relief of "Man my contemporary."

2

At two earlier points in this study I have called attention to Thoreau's use of the first-person-plural pronoun. There is the "we" which means "Channing and I" ("We laughed well at our adventure"); and there is the "we" which identified Thoreau with the Concord community ("We say [the rain] is going down the river, and we shall not get a drop," "We can afford . . . not to be provincial at all.") The latter and more inclusive "we" was perhaps made easier for Thoreau by his repeated use of the former—by his comradeship with Channing over the years. And surely his willingness to identify with the "communal we" is the ground from which sprang his philosophical humanism—the third and most inclusive "we," which placed him squarely among "the mass of men" and which made possible that impressive passage on "Man the crowning fact, the god we know."

The *Journal* contains many other instances of fellow feeling, stated or implied, in passages which have little or nothing to do either with Nature or the super-natural.

We cannot pronounce upon a man's intellectual and moral state until we foresee what metamorphosis it is preparing him for. (*J*, III: 71; 1851.)

I love ... to be convinced that the earth has been crowded with men, living, enjoying, suffering, ... I am the more at home. (*J*, III: 334; 1852.)

Myriads of arrow-points lie sleeping in the skin of the revolving earth, while meteors revolve in space. The footprint, the mind-print of the oldest men. ... Each one yields me a thought. I come nearer to the maker of it than if I found his bones. His bones would not prove any wit that wielded them, such as this work of his bone does. It is humanity inscribed on the face of the earth.... (*J*, XII: 90–92. See again note 1 to this chapter.)

Nothing has got built without labor. Past generations have spent their blood and strength for us. They have cleared the land, built roads, etc., for us. In all fields men have laid down their lives for us. (*J*, XII: 242; 1859.)

A man receives only what he is ready to receive, whether physically or intellectually or morally.... We hear and apprehend only what we already half know.... By and by we may be ready to receive what we cannot receive now. (*J*. XIII: 77; 1860.)

In all these brief examples, written during the last decade of Thoreau's life, the emphasis falls on the collective past of mankind, or upon its future, on human potentialities, while they vary in tone from a relative detachment to deep personal involvement.

In at least one *Journal* entry Thoreau very explicitly placed himself within the family of Man: "I only know myself as a human entity, the scene, so to speak, of thoughts and affections...."

(*J*, IV: 291; 1852). At a few other times, he seems somehow to have conceived for himself a non-human identity; the reader may recall such an instance, from *A Week:* "This, then, is that mankind. . . ." Something of the same sort was surely implied on those occasions when, in the earlier journals and letters, he compared himself to the god Apollo, tending the flocks of King Admetus[3]—that is, taking part in the mundane affairs of men, whether as school-teacher, pencil-maker, or surveyor. Yet even his uses of that myth, which were for the most part highly egocentric and anti-communal, occasionally admitted the identification of other men in the role of Apollo.* And once, in a letter to Richard Fuller, he actually referred to himself and his friend as "us Admetuses"—specifically, as undeserving recipients of the divine gift of music.[4]

The context of the *Journal* sentence in which he so emphatically identified himself as "a human entity" describes Thoreau's sense of kinship with thinkers and writers of other periods—especially with the Persian poet Sadi; and this kind of kinship is forcefully claimed for all mankind: "The entertaining of a single thought of a certain elevation makes all men of one religion. It is always some base alloy that creates the distinction of sects. . . . The difference between any man and that posterity amid whom he is famous is too insignificant to sanction that he should be set up again in any world as distinct from them." And now Thoreau posits still another basis for feelings about human solidarity—the complexity, the non-integrality, of the Self:

I only know myself as a human entity, the scene, so to speak, of thoughts and affections, and am sensible of a certain doubleness by which I can stand as remote from myself as from another. However intense my experience, I am conscious of the presence and criticism of a part of me which, as it were, is not a part of me, but spectator, sharing

---

* "I hear now from Bear Garden Hill . . . the sound of a flute, or a horn, or a human voice. It is a performer I never see by day; should not recognize him if pointed out; but you may hear his performance in every horizon. . . . He is a slave who is purchasing his freedom. He is Apollo watching the flocks of Admetus on every hill, and this strain he plays every evening to remind him of his heavenly descent." "Ah, yes, even here in Concord Apollo is at work for King Admetus! Who is King Admetus? It is Business, with his four prime ministers Trade and Commerce and Manufactures and Agriculture." "I hear a man playing a clarionet afar off. Apollo tending the flocks of King Admetus. . . . What a contrast this evening melody with the occupations of the day" (*J*, II: 373, 378; 1851; IV: 114; 1852.)

no experience, but taking note of it, and that is no more I than it is you. When the play—it may be the tragedy of life—is over, the spectator goes his way. It was a kind of fiction, a work of the imagination only, so far as he was concerned. (*J*, IV: 290–91; 1852.)

This is a puzzling passage, not so much in its assertion of the duality of a human personality as in the implied functioning of the respective "selves." For Thoreau writes that the "spectator" is a dispassionate critic, "sharing no experience" (not even the experience of love, presumably, nor of mystical joy), and yet this spectator in some sense antedates and survives the other, the active, enjoying and suffering self. "He" has "imagined" it all. These statements seem uncharacteristic of Henry Thoreau. They are echoed at least twice, however, in letters of 1853. There he stresses not the "doubleness" but the elusiveness of the self—the tenuousness, at times, of his sense of his own identity—although a double is clearly implied at certain points:

It is wonderful [he wrote to Blake] that I can be here, and you there, and that we can correspond, and do many other things, when, in fact, there is so little of us, either or both, anywhere. . . . Suddenly I can come forward into the utmost apparent distinctness, and speak with a sort of emphasis to you; and the next moment I am so faint an entity, and make so slight an impression, that nobody can find traces of me. I try to hunt myself up, and find the little of me that is discoverable is falling asleep, and then I assist and tuck it up.

In another letter to Blake (cited above, pp. 48–49) he had—rather coyly—voiced something of the same thought, with the added implication that there might be less distinction between one human identity and another than is ordinarily assumed: "Your words [in Blake's latest letter] make me think of a man of my acquaintance whom I occasionally meet, whom you too appear to have met, one Myself, as he is called. Yet why not call him *Yourself*? If you have met with him and know him [it] is all I have done. . . ."[5] This is reminiscent of the *Journal* passage's "a part of me . . . that is no more I than it is you," although in the latter, of course, Thoreau uses the nonspecific "you," equivalent to "any other human being." These sentences reappear in chapter 5 of *Walden*, with this addition: "This doubleness may easily make us poor neighbors and friends sometimes" (p. 135).

It was this "doubleness," surely, which made possible such a self-undermining gesture as that of Thoreau's including the Carew poem ("Thou dost presume too much, poor needy wretch"), which he himself titled "The Pretensions of Poverty," at the end of *Walden's* chapter 1. And it was no doubt this doubleness which underlay all of his manifest ambivalences—about himself, Nature, and other people. As Richard Lebeaux has helped to make clear, Thoreau's famous "ego" was not so well-defined, so overbearing or so exclusive of others as some critics have suggested—or as some *Walden* pronouncements might lead one to believe.* The thought of a diminished, or diminishable, identity, which is implied in the letters just quoted, might have served both to open Thoreau to others (increased humility fostering a receptivity), and to inhibit him by suggesting a frightening submergence of the self. Similarly, the double identity described in the *Journal* paragraph can suggest either a "slipperiness" which would render him "a poor neighbor," or a liberalizing detachment, which would better enable him to imagine other persons' points-of-view, as well as to see himself as others saw him. In any case, I suggest that this paragraph, whose first sentence so forthrightly proclaims its author to be "only . . . a human entity," is an important document, a kind of basic reference point, in any discussion of Thoreau's attitudes toward other human beings.

3

Still another such document exists in two short paragraphs of 1854, which occur without any obvious preamble in a *Journal* context of nature observations. These too are surprising. The first paragraph consists of one sentence: "In my experience, at least *of late years*, all that depresses a man's spirits is the sense of remissness,—duties neglected, unfaithfulness,—or shamming, impurity, falsehood, selfishness, inhumanity, and the like" (*J*, VI:

---

* At one point Thoreau himself responded specifically to that charge: "Now if there are any who think that I am vainglorious, that I set myself up above others and crow over their low estate, let me tell them that I could tell a pitiful story respecting myself . . . if my spirits held out to do it; I could encourage them with a sufficient list of failures, and could flow as humbly as the very gutters themselves; I could enumerate a list of as rank offenses as ever reached the nostrils of heaven; that I think worse of myself than they can possibly think of me, being better acquainted with the man" (*J*, III: 293; 1852).

483). My impression, from earlier journals, is that the things which most often depressed Thoreau's spirits were (1) a sense of isolation, of friendlessness; (2) a sense of lost vision, of his failure, as he grew older, to experience the "intoxications" of his youth; and (3) a sense—this one seldom voiced, but all the more bitter when it was—of having gained little or no recognition as a writer. But the sources of depression he named here, in 1854 (and the stress Thoreau placed upon "of late years" suggests his own awareness of a change in his attitudes), all—with the possible exception of "impurity"—have a *social* connotation. We describe as "duties," most commonly, those obligations which we owe to other people; one may speak of being "unfaithful" to an ideal, or to the best in oneself, but "shamming, falsehood, selfishness, inhumanity" all have to do with one's conduct and attitude toward other men and women.

The succeeding paragraph is yet more surprising:

From the experience of late years I should say that a man's seed was the direct tax of his race. It stands for my sympathy with my race. When the brain chiefly is nourished, and not the affections, the seed becomes merely excremental. (*J*, VI: 483; 1854.)

The word "seed" is not here—as it is in several other places—a metaphor for the truths a man utters or anything else of the kind; it means, quite literally, semen. The seed of an individual, then, is the "tax" of his race—in that it can serve to maintain the life of the race. And what has the brain, the intellect, to do with the seed? Presumably an intellect nourished at the expense of the emotions ("affections") might impede the flow of the seed, prevent the payment of the tax. But the tax must be paid, Thoreau implies, and paid with "sympathy," not merely for a sexual partner, but for all of the human race. If the seed is not employed as Nature designed, or even if the affections are not engaged in the sexual encounter, the seed might be considered "excremental." But what of the middle sentence? There the subject, "it," is no longer "a man's seed," but the writer's: Thoreau says that he feels *his* semen "stands for my sympathy with my race." Whether or not he had begun this paragraph with a sense that his own seed was "excremental" (possibly after an experience of night loss or masturbation), the implication here is that the seed's mere existence has this symbolic significance. And note that the two personal possessives are reinforced by this paragraph's beginning clause,

"From the experience of late years I should say. . . ." This is not a detached philosophical observation, but a personal testimony.

This paragraph calls to mind at least two other *Journal* passages. One is that of 1851 in which Thoreau pondered the possibility of "another relation to woman than leads to marriage, and yet an elevating and all-absorbing one, perhaps transcending marriage," and which expressed his certainty that "the design of my maker when he has brought me nearest to women was not the propagation but the maturation of the species." (See above p. 28.) In dealing with such passages as these the critic must proceed with great caution. It is possible, of course, to read the lines just quoted as a rationalization of sexual impotence, or as evidence of an extreme puritanical inhibition. One could cite the numerous passages which brood over the idea of "impurity" to support either of these readings. On the other hand, we must remember that, to the best of our knowledge, the woman to whom Thoreau at that time felt most closely drawn was physically inaccessible to him,—the loyal wife of a man who had befriended him. In view of this fact, his rationalizations and self-admonitions may seem more natural. As a whole, this *Journal* entry suggests that he had, for the moment, successfully sublimated his feeling for Lidian Emerson, that the relationship had reached a delicate equilibrium. ("By our very mutual attraction, and our attraction to all other spheres, kept properly asunder.") But it is obvious that the feeling was still intense, and that he must have felt confident of a reciprocal feeling on her part: "Our very mutual attraction"; "The one I love surpasses all the laws of nature in sureness." His reference in this context to "the history of chivalry and knight-errantry" indicates that by "another relation to woman" he certainly meant a relation of intense devotion, and not the strictly cerebral or pedagogical one that "elevation" and "maturation" might imply. And indeed, man's "love of woman" is the subject of the concluding sentence.

Another relevant passage, dated in the same year, involves the complex dream which ended with Thoreau feeling his body a musical instrument, then waking to find it an object grotesque and unclean. The report of that dream, it will be remembered, is followed by a brief, desolate paragraph on the ending of a relationship with a woman (Lidian Emerson, we must again assume) "who was as the morning light to me." (See above p. 29.) Reading that entry, I have suggested, it is easy to suppose that

Thoreau was leading an intense fantasy life, which may have prompted certain sexual manifestations. And when this possibility is granted, the various passages in which he accuses himself of "impurity" can be called in to support quite another assumption: that he knew himself capable of sexual excitement and sexual activity.

A number of other passages, especially in the *Journal*, can afford insights into Thoreau's attitudes toward sex. Quite predictably, there are as many contradictions in these attitudes as there are in his general responses to other human beings. At one extreme, he seems obsessed by the idea of "purity" or chastity; he praises Chaucer's repudiation of his writings which dealt with " 'the base and filthy love of men toward women' "; he asserts that "he is blessed who is assured that the animal is dying out in him day by day. . . ." [6] At another extreme he deplores the "grossness" and levity with which other men speak of the sexual relation; he writes that "to be married at least should be the one poetical act of a man's life" (*J*, V: 369; 1853); and he marvels "that men will talk of miracles [and] revelation . . . as things past, while love remains."

The last statement comes from the "thoughts" on "Love and Marriage" which Thoreau sent, with the companion piece on "Chastity and Sensuality," to Harrison Blake in 1852. These letter-essays are remarkable both for their ambivalence and their frankness, as well as for their revelation of very personal sexual longings. The second essay, which contains repeated warnings against "sensuality" and "lust," concludes, nevertheless, with this striking affirmation: "The intercourse of the sexes, I have dreamed, is incredibly beautiful, too fair to be remembered. . . . No wonder that, out of such a union *not as end, but as accompaniment* [my italics], comes the undying race of man." [7]

Several critics have overemphasized Thoreau's use of the word "impurity" in connection with sex, and the other instances of prudishness or anxiety which are certainly evident. [8] They ignore the fact that between the two extremes of repudiation and idealization there are many passages which reveal a simple acceptance of sexual love, and often a lively interest. We have seen how Thoreau more than once inveighed against "false modesty"; in both the *Journal* and *Walden* he welcomed the "calmness and gentleness" with which the Hindu writers discoursed upon physical love, and in the essay-letter to Blake he expressed surprise that "one of the most interesting of all human facts is veiled more completely than any mystery. . . . treated with secrecy . . . avoided,—from shame." [9]

In the early notebooks an erotic excitement often becomes overt: "the maiden waiteth patiently . . . for the slow moving years to work their will with her,—perfect and ripen her. . . . These young buds of manhood in the streets are like buttercups in the meadows,—surrendered to nature as they" (J, I: 94; 1839). "Every maiden conceals a fairer flower and more luscious fruit than any calyx in the field, and if she go . . . confiding in her own purity and high resolves . . . all nature will humbly confess its queen" (J, I: 292; 1841). While this passage may be somewhat overwritten, in 1852 Thoreau's impulse to identify maidens and young men with flowers resulted in a stylistically mature paragraph of great beauty, as well as erotic appeal:

Tomorrow, then, will be the first Sabbath when the young men, having bathed [in the river], will walk slowly and soberly to church in their best clothes, each with a lily in his hand or bosom,—with as long a stem as he could get . . . its odor contrasting and atoning for that of the sermon. We now have roses on the land and lilies in the water,—both land and water have done their best,—now *just* after the longest day. Nature says, "You behold the utmost I can do." And the young women carry their finest roses on the other hand. Roses and lilies. The floral days. The red rose, with the intense color of many suns concentrated, spreads its tender petals, . . . modest yet queenly, on the edges of shady copses and meadows, . . . surrounded by blushing buds, of perfect form; not only beautiful, but rightfully commanding attention; unspoiled by the admiration of gazers. And the water-lily floats on the smooth surface of slow waters, amid round shields of leaves, bucklers, red beneath, which simulate a green field. . . . How transitory the perfect beauty of the rose and lily! (J, IV: 148.)

"Gather ye rosebuds while ye may": *carpe diem* is the theme of this paragraph as surely as it is of Herrick's poem. When, ostensibly, the focus shifts from the men and women to the flowers themselves, we find that all the imagery for the roses is conventionally "feminine" ("spreads its tender petals . . . modest yet queenly"), while for the lilies it is "masculine" ("shields," "bucklers," "as long a stem as he could get"). Clearly the young men and women were also seen by Thoreau as representing Nature's "utmost," and are included in the final exclamation—"How transitory the perfect beauty of the rose and lily!" This exclamation in turn gives an added force to the two short brooding phrases in mid-paragraph (not sentences, but incantatory namings): "Roses and lilies. The floral days."

In *American Renaissance*, F. O. Matthiessen insisted upon Thoreau's "dislike of sensuality," and quoted his expressed desire for "a *purely* sensuous life" as evidence of "the mystical element that always remained part of his experience." Yet a paragraph of quotations he assembled actually reveals Thoreau's deep response to every kind of sense experience—to form and color, to fragrance, to the taste of berries, spring water, frozen apples, to an extraordinary range of sounds, to the tactile pleasure of strolling in the river with his clothes balanced on his head.[10] Joel Porte has seen Thoreau's reliance on his senses ("the perpetual instilling and drenching of the reality that surrounds us") as constituting the chief difference between his thought and that of Emerson and the other Transcendentalists.[11] Certainly his mystical bent was strong, as were his "Spartan" tendency and contempt for self-indulgence. Nevertheless, Porte is right in emphasizing Thoreau's absorption in the life of his five senses—an absorption that pervades all his writings. And, at many points, this general sensuality includes a specifically erotic awareness.

One unfailing source of excitement for Thoreau—as we have seen in the roses-and-lilies passage—was the color red.* Certain flowers are said to be "interesting, if only for their high color. Any redness is, after all, rare and precious. It is the color of our blood" (*J*, IV: 217; 1852). "I love to see any redness in the vegetation of the temperate zone. It is the richest color. I love to press these berries between my fingers and see their rich purple wine staining my hand. . . . It speaks to my blood . . . a feast of color. . . . Nature here is full of blood and heat and luxuriance." This is followed by the observation that "The grape-vines overrunning and bending down the maples form little arching bowers over the meadow, . . . like parasols held over the ladies of the harem, in the East" (*J*, II: 489–90; 1851).

Again and again in the *Journal* we find such erotic implications in Thoreau's responses to the vegetable world. Just as maidens could suggest flowers, so flowers and leaves often suggest maidens: "Even the dry leaves [upon snow] are gregarious. . . .

---

* For a fuller treatment of this topic, see Richard Colyers, "Thoreau's Color Symbols," *PMLA* 86 (1971): 999–1008.

How like shrinking maidens wrapping their scarfs about them they flutter along!" "There is a certain ... feminineness, suggested by the rounded lobes, the scalloped edge, of the white oak leaf. ..." (*J*, III: 223; 1852). And in the early spring:

The tobacco-pipe ... reminded me of a maiden in her robes of purity who has always been nurtured in a shady and vault-like seclusion. ... Pushing aside the doorway of dry leaves, three sisters of various heights issue from their hidden convent and stand side by side ... striving at first to conceal their nakedness and tenderness. A few loose, scanty, but beautiful, pearly sheaths alone invested them ... but soon, exposed to light and air, their virtue dried black. ... Their untried virtue cannot long stand the light and air. (*J*, V: 347–48; 1853.)

Another April entry involves synesthesia, as Thoreau exclaims upon "that early yellow smell. ... The odor of spring, of life developing amid buds, of the earth's epithalamium" (*J*, III: 432; 1852). For him any season was capable of prompting such reflections, although spring and summer were the most suggestive. "Methinks there is a male and female shore to the river," he wrote in mid-June, "one abrupt, the other flat and meadowy. ... The year is in its manhood now" (*J*, IV: 101–2; 1852).

Not surprisingly, we find that Thoreau's references to animal sexuality were sympathetic, and often prompted references to human love. For example, two fireflies, observed at length, were thought to be a female and a male—"both showing their lights that they might come together. It was like a mistress who had climbed the turrets of her castle and exhibited there a blazing taper for a signal, while her lover displayed his light on the plain" (*J*, II: 260; 1851). A peeping frog, when caught, "proved to be two coupled. They remained together in my hand. This sound has connection with their loves probably. ... My dreaming mid-summer frog" (*J*, III: 486; 1852). "I see ... by the Creek Brook, pretty chains of toad-spawn ... lines of black ova. ... This is what they were singing about" (*J*, V: 112; 1853). And as late as 1857 the sight of two birds moved Thoreau to one of the most poignantly personal utterances in the entire *Journal*:

two great fish-hawks ... slowly beating northeast against the storm, by what a curious tie circling near each other and in the same direction, as if you might expect to find the very motes in the air to be paired; two long undulating wings conveying a feathered body through the misty atmosphere, and this inseparably associated with another planet of the same species. . . . Damon and Pythias they must be. . . . Where is my mate, beating against the storm with me? (*J*, X: 126–27.)*

Finally, there are many instances of sexually suggestive imagery in the *Journal* which apparently had no specific source in Thoreau's daily experience. I have discussed (above, p. 18) a cluster of these images from an early (1841) passage, where the future was seen in terms of walled towns and gay pavillions in which "my own virtue would adventure" and "my future deeds bestir themselves . . . and move grandly toward a consummation." A paragraph whose focus is again on "future deeds" was entered in 1850: "My Journal should be the record of my love. I would write in it only the things I love . . . what I love to think of. . . . I feel ripe for something, yet do nothing. . . . I feel fertile merely. It is seedtime with me. I have lain fallow long enough" (*J*, II: 101). And in 1852 Thoreau wrote that the only worthy "themes" for the writer were those that "have kindled a flame in our minds. There must be the copulating and generating force of love behind every effort destined to be successful. The cold resolve gives birth to, begets nothing. . . . The poet's relation to his theme is the relation of lovers" (*J*, III: 253).

Elsewhere I have dealt more fully with this complex topic of Thoreau's sexuality.[12] Here I have attempted simply to suggest the range and the depth of his erotic responses, and to offer a frame of reference for the 1854 paragraph in which, in a context indicating that he had suffered from a "sense of . . . duties neglected . . . selfishness, inhumanity . . . ," he asserted that "a man's seed is the direct tax of his race," the payment of which must involve "the affections." If we imagine some kind of physical experience to have been in the back of his mind at this time, it would seem that he was not then troubled by any thought of "impurity"— or rather, not in the usual way. For this passage implies that it is the withholding of the seed, or the release of the seed without the affections that is "impure." If we view the year 1852 as a turning

---

* In 1859, coming upon two skaters on a frozen pond, Thoreau appears to have remembered the sight of the "paired" birds: "I saw a gentleman and lady very gracefully gyrating and, as it were, courtesying to each other. . . . their swift and graceful motions, their bodies inclined at various angles . . . reminded me of the circling of two winged insects in the air, or hawks receding and approaching" (*J*, XI: 453).

point in the *Journal*,[13] these two paragraphs of 1854 take on an added biographical significance. Their expression of a distrust of pure intellect has, as we have seen, many counterparts in the journals of the latter fifties, in which Thoreau frequently recoiled from the increasingly scientific character of his nature observations to emphasize the validity of intuition and emotion. In light of the regret expressed in the first paragraph at the thought of "remissness" and "selfishness," one might be led to assume that he was here accusing himself of having an overnourished brain and undernourished affections,* which rendered his own seed superfluous—"excremental."

But that is not precisely what the second paragraph says; and its tone, especially in the first two sentences, is not self-accusing, not bitter, but clearly positive. I suggest that what Thoreau was saying here, most basically, was that, "from the experience of late years," he felt his own sexuality as forming a link between him and "the mass of men," and that the thought was a welcome one: "It [my seed] stands for my sympathy with my race." The explicit derogation of the intellect in this context, and the emphasis on "the affections," suggest further that he then saw the individual's sexual nature as an acknowledged and valuable part of his total emotional nature, at the core of a sympathetic relatedness to other human beings.

---

* One remembers his distress in reporting the judgment (described as a "curse") of "a friend" in 1852: "I pray that if I am the cold intellectual skeptic whom he rebukes, his curse may take effect, and wither and dry up the sources of my life. . . ." (See above, p. 34.)

Seven

Experience, and 'Phil-anthropy'

Aᴛ a number of points in the *Journal*, and in *Walden*—most notably in the climactic chapter, "Spring"—Thoreau wrote glowingly of the idea of innocence, and of the possible recovery of innocence. And no doubt his profound sympathy for children (discussed above in chapter 4) was fed by this enthusiasm. But a somewhat more complex attitude is suggested elsewhere in *Walden*, in a description of some "brute neighbors," the newly-hatched partridges:

They are not callow like the young of most birds, but more perfectly developed and precocious.... The remarkably adult yet innocent expression of their open and serene eyes is very memorable. All intelligence seems reflected in them. They suggest not merely the purity of infancy, but a wisdom clarified by experience.[1]

—"Not *merely* the purity of infancy...." Surely it was in large part their qualities of freshness and relative purity which made children so attractive to Thoreau. Yet one description of the child who probably interested him more than any other recalls his rendering of the baby partridge: he saw in the expression of Johnny Riordan's "old-worthy" face "the tried magnanimity and grave nobility of ancient and departed worthies."

These paragraphs bring to mind Thoreau's consistently positive use of the word "experience," and his passion for "facts." His great respect for inevitable human experience has already been illustrated in this study ("What is Nature unless there is eventful life passing within her? Many joys and many sorrows...."; "I love to be convinced that the earth has been crowded with men, living, enjoying, suffering. . . .") But the challenge to innocence could be more direct: "I don't like people who are too good for this world. Let a man reserve a good appetite for his peck of dirt, and expect his chief wealth in unwashed diamonds. To know nature and ourselves well, we must have acquired a certain hardness and habitual equanimity." * The passage continues with a reference to the "last trump as I have heard foretold"—evidently a "crank" prediction of an early end to the world, which, he implies, was accepted with pious resignation by "the tender sex, and their hangers-on." "But," he concluded, "men of true mettle will prefer to buffet it here a spell longer." [2] Again and again this existential theme is sounded in the *Journal*, though perhaps never more vigorously than in that early colloquial phrase—"buffet it here a spell longer."

A significant statement of the theme occurs in a passage of 1851, in which "fact" and "experience" are key words, and in which Thoreau's frequent glorification of youth—a glorification which, for him as for Wordsworth, was intimately bound up with his mysticism—is seriously called into question. "It is a rare qualification," it begins, "to be able to state a fact simply and adequately, to digest some experience cleanly, to say 'yes' and 'no' with authority, to make a square edge, to conceive and suffer the truth to pass through us living and intact. . . . First of all a man must see, before he can say." It is apparent in "a man must see, before he can say" that Thoreau was thinking, at least in part, about the experience necessary to the writer. And it becomes apparent, as the passage proceeds, that it is not only youth but perhaps the mystical vision itself which is being disparaged:

A fact truly and absolutely stated is taken out of the region of common sense and acquires a mythologic or universal significance. Say it and have done with it. Express it without expressing yourself. See not with the eye of science, which is barren, nor of youthful poetry, which is impotent. But taste the world and digest it. . . . At first blush a man is not capable of reporting truth; he must be drenched and saturated with

---

* This entry belongs to the early—for a time lost—journal (of 1841) which came under the editorship of Perry Miller in 1958. But Miller made no comment on these statements, a full appreciation of which might have forced an alteration of his assessment of Thoreau as "a congenital misanthrope" and (quoting Stevenson) a " 'prig.' "

it first. What was *enthusiasm* in the young man must become *tempera-ment* in the mature man. (*J*, III: 85–86; 1851.)

The word "mythologic"—which we know Thoreau valued highly, but whose assigned meaning is not always clear and must indeed be assumed to vary—here is equated with "universal"; and, since it is contrasted with "common sense" (a phrase he usually deni-grates), it must also mean ultimately significant, philosophical. Two phrases insist that gaining this philosophical universality must in-volve a transcending of the individual ego: "Express it without expressing yourself"; "suffer the truth to *pass through us.* . . ." And the "us" functions, as I've suggested these plural pronouns often do, to implicate the rest of humanity in what is being said, to reinforce the idea of universality. Then, there is "world," a word which we know Thoreau often uttered contemptuously, con-trasting it with "earth" (non-human Nature) and asserting that immersion in "the world" can corrupt and stultify.* Here he asserts that it is necessary to *digest* the world. And the words "impotent" and "conceive" introduce sexual associations which confer a spe-cial urgency on the passage: to have digested the world, been "drenched and saturated" with experience (how vividly physical all these images are!), is to become potent. But what is "impotent"? We have met before the suggestion that science is "barren," but that Thoreau could disparage "youthful poetry"—call *that* "im-potent—is hard to believe. He does, however, seem to acknowledge its potential worth in the last sentence: what was (an intermittent or somewhat frenzied) "enthusiasm" in youth—whether poetic perception, mystical awareness, ardor for friendship, or zeal to serve mankind—must become "temperament," the settled habit of mind, the steady life-pervading force of maturity.

Clearly this passage has a personal significance. Thoreau was thirty-four years old in 1851. He had, during the preceding four or five years, been expressing regret at the passing of his own youth and the diminution of his poetic awareness, his "intoxica-tions"; this passage may in part represent a comforting rationaliza-tion. Here, at any rate, he was surely addressing himself *as a*

---

* "Ah! the world is too much with us, and our whole soul is stained by what it works in, like the dyer's hand. A man had better starve at once than lose his innocence in the process of getting his bread. . . . If within the old man there is not a young man,—within the sophisticated, one unsophisticated,— then he is but one of the devil's angels" (*J*, V: 454; 1853).

writer, and charging himself to digest the world, to immerse himself in a rich and varied experience, as he did in *Walden*'s last chapter, when he expressed his decision to "go before the mast and on the deck of the world." There is no doubt that these are serious and considered statements of his doctrine of experience, and they are supported not only by the passage from his youth— "we must have acquired a certain hardness and habitual equanimity"—but by others written throughout his life. It is a doctrine which ultimately rested on Thoreau's inexhaustible curiosity, on his craving for facts, for "reality." This craving was never more strikingly expressed than in the following passage from a notebook of 1852: "There is something invigorating in this air, which I am peculiarly sensible is a real wind, blowing from over the surface of a planet. I look out at my eyes, I come to my window, and I feel and breathe the fresh air. It is a fact equally glorious with the most inward experience. Why have we ever slandered the outward?" (*J*, IV: 312–13). This climax was prepared for by the reflection that "I live so much in my habitual thoughts, a routine of thought, that I forget there is any outside to the globe.... Yet it is salutary to deal with the surface of things." And all these injunctions to seek fresh experience are prefaced by a phrase— "Now I sit on the Cliffs and look abroad over the river and Conantum hills"—which proves, what could be surmised, that when Thoreau went on to speak of going to his "window" he meant to so attenuate and stress the phenomenon of seeing that it could not possibly be taken for granted: "I *look out at* my eyes" upon the world, as from a window. In the same period he had already sounded the experiential theme in relation to the writer: He "who does not speak out of a full experience uses torpid words, wooden or lifeless words, such words as 'humanitary,' which have a paralysis in their tails" (*J*, IV: 225).

This theme gained reinforcement in his contemplation of natural phenomena. The hawk is "a very handsome bird, . . . not fitted to walk much on the ground, but to soar.... Yet there is a certain unfitness in so fair a breast, so pure white, made to breast nothing less pure than the sky or clouds.... Never bespattered with the mud of earth" (*J*, IV: 332). In the passage which compared the tobacco-pipe plant to "shrinking maidens . . . reared in a vault-like seclusion," Thoreau twice reiterated the point that "their untried virtue cannot long withstand exposure to the light and air"— perhaps unconsciously echoing Milton: "I cannot praise a fugitive and cloistered virtue." A sunset prompted a similar reflection (which is rather surprising in view of Thoreau's morning mystique): "This is the most glorious part of this day, the serenest, warmest, brightest part, and the most suggestive. . . . It is chaste eve, for it has sustained the trials of the day, but to the morning such praise was inapplicable" (J, IV: 33; 1852). And this conviction about the superiority of evening to morning found one of its human exemplars in an old man, "Brooks Clark, who is now about eighty," whom Thoreau met on a woodland path in the autumn of 1857, hurrying along barefoot in a cold wind, carrying his shoes full of wild apples. His response to Brooks Clark is reminiscent at several points of Wordsworth's "Leech-Gatherer":

It pleased me to see this cheery old man, with such a feeble hold on life; bent almost double, thus enjoying the evening of his days. . . . This old man's cheeriness was worth a thousand of the church's sacraments and *momento mori's*. . . . If he had been a young man, he would probably have thrown away his apples and put on his shoes when he saw me coming, for shame. But old age is manlier; it has *learned to live*, [my italics] makes fewer apologies. . . . This seems a very manly man." (J, X: 109–10; 1857.)

But the principal statement of Thoreau's doctrine of experience, his reverence for maturity, is a poem, "Manhood"—by no means his most deft or polished but surely one of the most interesting—which in substance and tone closely resembles the 1852 reflections about the hawk's white breast, and the serenity of evening. "I love to see the man, a long-lived child," it begins, "As yet uninjured by all worldly taint / As the fresh infant whose whole life is play. / . . . But better still I love to contemplate / The mature soul of lesser innocence. . . ." The next few lines make it clear that "lesser innocence" is not merely a synonym for "experience" abstractly conceived. Rather Thoreau meant to emphasize the necessity of some exposure to evil, including some confrontation of evil in the self (—a man must eat "his peck of dirt," as he had put it elsewhere):

. . . The mature soul of lesser innocence,
Who hath travelled far on life's dusty road
Far from the starting point of infancy
And proudly bears his small degen'racy
Blazon'd on his memorial standard high

Who from the sad experience of his fate
Since his bark struck on that unlucky rock
Has proudly steered his life with his own hands.

This sounds like one of Melville's suffering and defiant heroes
(just as the characterization of his opposite, "as yet uninjured by
all worldly taint," may remind us of Ishmael's regretful assessment of Starbuck, or of the elder Henry James's reference to
Emerson as "my unfallen friend"). But above all, as the poem proceeds, I am reminded of Thoreau's descriptions of John Brown: *

Though his face harbors less of innocence
Yet there do chiefly lurk within its depths
.　.　.　.　.　.　.　.
Noble resolves which do reprove the gods[;]
And it doth more assert man's eminence
Above the happy level of the brute
And more doth advertise me of the heights
To which no natural path doth ever lead
No natural light can ever light our steps,
—But the far-piercing ray that shines
From the recesses of a brave man's eye.[3]

The poem widens at the last from a celebration of experience and
maturity into a resolute declaration of humanistic faith. The contemplation of a brave and noble individual asserts the "eminence"
of mankind, not only above the level of other animal life, but in a
Promethean sense above "the gods"; and it is this contemplation
alone (rather, even, than the contemplation of Nature) which can
yield an awareness of "the heights"—ultimate truth, ultimate good.
The date of this poem is not known; Professor Carl Bode has
offered the "guess" that it has no connection with John Brown,
but was composed in the forties.[4] In any case, taking it together
with the *Journal* paragraph which dismisses "people who are too
good for this world," and with the passages just cited from the
late fifties, we must conclude that this profound respect for ex-

---

* "A man of Spartan habits, who at sixty... is ever fitting himself for difficult enterprises. A man of rare common sense and directness of speech, as
of action; a Transcendentalist above all, a man of ideals and principles....
Of unwavering purposes, not to be dissuaded but by an experience and wisdom greater than his own. Not yielding to a whim or transient impulse, but
carrying out the purpose of a life" (J, XII: 420; 1859); and see "A Plea for
Captain John Brown," (*Writings*, IV, p. 413).

perience and maturity, and the humanism which informed and was informed by it, were fundamental elements in Thoreau's thought from first to last.

2

The focus on "the mature soul" in the poem "Manhood" recalls a statement from a passage discussed at length in chapter 6,—the statement that "the design of my maker when he has brought me nearest to women, was not the propagation but the maturation of the species." Whatever this may reveal of Thoreau's attitude toward himself (his disclaiming a role in "propagation," for instance), it tells us something about an underlying attitude toward "the species"—that he believed it capable of maturation. There is evidence elsewhere that this sometimes vehemently misanthropic Thoreau—together with most of his contemporaries—held a deep, though perhaps not always conscious, conviction that mankind was inevitably destined to mature. "By and by we may be ready to receive what we cannot receive now," he wrote (J, XIII: 77) in 1860. And in *Walden's* chapter on "Higher Laws," his discussion of dietary practice ends thus: "I have no doubt that it is a part of the destiny of the human race, in its gradual improvement, to leave off eating animals, as surely as the savage tribes have left off eating each other when they came in contact with the civilized." [5] The sentence's assertion—its only controversial element—is that vegetarianism will form a part of the race's improvement; the improvement itself is taken completely for granted.

But what did Thoreau mean in claiming for *himself* a role in "the maturation of the species"? Or, indeed, to what extent did he see himself in such a role at all? We remember numerous barbed remarks he made about philanthropy, and reformers, including his statement, in a letter to Blake, that he "very rarely" felt "any itching to be what is called useful to my fellowman." Yet this statement to Blake should alert us once again to the necessity of giving due weight to *every* element in a sentence written by Thoreau. Here "what is called useful" no doubt meant "what the self-proclaimed reformers and the self-righteously charitable call useful." And this in turn recalls still another statement, from the *Week:* "Use me then, for I am useful in my way." He would be very useful indeed, he told the world repeatedly, in *his* way.

In dealing with his attitudes toward the community in which

he lived I have already pointed out various kinds of services, neighborly and practical, performed by Thoreau over the years. It is also important to remember that, despite the contempt he frequently expressed for politics and politicians, and despite his disclaimers of involvement, he was a political activist. In the long struggle against slavery—from his jail experience of 1846 to his defense of John Brown in 1859—he was no less committed, and perhaps in the long run no less effective, for being independent of organized movements. "I have no private good," he had written in 1842, "unless it be my peculiar ability to serve the public" (*J*, I: 350). Another interesting commentary on the individual's relationship to society (and on political activism) occurs in a notebook of 1851, where he questioned the wisdom of Mirabeau's having taken to "highway robbery" in order to test the demands of a "formal opposition to . . . society" and to point up a parallel with imperialist wars which were sanctioned by society. "This was good and manly," Thoreau commented, "as the world goes; and yet it was desperate. A saner man would have found opportunities enough to put himself in formal opposition to the most sacred laws of society, . . . in the natural course of events, without violating the laws of his own nature. . . . Let us not have a rabid virtue that will be revenged on society,—that falls on it, not like the morning dew, but like the fervid noonday sun, to wither it" (*J*, II: 332–33).

This passage was incorporated almost verbatim into *Walden's* last chapter (pp. 322–23), although without the final striking simile. At several other points in *Walden*, most memorably in the chapter 1 paragraph on "lives of quiet desperation" (p. 8), Thoreau fully confronted the demon of personal—and national—despair. "Let us spend one day as deliberately as Nature," he urged, "gently and without perturbation" (p. 97). In the *Journal* passage on Mirabeau he at first, and characteristically, dwells on the injury which a "desperate" stance can do to the individual's own integrity. But at the end his concern is for society—the responsible individual's mission in society must not be to "wither" it, but, "like the morning dew," to cleanse and refresh.

Stanley Cavell, viewing *Walden* as "a heroic book," sees Thoreau as "aligning himself with the major tradition of English poetry, whose most ambitious progeny, at least since Milton, had been haunted by the call for a modern epic, for a heroic book which was . . . a renewed instruction of the nation in its ideals. . . ." Citing Thoreau's reference (in an early essay on Carlyle) to "the promise of England," Cavell adds: "As against the usual views about Thoreau's hatred of society and his fancied private declaration of independence from it, it is worth hearing him from the outset publicly accept a nation's promise, identify the significant news of a nation with the state of its promise, and place the keeping of that promise in the hands of a few writers." [6] Ultimately, usefulness "in my way" meant for Thoreau something less timely, less specific and more fundamental than any political or philanthropic activities, something of which they were but outgrowths and emblems.

In introducing my discussion of Thoreau's commitment to community, I cited the passage at the end of *Walden*'s chapter 3 which asserts "it is time that villages were universities." In fact, the whole of *Walden* is an expression of Thoreau's essential humanism, of his determination to "serve the public good"; and this is fully evident despite, or even because of, those instances of cynicism and scathing criticism which were surveyed in chapter 1 of this study. Some readers, in his time and in ours, have claimed to be offended by the book's "egotism," its "brag," as of Chanticleer, as well as by its occasional misanthropic gibes. But Thoreau salutes the cockerel's shrill cry for its awakening and inspiriting quality, for its *social* function: "I propose to brag as lustily as Chanticleer in the morning . . . if only to wake my neighbors up"; —"think of it! It would put nations on the alert. Who would not be early to rise, and rise earlier and earlier every successive day of his life, till he became unspeakably healthy, wealthy and wise?" * [7] This mocking paraphrase of Benjamin Franklin's mun-

---

* Note "my neighbors" in the first sentence, and "nations" in the second. And note how Thoreau in this passage insists on the *American* pedigree of this cockerel with which he identifies himself: "This once wild Indian pheasant . . . He is more indigenous even than the natives" (p. 127). In *The Senses of Walden*, Stanley Cavell emphasizes Thoreau's awareness of the American roots of this passage, as of the entire book: "This smack at Benjamin Franklin's prophecies for America continues the writer's call for 'a little Yankee shrewdness' [*Walden* 1, p. 28], and acknowledges the American location from which his calls and songs will have to make their way. . . . Through *Walden*'s Chanticleer, in his bragging, and in his devotion to philosophy and to the tallest tales of the race, its writer takes upon himself the two archetypes of American folklore distinguished by Constance Rourke: The Yankee, and the Gamecock of the Wilderness" (Cavell, *Senses of Walden*, p. 36). Throughout his book Cavell comments directly on Thoreau's deep involvement with this country—its origins, its hopes and "promises," its hypocrisies and failures (see, for example, pp. 6–11, 23–24, 58, 82–92, 114).

dane prescription for success echoes other sardonic references in the first chapter, "Economy." The word "unspeakably" here again reflects Thoreau's mystical tendency: the experience of the cock's clarion cry brings awareness (to those who are ever on the alert for such awareness) of Life on a transcendent plane, and the possibility of ineffable "health," "wealth," and wisdom, which he believed accessible to all, but of which the Benjamin Franklins of the world are unaware. "But," Thoreau added, "its shrill sound never roused me from my slumbers." This was so precisely because *he* was not "asleep," not oblivious to "the actual glory of the Universe," as he put it elsewhere, not "dead"; because, of course, he did see himself as Chanticleer, a herald of dawn, and his book as an awakening and inspiriting appeal, addressed to all who have ears to hear. He states this explicitly in a great number of passages, and most resoundingly in the first and last chapters:

I would fain say something, not so much concerning the Chinese and Sandwich Islanders as you who read these pages, who are said to live in New England; something about your condition . . . in this world, in this town, what it is, whether it is necessary that it be as bad as it is, whether it cannot be improved as well as not. I have travelled a good deal in Concord. . . . [note "*said to* live."]

I desire to speak somewhere *without* bounds; like a man in a waking moment, to men in their waking moments. . . .[8]

There is not much egotism, I think, in these two statements. Both of them voice a hope, an intention, the achievement of which may be uncertain. The tone of the first is one of high seriousness, of an earnestness which becomes urgent in the sentence's prolongation—in the rhythmic repetitions of "in this world, in this town, what it is, whether it is . . . whether it cannot be improved." And in the second statement I hear a profoundly tender concern: in its simplicity and humility ("I desire to speak," "like a man," "a waking moment"), in the association of "a man . . . to men" (not "to *other* men"), and perhaps even in the comma, which creates a tiny suspense—first, "I desire to speak" in a given way, then the comma, then "to men . . ."; the pause suggests "I dare to hope that I may be speaking *to* someone."

Speaking about what? There can be as many answers to that question—or as many variants of a few basic answers—as there are serious readers of *Walden*. Let us say, as basically and briefly as possible, speaking about the difference between mere existence and Life, or about the necessity of growth, of "renewal." ("I grew in those seasons like corn in the night"; " 'Renew thyself completely each day; do it again, and again, and forever again.' ") [9] The 1842 *Journal* entry in which Thoreau declared that he had "no private good, unless it be my peculiar ability to serve the public" can help to clarify the relationship between this thematic core and the urgently repeated desire for communication. "I must confess," he continued, "I have felt mean enough when asked how I was to act on society, what errand I had to mankind. Undoubtedly I did not feel mean without a reason, and yet my loitering is not without defense. I would fain communicate the wealth of my life to men, would really give them what is most precious in my gift. . . . I will sift the sunbeams for the public good. I know no riches I would keep back" (*J*, I: 350). "My peculiar ability" echoes again the "in my way" discussed earlier.

Thoreau returned to this theme two days later: "If I could help infuse some life and heart into society, should I not do a service?" And a lyrical expression of the same impulse appears in a *Journal* passage entered ten years later: "March 15. . . A mild spring day. . . . The air is full of bluebirds. . . . The villagers are out in the sun, and every man is happy whose work takes him outdoors. . . . I wish to begin this summer well, to do something in it worthy of it and of me; . . . May my melody not be wanting to the season! May I gird myself to be a hunter of the beautiful, that naught escape me! . . . I am eager *to report* [my italics] the glory of the universe. . . ." (*J*, III: 350–51; 1852).

Thoreau voices this same commitment to *communicate* what he felt to be the essence of experience ("the quality of my daily life" —*J*, III: 351) in one of the most memorable passages of *Walden's* most explicitly "thematic" chapter: "I went to the woods because I wished to live deliberately, to front only the essential facts of life, . . . to live deep and suck out all the marrow of life. . . . to drive life into a corner, and reduce it to its lowest terms, and, if it proved to be mean, why then to get the whole and genuine meanness of it, and *publish its meanness to the world*; or if it were sublime, to know it by experience, and *be able to give a true account of it*. . . . [my italics]." This is followed, near the end of the chapter, by a paragraph in which the plural pronoun is repeated with an almost bullying insistence: "Let us spend our lives in conceiving. . . . Let us spend one day. . . . Let us rise early. . . .

Why should we knock under . . . ? Let us not be upset and over-whelmed . . . . We will consider. . . . Let us settle ourselves. . . . We crave only reality." [10] And it was preceded, in chapter 1, by an equally explicit avowal: "I have been anxious . . . to stand on the meeting of two eternities, the past and future, which is precisely the present moment; to toe that line. You will pardon some ob-scurities, for there are more secrets in my trade than in most men's, and yet not voluntarily kept, but inseparable from its very nature. I would gladly tell all that I know about it, and never paint 'No Admittance' on my gate." [11] The conjunction of "obscurities" and "secrets" with the phrase "two eternities" suggests that Thoreau was here again referring to an essentially mystical view of life, which, he emphasizes, he is eager to share. Again he stresses communication.

The humanistic and communal impulses that prompted this reiterated desire of Thoreau's—to communicate the "wealth" of his life and the truth he had perceived—are revealed in several other ways in *Walden*. Not only is there evidence of his belief that the human species is improvable in an evolutionary sense, but also of a belief that the life of any individual is capable of regeneration at any time (" 'Renew thyself . . . each day; do it again. . . .' ") "No man knoweth the hour in which his life [as distinguished from mere existence] may come," he had written in the *Journal*; and similarly, near the beginning of *Walden*, "But man's capacities have never been measured; nor are we to judge of what he can do by any precedents. . . . Who shall say what prospect life offers to another?" At other points he dwells on the idea of community, or on a simple everyday interaction with other people:

At length, in the beginning of May, with the help of some of my ac-quaintances, . . . I set up the frame of my house. No man was ever more honored in the character of his raisers than I. They are destined, I trust, to assist at the raising of loftier structures one day.

What recommends commerce to me is its enterprise and bravery. . . . I see these men every day go about their business with more or less cour-age and content, doing more even than they suspect. . . . I am less af-fected by their heroism who stood up for half an hour in the front line at Buena Vista, than by the steady and cheerful valor of the men who in-habit the snow-plough for their winter quarters. . . .

I think that I love society as much as most, and am ready enough to fasten myself like a bloodsucker for the time to any full-blooded man

that comes in my way.... I had three chairs in my house; one for solitude, two for friendship, three for society. When visitors came in larger
... numbers there was but the third chair.... It is surprising how many
great men and women a small house will contain.

We made that small house ring with boisterous mirth and resound with
the murmur of much sober talk.... Broadway was still and deserted in
comparison.[12]

Finally there is that revealing paragraph near the end of the
book which begins "I left the woods for as good a reason as I went
there. Perhaps it seemed to me that I had several more lives to
live, and could not spare any more time for that one." At first the
point seems to be that he feared a kind of stagnation—had been
distressed to find that in only one week his feet had worn a path
from house to pond, which prompted him to exclaim "how deep
the ruts of tradition and conformity!" At the end of the paragraph,
however, Thoreau suggests that the greater part of his motive was
a desire to function again, more directly, in the community of men,
and—having confronted the "essential facts," and prepared his
testament of Simplicity—to expose himself more thoroughly to the
complexities of family, village, American life: "I did not wish to
take a cabin passage, but rather to go before the mast and on the
deck of the world.... I do not wish to go below now."[13] It is
clear that by taking "cabin passage" ("going below") Thoreau
meant an extended stay at Walden, and that "before the mast and
on the deck of the world" was his metaphor for a thorough rein-
volvement in human society. This is even clearer in the *Journal*
entry from which this passage derives:

But why I changed? why I left the woods? I do not think that I can
tell. I have often wished myself back.... Perhaps if I lived there much
longer, I might live there forever. One would think twice before he accepted heaven on such terms. A ticket to Heaven must include tickets to
Limbo, Purgatory, and Hell.... No, I do not wish for a ticket to the
boxes, nor to take a cabin passage. I will rather go before the mast and
on the deck of the world. (*J*, III: 214–15; 1852.)

Here the whole idea is set forth in terms more extreme than those
of the *Walden* version—here the woods were "Heaven" and the
implication is that life away from the woods, in society, may be
"Limbo, Purgatory, and Hell," all three. But Thoreau added (in both
versions) that he did not wish again to repeat the Walden experi-

ence: "I do not wish to go below now."—that is, at the time of this writing, 1852, five years after his having left the woods. There follows, in *Walden*, a summing up of persuasive simplicity: "I learned this, at least, by my experiment; that if one advances confidently in the direction of his dreams, and endeavors to live the life which he has imagined, he will meet with success unexpected in common hours." And this paragraph concludes with one of many direct addresses to the reader: "If you have built castles in the air, . . . that is where they should be. Now put the foundations under them." [14]

Eight

"A Certain Doubleness"

I will not plant beans another summer, but sincerity, truth, simplicity, faith, trust, innocence. and see if they will not grow in this soil. . . . I would not forget that I deal with infinite and divine qualities in my fellow. All men, indeed, are divine in their core of light, but that is indistinct and distant to me, like the stars of the least magnitude, or the galaxy itself, but my kindred planets show their round disks . . . to my eye. (*J*, I: 382–83.)

So wrote the hopeful Thoreau in his *Journal* in 1845. But when the passage reappeared near the end of *Walden's* seventh chapter, "The Bean Field," it was considerably altered. The cluster of celestial images is missing. There is a more negative note in the first sentence—"[I will plant] such seeds, *if the seed is not lost* [my italics], as sincerity, truth. . . ."—and a clear confession of discouragement farther on: "Alas! I said this to myself; but now another summer is gone, and another, and another, and I am obliged to say to you, Reader, that the seeds which I planted, if indeed they *were* the seeds of those virtues, were wormeaten or had lost their vitality, and so did not come up. Commonly men will only be brave as their fathers were brave, or timid." [1] Such frankly disheartened statements as this are rare in *Walden,* but all the more striking for that reason. They remind us that Thoreau's ultimate commitment to the service of humanity was not hastily nor lightly made, that *Walden's* affirmations were hard won.

Thoreau's misanthropy—ultimately rooted, I believe, in his idealism, his great expectations for humanity—was never completely exorcised, although it may have diminished somewhat toward the end of his life. We cannot shrug off those blatant expressions of hostility which we examined in chapter 1, any more than we can disregard their opposites—the profoundly humanistic statements discussed in chapters 6 and 7. Throughout his life, Thoreau's utterances on the subject of particular persons or of people in general were often marked by extreme contradictions, polarities of feeling. In the first chapter my aim was to present and discuss the purest, least diluted instances of his misanthropy that could be found. Yet I had very early in that chapter to point out certain ambiguities and implicit contradictions within passages which at first glance seemed to express unqualified disapproval or contempt. In this chapter and the following ones, I will examine several key passages in which this kind of contradiction, or ambivalence, is much more evident; and in treating these passages, I shall give still more detailed attention to style and to nuances of tone than I have before attempted.

Obviously the two passages cited above chronicle a major shift in feeling, of which their author was painfully aware—from the optimism of 1845 to the disillusionment ("Alas . . . I am obliged to say to you, Reader") of the corresponding paragraph in *Walden*. Probably the latter was written during one of those unhappy periods of 1851 or 1852 when Thoreau was driven to question his own ability, and that of every other person, to communicate sincerely with his fellows, and when he accused his acquaintances of "cowardice" in their relationships. But the beginnings of disillusionment and failure are visible in the earlier *Journal* paragraph, not only in the admission that the "divinity" of other people is "indistinct and distant," but also in the way in which Thoreau's purpose is formulated: "[I will plant] sincerity . . . faith, trust . . . and see if they will not grow in this soil"; "*I would not forget* [my italics] that I deal with infinite and divine qualities in my fellow." He was here stating a seemingly tentative humanist position, which necessitated a resolution—not to forget.

This recalls the 1852 passage in which he admonished himself to "do the things which lie nearest. . . . Live a . . . life more true to your friends and neighbors, more noble and magnanimous," but in which he also confessed that these are the things "which are difficult to do." (See above p. 98.) Again and again one comes upon these self-exhortations in the *Journal*, passages in which Thoreau urged himself to take more interest in his fellow men, to think well of them, to love them.

We must have infinite faith in each other. If we have not, we must never let it leak out that we have not. . . . There is the same ground for faith now that ever there was. It needs only a little love in you who complain to ground it on. (*J*, III: 258; 1852.)

I sometimes reproach myself because I do not find anything attractive in certain mere trivial employments of men,—that I skip men so commonly, and their affairs. . . . I will not avoid, then, to go by where these men are repairing the stone bridge,—see if I cannot see poetry in that. . . . It is narrow to be confined to woods and fields and grand aspects of nature only. The greatest and wisest will still be related to men. (*J*, II: 420–21; 1851.)

The sight of another laborer, a stone-mason, gave rise to thoughts about the knowledge and skills associated with every craft. Such observations rarely failed to arouse Thoreau's interest, and at first the characteristics attributed to the mason are favorable ones—skill, patience, and "cunning" deliberation. But his successes soon prompted the reflection—typically Thoreauvian—that "mankind [has] much less moral than physical energy . . . any day you see men following the trade of splitting rocks, who yet shrink from undertaking apparently less arduous moral labors, the solving of moral problems." That is a reflection which no serious reader would dispute—least of all in our time, when technology has made possible all but incredible advances in manufactures, in warfare, and the conquest of space, while the "moral problems," augmented, continue to defy solution; it is the now familiar perception of "cultural lag." In this instance, however, the perception signals a subtle shift in Thoreau's attitude toward the mason: "He fights with granite. He knows the temper of the rocks. He grows stony himself. His tread is ponderous and steady like the fall of a rock." By itself this could be regarded as creative hyperbole, and it may even be an apt description of that particular workman. But it soon becomes obvious that Thoreau's feeling toward the man had grown distinctly negative:

The habit of looking at men in the gross makes their lives have less of human interest for us. But though there are crowds of laborers before us, yet each one leads his *little* epic life each day. There is the stone-mason, who, methought, was simply a stony man that hammered stone. . . . *But he, I find, is even a man like myself*, for he feels the heat of the sun and has raised some boards on a frame to protect him. And now, at mid-forenoon, I see his wife and child have come and brought him drink and meat for his lunch and to assuage the stoniness of his labor, and sit to chat with him. (*J*, II: 491–92; 1851. My italics.)

Here again is the note of self-admonition—one of Thoreau's reminders to himself to respect other men, to appreciate the individual humanity of each one. Yet in the midst of it he made that tacit admission that for a time this other man *had not seemed human*. There is no clearer example in all the *Journal* of a statement that is *ostensibly*—and is obviously *intended* to be—sympathetic, whose tone, nevertheless, is markedly condescending, even cold.

Still another instance of self-exhortation occurs in a poem titled "The Hero." At the beginning and the end it voices the same aspirations found in Thoreau's early essay, "The Service"—commitment to a strenuous life of unceasing alertness and unflinching bravery, and to goals forever challenging because forever unreachable. There is an allusion to Wordsworth (to his "serene and contented" old age) immediately following this poem in the *Journal*. And a passage in the heart of the poem is reminiscent of Wordsworth's "still sad music of humanity":

Yet some mighty pain
He would sustain,
So to preserve
His tenderness.
Not be deceived,
Of suff'ring bereaved,
Not lose his life
By living too well,
And so find out heaven
By not knowing hell.

.   .   .

Yet some Aaron's rod,
Some smiting by God,
Occasion to gain
To shed human tears. . . .[2]

Thoreau did not often voice this idea—that one must undergo great pain in order to nurture his capacity for sympathy. This study has already included several expressions of intense suffering from the *Journal*; there are others. But Thoreau did not dwell upon his sorrows—not even after the horrifying illness and death of his brother, not even during his own worst periods of isolation and apparent failure, nor when he felt most convinced of the shallowness or falsity of other people. He was not a man who placed a high value upon suffering, and if he occasionally suggested that it might have a useful effect—in the strengthening of character or in rendering the sufferer more sympathetic to others—the thought is set down in matter-of-fact terms, never insisted upon. Such an effect must have been in his mind when he wrote, following John's death, "For my own part, I feel that I could not have done without this experience." The statement has shocked many readers, and may have shocked Isaiah Williams, to whom it was written, even in its context[3] and despite several years' acquaintance. On the basis of what we know about his feeling for John and his immediate reaction to that death, we must assume Thoreau meant that, having undergone the experience, he was determined to assimilate it and to learn from it. This interpretation gains support from a *Journal* entry of the same month: "Whatever I learn from any circumstance, that especially I needed to know. Events come out of God, and our characters determine them [or at least our response to them?], as much as they determine the words and tone of a friend to us. Hence are they always acceptable as experience, and we do not see how we could have done without them" (J, I, 323–24; 1842).

All this is consistent with the import of numerous other statements, both those which stress the value of experience in general and those which celebrate the "joy" inherent in everyday life. "I do not propose to write an ode to dejection, but to brag as lustily as chanticleer in the morning, standing on his roost, if only to wake my neighbors up." We should remember that Thoreau excerpted this *Walden* sentence for the first edition's title page.[4] In minimizing the usefulness of suffering, and refusing to dwell upon it, he was to some extent the child of his age and of his young, still hopeful nation; and to some extent, of course, he was voicing a tenet of Transcendentalism, the "unshakable optimism" of Alcott, and of Emerson. But Thoreau's resolute refusal to despair, his repeated assertions of satisfaction with his life—LIFE—were intrinsic, the result of a complex conjunction of elements fundamental to his being: both his stoicism and his mysticism, his aesthetic sensibility, his profound response to Nature, to wilderness, and also, surely, his faith in "the gradual improvement of the human race."

One senses, moreover, his shrewd awareness that those who

celebrate the value of suffering may become bewitched by it, may even unconsciously cultivate it. "I believe that what so saddens the reformer," he wrote in *Walden*, "is not his sympathy with his fellows in distress, but, though he be the holiest son of God, is his private ail." [5] It is a perception experienced, or a question asked, in every generation by sensitive people who are aware of the events around them: how much is one's vague depression a *Weltschmerz*, a concern about injustice and one's "fellows in distress," and how much some personal malaise which actually subverts one's ability to act worthily in society? Thoreau liked at times to take a lofty, eagle's-eye view of human society and history. Nevertheless, considering how deeply he was troubled by the evils of slavery (all kinds of slavery), the fate of John Brown, and the cynicism or indifference of many "Christians" around him, one suspects that his adopting that lofty view was a form of self-preservation—as was, no doubt, his assertion after John's death that everything was "acceptable as experience." Presently we shall examine in detail other passages which reveal Thoreau's feelings when he was obliged to confront the sufferings of others at close range—passages which are at least as ambivalent, as fraught with radical inner contradictions, as the self-admonishing ones discussed above.

At times, of course, a close-range confrontation with any "other" could be something of a problem for Thoreau. Now and then, he confessed in his *Journal*, other human beings seemed unreal to his perception, and sometimes it is obvious that they became the more attractive for this seeming unreality:

There was [a] man in a boat in the sun, . . . lifting high his arms and dipping his paddle as if he were a vision bound to [the] land of the blessed—far off as in a picture. When I see Concord to purpose I see it as if it were not real but painted. (*J*, II: 423; 1851.)

As I stood on the bank of the pond . . . I saw not more than thirty rods off a chopper at his work . . . against the snow on the hillside beyond. It was perhaps one of those effects which have made men painters. I could not behold him as an actual man; he was more ideal than in any picture I have seen. He refused to be seen as actual. (*J*, III: 254; 1852.)

I have cited in chapter 1 another such passage, in which ice fishermen, seen through a mist, were said to be "as ill-defined and great as men should always be." This idea, that other people are rendered more tolerable when distant, is echoed in yet another curious passage of this period, along with a note of personal grievance, but also with a hint, once again, of commitment to public service:

My practicalness is not to be trusted to the last. To be sure, I go upon my legs for the most part, but, being hard-pushed and dogged by a superficial common sense which is bound to near objects by beaten paths ... I begin to be transcendental and show where my heart is. I am like those guinea fowl which Charles Darwin saw at the Cape de Verde Islands.... Keep your distance, do not infringe on the interval between us, and I will pick up lime and lay real terrestrial eggs for you, and let you know by cackling when I have done it.

"When I have been asked to speak at a temperance meeting," he added, "my answer has been, 'I am too transcendental to serve you in your way.' "—There it is again: "Use me, for I am useful in *my* way." Here the target of Thoreau's impatience is the often superficial, common-sensical "mass of men," who are addressed with the generalized "you." Yet an ambivalence of attitude is implied —Thoreau is clearly saying, "I cannot conform to your expectations, but I would like to serve you ... in my way." (Note that the "cackling" here corresponds to the "crowing" of Thoreau-Chanticleer in *Walden*.) And the positive aspect is still more evident in the following two paragraphs. There a celebration of the beauty of the earth and the exhilaration of walking comes, quite surprisingly, to focus on the idea of a welcome interaction with other people: "You may walk out in any direction ... and everywhere your path leads you between heaven and earth, not away from the light of the sun and stars and the habitations of men. I wonder that I ever get five miles on my way, the walk is so crowded with events and phenomena. How many questions there are which I have not put to the inhabitants!" The passage closes with a striking instance of the communal "we": "With reference to the near past we all occupy the region of common sense, but in the prospect of the future we are, by instinct, transcendentalists" (*J*, II: 228–29; 1851).

But Thoreau again strikes out at the common-sense mediocrity of the average man in a highly ambivalent passage whose starting point was that one of all of Nature's phenomena most troubling to him: "When I saw the fungi in my lamp I was startled and awed, as if I were stooping too low, and should next be found classifying carbuncles and ulcers. Is there not sense in the mass of men who ignore and confound these things, and never see the cryptogamia on the one side any more than the stars on the other?" Such a question is a measure of the degree to which Thoreau was troubled by all evidences of parasitism and disease in Nature (as, of course, in the moral sphere). But the question is more tentative than genuine, and the tribute to common sense is grudging at best. This becomes clear in the following sentence, which restates the terms of the question, attributing to the mass of men, not "sense," but rather venality: "they," no more conscious of the sublime than of the extremely sordid, can nonetheless "all read the pillars on a Mexican quarter." The sharpness of this is somewhat mitigated by a final restatement, whose tone is fairly neutral: "They ignore the worlds above and below, keep straight along, and do not run their boots down at the heels as I do."—And the paragraph trails off into a lengthy complaint about the non-durability of boots and the cupidity of cobblers who scant the heel pegs (*J*, V: 51–52; 1853).

A salute to one of the natural phenomena best beloved by Thoreau suddenly involves a seemingly unprovoked attack on human civilization, or a dismissal of it: "I love that early twilight hour when the crickets still creak right on with such dewy faith and promise. . . . While the creak of the cricket has that ambrosial sound, no crime can be committed. It buries Greece and Rome past resurrection. The earth-song of the cricket! Before Christianity was, it is. Health! health! health! is the burden of its song." Certainly a strong and growing emotion is obvious here—in the words "dewy" and "earth," the curious tense transposition of "Before Christianity was, it *is*," the grammatical incompletion of the first exclamation, and, of course, in the exclamation points themselves. Therefore we cannot but take seriously the implied denigration of usually respected human societies and institutions, the more so as Thoreau's introduction of them seems completely gratuitous. The odd change of tense conveys, literally, "Before Christianity existed the cricket existed, as it now exists"; but it has the suggestive effect of relegating Christianity entirely to the past while magically underscoring the timeless durability of the cricket's song. There is also the association of Greece, Rome, and Christianity with "crime," and, by implication, with disease, since the interpretation of the cricket-sound as "health!" appears to be offered as an alternative. The next sentences, however, introduce the familiar note of ambivalence. The morning sound of the cricket is heard as "Health! health!" because "man, refreshed with sleep, is thus innocent and healthy and hopeful."—Not "I am"; "man is." The fellow-feeling implied in "man" is echoed once again in a communal "we" at the paragraph's end. But there is also an echo of the earlier thrust at society and its institutions, in a reference to a familiar line from Wordsworth–the line that was probably most often quoted by Thoreau: "When we hear that sound of the crickets in the sod, the world is not so much with us" (J, IV: 109–10; 1852).

Thoreau's tone and underlying attitudes in these passages can be better understood when considered together with another entry of the early fifties. There a paragraph in the midst of copious and seemingly untroubled field notes suddenly reveals a deep mistrust of the scientific orientation. "Man cannot afford to be a naturalist, to look at Nature directly," it begins, "but only with the side of his eye. He must look through and beyond her. To look at her [analyzing and classifying] is fatal as to look at the head of Medusa. It turns the man of science to stone." To look "through and beyond" Nature, we know, was for Thoreau to look with the eyes of the poet, the philosopher, the mystic. There follows here one of the earliest of many lamentations, in the *Journal*, that he felt himself increasingly bound to analysis and classification, amassing notes compulsively, as if against his will. Having rasped his hand against a rough rock, he says, he realized that his attention was immediately diverted from the pain to an examination of the lichens growing there. (In other words, intellect superseded feeling.) And yet, he confessed, "I have almost a slight, dry headache as the result of all this observing." It is just before that confession that this startling sentence occurs: "I look upon man but as a fungus" (J, V: 45; 1853). First "man," an agent, presumably capable of choice, is warned against a literal, scientific view of Nature; then "man" suddenly becomes an object—and of all objects, the most disagreeable!—within that view. The drift of several of these passages suggests that whatever misanthropic vein was native to Thoreau's temperament was fed and accentuated by his scientific preoccupations; and, also, that part of his resistance to this growing preoccupation came from his perception that it might involve a further diminishing of mankind in his total perspective. This, the fungus passage suggests, was, after all, a thing greatly to be feared.

2

As I stand under the hill beyond J. Hosmer's and look over the plains westward toward Acton and see the farmhouses nearly half a mile apart, few and solitary, in these great fields between these stretching woods, out of the world, where the children have to go far to school;

the still, stagnant, heart-eating, life-everlasting, and gone-to-seed country, so far from the post-office where the weekly paper comes, wherein
the new-married wife cannot live for loneliness, and the young man
has to depend upon his horse for society ... the world in winter for
most walkers reduced to a sled track winding far through the drifts,
all springs sealed up and no digressions; where the old man thinks he
may possibly afford to rust it out, not having long to live, but the
young man pines to get nearer the post-office and the Lyceum, is restless and resolves to go to California, because the depot is a mile off (he
hears the rattle of the cars at a distance and thinks the world is going
by and leaving him); where rabbits and partridges multiply, and muskrats are more numerous than ever, and none of the farmer's sons are
willing to be farmers, and the apple trees are decayed and the cellar
holes are more numerous than the houses, and the rails are covered with
lichens, and the old maids wish to sell out and move into the village,
and have waited twenty years in vain for this purpose and never finished
but one room in the house, never plastered or painted, ... lands which
the Indian was long since dispossessed [of], and now the farms are run
out, and what were forests are grain fields, and what were grain fields,
pastures; ... where some men's breaths smell of rum, having smuggled
in a jugful to alleviate their misery and solitude; where the owls give
a regular serenade;—I say, standing there and seeing these things, I
cannot realize that this is that hopeful young America, which is famous
throughout the world for its activity and enterprise, and this is the most
thickly settled and Yankee part of it. What must be the condition of
the *old* world! (*J*, III: 237–38.)

This remarkable passage, which the *Journal*'s editors headed
"The Gone-to-Seed Country," occurs in an entry of 1852, dated
January 27. It begins matter-of-factly, "Mill Road, south of Minis-
terial swamp, 3 p.m.," and then sweeps on in a single sentence
(here necessarily shortened) for a page and a half, or about 475
words. One is struck first of all by the sheer length of the sentence,
and next by its tonal variations. Its overall effect is one of gathering intensity, achieved by the accumulation of dependent clauses,
by abrupt changes of focus, and by certain ellipses and omissions
—all of which suggest that the passage was written quickly,
urgently, and (though possibly augmented) not substantially re-
vised.* It was this sentence which formed the starting point for

---

* Such an assumption is borne out by an acquaintance with this passage in
the original manuscript notebook. (MA 1302, number 15, Morgan Library,

this study, which alerted me to other passages equally complex in tone, and led me to ponder the question of Thoreau's relationships —his humane sympathies and his misanthropy, and their often close conjunction.

In this passage the tone seems to fluctuate between compassion and a critical detachment laced with scorn. There is pity, even empathy, for frustrated and lonely people, in such terms as "heart-eating," in the glimpses of the far-journeying children, the new-married wife, the old man who merely endures life, and even the "misery and solitude" of the rum-drinkers. Near the beginning Thoreau mentions two farmers by name, and with sympathy: "Young J. Hosmer," who has returned with his wife "in despair, after living in the city," and one Tarbell, who cannot, single-handed, "break out" of his snow-filled road in winter. But we are aware all the while of a cool countercurrent running through the paragraph—the coolness of a critical observer or satirist. The young man's restlessness is reported in an unmistakably satirical way: he "pines" for mere proximity to the post office; the depot is too far away to serve for daily diversion, yet too near—the sound of the trains evokes for him the world, which he feels himself

---

New York.) The quality of Thoreau's always difficult script seems here even more swift and slanting than in the immediate context; at several points a word or fragment of a word was impatiently crossed out, and there are a number of fine-script insertions between lines. Most of these insertions are in the same ink and the same headlong script that cover the page (e.g., "and the rails are covered with lichens," "never plastered or painted inside or out"); but a few which are in pencil (e.g., "he hears the rattle of the cars . . . and thinks the world is going by and leaving him"; "where some men's breaths smell of rum . . . their misery and solitude") suggest a subsequent effort on Thoreau's part to round out his description. In some instances the beginnings of short dependent clauses are capitalized as if they were independent sentences, but at other points not only words but two or three clauses are linked together in a single sustained scrawl, in which he did not lift his pen until it reached the very edge of the page. A look at the manuscript reinforces for the reader a sense both of the urgency with which the passage was first composed, and (on the evidence of the pencil insertions) the importance which it continued to have in Thoreau's eyes. Its importance, and—however troubled he may have been in the rendering—the artistic satisfaction that he may have felt in having fully and successfully rendered the gone-to-seed landscape, is perhaps reflected in the final short paragraph which ends the entry under this date: "I do not know but thoughts written down thus in a journal might be printed in the same form with greater advantage than if the related ones were brought together into separate essays. . . ." (J, III: 239).

somehow outside; and might he not still feel bypassed in California? His restlessness recalls Thoreau's light satires on compulsive travelling, in the final chapter of *Walden* and elsewhere ("Our voyaging is only great-circle sailing . . . explore your own higher latitudes. . . .") The old maids are pitiable, yes, yet they are also made in a very few words to seem ridiculous. Their designation is abrupt and uncompromising—"the old maids"; they "wish," still, to bring off a real-estate transaction which has been frustrated for twenty years. Indeed, there is a touch of scorn in the hyperbolic statement that the new-married wife "cannot *live* for loneliness."

When the impulse that piled up this astonishing series of dependent clauses had spent itself, when Thoreau at last reined in, to repeat "standing there," and deliver the main clause of his sentence, he dropped back into the relatively matter-of-fact tone of the passage's beginning. And we gather from the socioanalytical sentences which follow that (as we should expect) he did indeed deplore what seemed to him the weakness and the herd instinct of such gone-to-seed Americans, their lack of energy and of Self-Reliance. Yet in the body of that very long sentence (where he was contemplating individuals rather than the mass of men), there is compassion, there is an awareness of people suffering. And—since his attitude is ambivalent, since he is also the cool observer, satirist, judge—there is great tension; the paragraph achieves a memorable tension and vitality.

Whatever his assessment of the weakness of these individuals, it is important to recognize that Thoreau's basic concern here was for a community, for "civilization." The reference to his "hopeful young" nation's (supposed) "activity and enterprise" recalls those passages in which he praised the "sturdy uplandish vigor" of certain New Hampshire towns, or in which he urged a broad educational-cultural program for Concord and similar communities. The gone-to-seed country is "stagnant, heart-eating," and its remaining inhabitants are miserable, because human habitations are ever fewer—"the cellar holes are more numerous than the houses." This passage describes an instance of a decaying community's gradually being reclaimed by Nature, but Thoreau, the apostle of Wildness, does not seem here to have felt any satisfaction on witnessing that reclamation. If his tone in dealing with the remaining inhabitants is now compassionate, now ironic, his description of the gone-to-seed country itself is broodingly elegiac in tone. The natural details selected do not illustrate exuberance or beauty but a seeming fatigue and impoverishment in Nature herself—sealed-up springs, decaying apple trees, lichens—and these details are interwoven throughout with the instances of human dissatisfaction and distress.

The passage reveals once again how, in the expanding America of the early fifties, when—despite the sectional quarrel—many of his contemporaries still felt only confidence in the country's enterprise and its future, Thoreau, looking near at hand, perceived signs of exhaustion, fear, and decadence. These are perceptions more commonly recorded in the later nineteenth century and the twentieth; and the vignette portraits in this passage may remind us of the wistful, mildly eccentric farm dwellers and villagers of Sarah Orne Jewett and Mary Wilkens Freeman, or of O'Neill's "Desire Under the Elms." I am especially reminded of several poems by Frost, which depict lonely, deteriorating New England habitations and lives discouraged and thwarted—among them, "The Hill Wife," "An Old Man's Winter Night," "A Servant to Servants," "Directive," "A Cabin in the Clearing."

And when Thoreau attempted to express these insights, and his feelings about them, his style became highly complex and unconventional, little resembling the neat Addisonian ideal still cherished by many Americans of his time. It does resemble the solemn paratactic cadences of the last chapter of Ecclesiastes ("In the day when the keepers of the house shall tremble, and the strong men shall bow themselves, and the grinders cease because they are few, and those that look out of the windows be darkened, / And the doors shall be shut in the streets, when the sound of the grinding is low, / . . . and the almond tree shall flourish, and the grasshopper shall be a burden, and desire shall fail. . . .") Apparently Thoreau had an intimate acquaintance with that chapter, whose beginning, "Remember thy Creator in the days of thy youth," is echoed once in *Walden* and at least twice in the *Journal*. In this passage, whether consciously or unconsciously echoing, he may have felt himself in an analogous role, of "preacher" or prophet. And at times the "Gone-to-Seed" passage approaches the density and apparent disorder that characterize a dominant idiom of twentieth-century literature. To my ear, this lengthy, cumulative sentence, syntactically strained, with its parenthetic asides and chains of dependent clauses, suggests the style of no other writer so much as Faulkner. In the rhythm of such passages as "and the apple trees . . . and the cellar holes . . . and the rails . . . and the old maids wish to sell . . . ," and above all in "lands which the Indian was long since dispossessed [of]," the similarity is especially striking.[6]

Some years later Thoreau wrote another paragraph about a gone-to-seed farm. An entry in 1859, which begins with cheerful botanical notes, moves on to a long meditation on the smoking chimneys of farm-houses. This time the point is that charm is lent to the scene by distance and by ignorance; the passage illustrates Thoreau's perennial impulse to glorify Man, an impulse perennially frustrated: "When I see only the roof of a house above the woods . . . I presume that one of the worthies of the world dwells beneath it. . . . But commonly, if I see or know the occupant, I am affected as by the sight of the almshouse or hospital." Here, as if unwilling to pursue such thoughts, he shifted to five more short paragraphs of random botanizing, but then, compulsively, returned to the earlier subject: "Consider the infinite promise of a man, so that the sight of his roof at a distance suggests an idyll or a pastoral. . . . How all the poets have idealized the farmer's life!" There follows this haunting paragraph, concluding the entry for that date:

As I come by a farmer's to-day, the house of one who died some two years ago, I see the decrepit form of one whom he had engaged to "carry through," taking his property at a venture, feebly tying up a bundle of fagots with his knee on it, though time is fast loosening the bundle that he is. When I look down on that roof I am not reminded of the mortgage which the village bank has on that property,—that that family long since sold itself to the devil and wrote the deed with their blood. I am not reminded that the old man I see in the yard is one who has lived beyond his calculated time, whom the young one is merely "carrying through" in fulfillment of his contract; that the man at the pump is watering the milk. I am not reminded of the idiot that sits by the kitchen fire. (J, XII: 368–69.)

Again we see a complication of style, and sense a growing urgency. In fact, Thoreau's feeling here apparently became so intense that he failed to make clear the number and roles of the personae (old men, young men) figuring in the passage.* Again, for twentieth-century readers, there are Faulknerian portents, both of style and

---

* The manuscript original of this passage proved to be among the most difficult—least legible—of the fifty or so passages (dated between 1850 and 1860) which I have examined at the Morgan Library.

of subject—the physical and moral disintegration of a family, the idiot by the kitchen fire. Most striking, however, is a shift in tone as the paragraph develops. The first "I am not reminded" may be taken simply as underscoring, ironically, what has just been said about the poet's habitual idealization of the farmer; but the second and third carry a note, increasingly insistent, of dread, as if Thoreau had literally tried to resist pondering this scene of suffering and decay.

Coming to these *Journal* passages with a prior knowledge of *Walden*, one is likely to recall a passage in chapter 14, "Former Inhabitants and Winter Visitors." This passage treats another portion of gone-to-seed country—the defunct Brister's Hill community and other abandoned dwelling-sites near Walden Pond, once occupied by a scattering of freed slaves, by Wyman the potter "squatting" in a rude hut, Hugh Quoil, the alcoholic Irishman who had seen better days, the rum-ruined Breed family, and others. In Thoreau's dealings with these vanished shades there are no all-but-unparseable, highly charged sentences comparable to the *Journal* passages discussed above. The tone, for the most part, is that of an inquisitive antiquarian. At the end—in what I feel to be one of the less attractive passages in *Walden*—the antiquarian turns moralist, coldly censorious. Querying why this community failed to survive, he mutters "degeneracy," fixes upon the demon Rum ("they were universally a thirsty race"), and finally exclaims, "Alas! how little does the memory of these human inhabitants enhance the beauty of the landscape!" [7]

Once in his *Journal* Thoreau instructed himself to rid his prose of "Alas." It was sound advice, but he continued now and then to fall back on this "literary" prop—usually, it seems, when he was trying to escape from a painful emotion. I think that is what happened at the end of this passage in *Walden*. Although the style is relatively calm and controlled throughout, there are three points at which (as Emerson put it) "the temperature of thought" rises and the tone becomes more emotional, the phrasing more rhythmic, the language richer.

In each case the emotion, implied or overtly expressed, is pity. In the first of these, Thoreau tells how he one night encountered the sole surviving Breed, "moaning" beside the blackened cellar hole of his family's burned-out house. "Soothed by the sympathy which my mere presence implied," he groped in darkness for the well-sweep his father had made, begging Thoreau to admire its weight and workmanship. The second instance concerns the pathetic remains—"curled-up" clothing, pipe, soiled playing cards—he discovered in the dead Hugh Quoil's shanty. The third is a descriptive meditation upon the entire gone-to-seed landscape, with its over-grown cellar holes ("dents in the earth"), covered wells and choked springs ("dry and tearless grass"), and the once-domesticated lilac bushes, which have long out-lived their youthful human planters and still flourish, "tender, civil, cheerful," among the rank returning natural foliage.* It was immediately following this sympathetic passage on the children and the lilac that Thoreau pulled himself up ("Alas!") and became the censorious judge.

The *Journal* contains at least one other passage in which he describes a section of his native Middlesex as gone-to-seed country. This time one Isaiah Green of Carlisle, a town selectman whom he had encountered when "perambulating the bounds" of Concord, is in the foreground. At first Thoreau expressed genuine pity at the thought of "the retirement in which Green has lived for nearly eighty years." The old man "can remember when there were three or four houses around him," but the "billows of migration," now

---

* This last passage, in the landscape details selected—closing cellar holes, water springs, lilacs—in its tender evocation of vanished children, and in the complexity of its tone (melancholy, detachment, wry humor, tenderness, in rapid succession) bears a striking resemblance to one of Frost's finest poems, "Directive." Although "Directive"—with its journey framework, its direct address to the reader, and its suggestions of myth and ritual—has a greater richness and force than Thoreau's paragraph, it is quite possible that the poem was suggested to Frost by this passage in *Walden*.

Although he does not mention this *Walden*-"Directive" correspondence, Reuben Brower has discussed certain temperamental and artistic affinities between Frost and Thoreau in *The Poetry of Robert Frost: Constellations of Intention.* ([New York: Oxford University Press, 1963], see especially pp. 69–74, and 102.) Recently, reviewing *Walden*, I noticed one other interesting correspondence, this one to Frost's "Fire and Ice." In chapter 13, "House-Warming," Thoreau told how his usually "trustworthy housekeeper—Fire" had one day shot a spark which partially burned his bed. In the next paragraph he remarked on the inability of mankind to withstand cold, concluding that we need not "trouble ourselves to speculate how the human race may be at last destroyed. It would be easy to cut their threads any time with a little sharper blast from the north" (pp. 253–54). ("Some say the world will end in fire, / Some say in ice" ... "I know that for destruction ice / Is also great / And would suffice.") I think it will be agreed that of these two meditations on the end of humanity Thoreau's is a little less coldly misanthropic in tone than Frost's. Both appear to have accepted the idea of the world's end—simply pondering the manner in which it could occur.

populating the American West, have "long since swept over the spot which Green inhabits, and left him in the calm sea"—in an exhausted, all-but-abandoned region. "There is somewhat exceedingly pathetic to think of in such a life as he must have lived. . . . such a life as an average Carlisle man may be supposed to live drawn out to eighty years. And he has died, perchance, and there is nothing but the mark of his cider-mill left. . . . and so men lived, and ate, and drank, and passed away. . . ." (*J*, III: 4; 1851). But here, once again, Thoreau was ambivalent. As the focus widened from Green to include others of his kind, a pronounced shift in feeling occurred, from pity to contempt: ". . . and so men lived and ate, and drank, and passed away—like vermin. Their long life was mere duration. . . . That is the life of these *selectmen* (!) spun out. They will be forgotten in a few years, even by such as themselves, like vermin. . . . We only know that they ate and drank, and built barns, and died, and were buried, and still, perhaps, their tombstones cumber the ground." (*J*, III: 4, 9–10; 1851).

On a few pages before and after this Thoreau complained bitterly, as we have seen, of certain unnamed selectmen and landowners whom he had met or observed in the course of his surveying work. It is not clear whether he saw Green as one of those— "commonplace and worldly-minded . . . mean and narrow-minded . . . grovelling, coarse, and low-lived" (*J*, III: 5, 23); or whether this particular shift from pity to contempt reflected a more general, though unconscious, class prejudice, felt instinctively by a highly educated man for the mass of mere land-tillers whom he did not know well—not Minott, Hosmer or Rice, but the "typical" property-conscious owners (whose fences impeded his own poetic-scientific perambulations). At any rate *these* farmers, and the Brister's Hill squatters in *Walden*, are the ancestors of Eliot's "hollow men." They belong to that great "mass of men" of whom Thoreau wrote so searingly (in "A Plea for John Brown") that they *could not die*—they "hadn't got it in them"; their "lives" seemed to him so lacking in true vitality that the eventual transition to physical death would make little difference.

Nine

The Problem of Death

Bitter though it is, Thoreau's assertion in "A Plea for John Brown" that most men are incapable of dying, because never sufficiently alive, is surely one of the most ineffably comic passages in American literature. Many readers must have laughed aloud— briefly—at this memorable instance of Thoreauvian extravagance. Already unnerved by the depth of his distress at Brown's fate and his furious condemnation of all who did not share his admiration, they can find a momentary release from tension in the section which begins "This event advertises to me that there is such a fact as death," and which goes on, "piling Pelion upon Ossa," for a full page.* Surprised by its wit and flourish, the reader may at first miss the intense, unabated anger that surges through this passage, and the complexity of attitudes it reveals. A closer inspection suggests that while Thoreau was indeed enraged by the timidity or the indifference of most of his contemporaries in this crisis, he was also, then as always, angry at the thought of death—Brown's imminent death, and Death. Yet in this passage he uses—exploits— the idea of death, with an "insolent familiarity,"[1] to discredit, indeed, to dismiss, the mass of men: death is treated as a *distinction*

---

* "It seems as if no man had ever died in America, for in order to die you must first have lived.... I hear a good many pretend that they are going to die.... Nonsense! I'll defy them to do it. They haven't got life enough in them.... Do you ... think you are going to die, sir? No! There is no hope of you, sir, you haven't got your lesson yet. You've got to stay after school.... Franklin,—Washington,—they were let off without dying; these were merely missing one day." See below for the passage's climax, and above, chapter 1, p. 5, for its preceding context.

conferred only upon those, like John Brown—"half a dozen or so since the world began"—who have been truly alive. And here, at what is surely the comic climax, we again encounter that terrible apparition, the fungus. Those (supposed) worthies who "haven't got life enough in them" to die, will simply "deliquesce like fungi, and keep a hundred eulogists mopping the spot where they left off." [2] The "deaths" of such as these are both trivial and repulsive. The reader can feel the full force of this statement, the blackness of its humor, only if he has read the *Journal* passage on the giant parasol fungus, which "defiled all it touched," and the bitter confession that "I look upon man but as a fungus", as well as the cold remark about the old man bundling fagots, that "time is fast loosening the bundle that he is," and the reiterated statement that Green of Carlisle and his kind merely eat, drink, build barns, and die, *"like vermin,"* and are forgotten, "like vermin."

Only a few commentators have discussed Thoreau's attitudes toward death at any length.[3] As the John Brown passage suggests, it is a predictably complex subject. For a man who so elevated and intensified the idea of *life*, that he habitually invested all the world's mutations with more than their original force, the thought of death would have to be a compelling and a powerfully repugnant thought. Just as he refused to dwell on the thought of suffering—or tried to evade it—so at times he attempted to evade the idea of death. His whole inclination was to concentrate on Life,* and, confronted by the fact of death, to try to "outface" it; perhaps his most characteristic response was one of anger.

Such an effort to outface death is apparent in the impatient, dismissive tone of a familiar passage from *Walden's* chapter 2: "Be it life or death, we crave only reality. If we are really dying [note the tentative "if"], let us hear the rattle in our throats and feel cold in the extremities; if we are alive [again, "if"; an awareness of the difference between mere existence and genuine living is vital here], let us go about our business." [4] We have seen Thoreau's attempt at a transcendental kind of acceptance, an effort to go about his business, in the letter to Williams following John's death.[5] A more characteristic reaction—in which (as in the John Brown passage) anger is expressed with defiant humor—is seen in a terse *non*

---

* "I would crow like Chanticleer in the morning ... without thinking of the evening, when I and all of us shall go to roost...." (J, V: 215–16). Note here the emphatic inclusion of the "communal" plural—"and all of us."

sequitur written years later, when, in the middle of a tranquil paragraph on the beauties of autumn, he suddenly remarked that "A man killed by lightning would have a good answer ready in the next world to the question 'How came *you* here?' which he need not hesitate to give" (*J*, IV: 306; 1852). However droll the tone,* he was then shaking his fist at fate.

An important question arises: what significance did Thoreau attach to that phrase, "the next world"? One remembers his reported reply to a pious visitor when he was in his last illness— "One world at a time." [6] There are other such hints in his writings that at times he might have believed—or at least greatly wished to believe—in the possibility of a personal immortality. One eloquent statement of such a belief, or hope, is treated farther along in this chapter. (See below, p. 165.) But at least as many passages suggest that he, like Melville, had "made up his mind to be annihilated." [7] The obsessive preoccupation with Life would certainly not contradict an acceptance of death as final.

The distress, the revulsion which Thoreau often felt in confronting the thought of that finality is nowhere more vividly shown than in a bitter "nocturne" of 1853, in which he described a period of personal barrenness—a time when "the Milky Way yields no milk" and the silence, at other times so greatly valued, was "not fertile" but "negative . . . a mere Sahara, where men perish of hunger and thirst. . . ." In a succeeding paragraph he described a dream of which, he asserted, "I easily read the moral": "Yesterday I was influenced with the rottenness of human relations. They appeared to me full of death and decay, and offended the nostrils. In the night I dreamed of delving amid the graves of the dead, and soiled my fingers with their rank mould. It was *sanitarily, morally, and physically* true" (*J*, IV: 472). This linking of disgust at the thought of death with an expression of misanthropy —again as in "A Plea for John Brown"—occurs in a number of other places in the *Journal*. Here, a confident interpretation of the last sentence quoted is probably beyond our grasp, except as it supports in a general way Thoreau's assertion that he could explain

---

* The jesting note in connection with death is heard at many other points, for example in the *Journal* remark: "Very nice; as the old lady said when she had got a gravestone for her husband." The relevance of this remark is obscure; it follows the statement that "A man tells me he saw a violet to-day," which Thoreau doubtless considered a "very nice" piece of information in December—but why *that* association? (*J*, IV: 427; Dec. 9, 1852).

the dream (that is, evidently, its relevance to "the rottenness of human relations") and that it was shockingly vivid. The somber emphasis on its "truth" is borne out by the (perhaps unconscious) shift from "dreamed of delving" to "soiled"—not "and of soiling," but "and soiled my fingers with their rank mould."

Something of the same repugnance is surely present, though more quietly expressed, in another passage of the same year, which once again refers to the—for Thoreau—most distressing growth in the natural world. Having just commented on the smell of decaying fungi, he fell to musing on "the earthiness of old people." Despite the fact that for this poet-naturalist the fungus was invariably associated with a cluster of ideas such as "corruption," decay, and death, the sequence of thoughts in this passage suggests that the specific idea of human mortality was often near the surface of his consciousness. Here, apparently triggered by an odor, is Thoreau's response to the very old—not to Minott nor Mary Emerson, nor Charles Dunbar nor Brooks Clark, but "the mass of" old people. They are described as "mouldy as the grave"; "their wisdom" is said to "smack of the earth." And although "earth" was normally a most positive word for Thoreau, it seems not to be so here, for the wisdom of old people is also said to have "no foretaste of immortality in it. They remind me of earthworms and mole crickets" (J, V: 377). Two days later he wrote that "the year is full of warnings of its shortness, as is life"; he felt that the August insects and flowers were all saying " 'For the night cometh in which no man may work' " (J, V: 379). At times the worth of man's entire life cycle seems to have been negated for Thoreau by the prospect of eventual extinction. In one of the earliest examples of Thoreauvian misanthropy cited in chapter 1, the fact of mortality is included as the climactic item in a calculatedly belittling caricature of humankind: "Such is man,—toiling, heaving, struggling ant-like to shoulder some stray unappropriated crumb . . . ; then runs out, complacent . . . ; there seen of men, world-seen, deed-delivered, vanishes into all-grasping night" (J, I: 34; 1838). Certainly there is "no foretaste of immortality" here. Indeed, this may have been one source of Thoreau's misanthropy: since all are sentenced to die, and if there is no hope of an after-life, he may at times have felt, both the drudgery and the self-vaunting of "the mass of men" seem pointless, even despicable.

Nevertheless, many of those passages in his work which are notably ambivalent, which are striking for a wide divergence of attitudes toward other human beings, have also to do with the fact of facts—the fact of death. In another early notebook (1840) there is a long outburst on burial customs which reveals a revulsion even more conscious than that revealed in the passage describing the dream of "delving amid the graves of the dead." It begins, "How may a man most cleanly and gracefully depart out of nature?" Although written before the death of John, and—so far as we know—before any other death had touched Thoreau closely, this passage nevertheless dwells obsessively upon the decomposition of the dead body (its "impurities" are linked to the vices its owner had had when alive: "It was no better than carrion before but just animated enough to keep off the crows"), and upon the "disgusting" thought of the earth becoming ever more encumbered with rotting human carcasses.[8] Though calm at the beginning, the passage's tone quickly becomes strident, bitter, and at times all but choked with repugnance. The point that it is man's unclean mode of life which accounts for his repulsiveness in death—as, often, for his death itself—is sounded repeatedly:

Disease kills him, and his carcass smells to heaven. It offends the bodily sense, only so much as his life offended the moral sense. It is the odor of sin.... The birds of prey which hover in the rear of an army are an intolerable satire on mankind, and may well make the soldier shudder. The mosquito sings our dirge.... He preaches a biting homily to us. He says put away beef and pork—small beer and ale, and my trump shall die away and be no more heard. The intemperate cannot go nigh to any wood or marsh but he hears his requiem sung—all nature is up in arms against him.

...Man lays down his body in the field and thinks from it as a stepping stone to vault at once into heaven, as if he could establish a better claim there when he had left such a witness behind him on the plain.... When we have become intolerable to ourselves shall we be tolerable to heaven?

...When nature finds man returned on her hands, he is not simply those pure elements she has contributed to his growth, but with her floods she must wash away and with her fires burn up the filth that has accumulated, before she can receive her own again. He poisons her gales and is a curse to the land that gave him birth—she is obliged to employ her scavengers in self-defence to abate the nuisance.

At this point the twentieth-century reader will inevitably think of mankind's present perils of air- and water-pollution, and it is easy to imagine Thoreau, faced with our situation, reacting in some such terms as these. But it is clear that he was then pondering both the literal decay of the human body and whatever struck him as "moral decay"—considering them together as if they were inseparable. His revulsion at the thought of rotting corpses had awakened a savage outburst of misanthropy, in which anger at death itself easily became anger directed against its victims. There is no suggestion that, since humanity is itself the creature of "heaven" and/or "nature," it might be unfair to condemn the creature alone. In this passage, man is held to be the author of his own dissolution and shame.

And yet the second half of the passage contains hints of Thoreau's humanism, of a tenderness and a yearning which do not mitigate, but which in fact account for his bitterness in the face of man's death and dissolution. "May we not," he wonders, "suffer our impurities gradually to evaporate in sun and wind, with the superfluous juices of the body, and so wither and dry up at last like a tree in the woods, which . . . still stands erect without shame or offence amidst its green brethren, the most picturesque object in the wood." Surely no realistic proposal for the disposal of the dead, this may be seen rather as a highly personal, metaphorical recommendation for the manner in which human beings ("we") should regard their lives and deaths, their bodies, their errors and their ("our") "impurities." Similarly, it is fairly certain—on the evidence of other *Journal* entries and the "Higher Laws" chapter of *Walden*—that Thoreau was not, in 1840, consistently following a vegetarian diet; nor can we suppose that he ever literally believed that such a diet, together with abstinence from alcohol, could yield immunity to malaria and yellow fever, or retard the decomposition of the corpse. But that he could, under the stress of strong emotion, indulge in such a fantasy is further evidence of the horror he then felt before the specter of death, and also of the intensity of his wish that men might both live and die "cleanly and gracefully."

The realistic recommendation that he did make here was for the substitution of cremation for burial: "The ancients were more tidy than we who subjected the body to the purification of fire before they returned it upon nature. . . ." This concludes the passage; and yet in a neighboring paragraph we find Thoreau again musing wistfully, this time upon the beauty of seashells, and asking rhetorically whether man might not somehow "cast his shell with as little offense as the muscle [mussel], and it perchance be a precious relic to be kept in the cabinets of the curious?" The expression of such a wish on behalf of mankind can only be viewed as evidence of a quixotic tenderness lurking at the core of Thoreau's misanthropy, underneath all his ironies and all his disgust—a tenderness further evident as this paragraph continues: "May we not amuse ourselves with it [man's "shell": his bones, we might translate], as when we count the layers of a shell, and apply it to our ear, to hear the history of its inhabitant in the swell of the sea—the pulsation of the life which one passed therein still faintly echoed?" [9] This has something of the quality of Thoreau's salute to the arrowhead, as "the foot-print, the mind-print, of the oldest men." Here he seems tacitly to acknowledge what he so sharply denied in the John Brown passage—the special significance of any individual lifespan. One senses his passionate desire to make *meaningful* both "the life which once passed therein" (in the human "shell") and, by implication, the fact of death itself.

The journal for 1852, that banner year, contains a fascinating long passage (J, IV: 155–58) which recalls Thoreau's wry suggestion about the entry of "a man struck by lightning" "into the next world." First, he devotes one and a half pages to a description of the destruction of a large tree by a lightning bolt, whose explosive force furrowed the surrounding earth and passed through the cellar of a nearby house, its concussion breaking windows and knocking down the inhabitants above. Thoreau's account of its apparent course and the resulting damage is typically systematic and clear. It is rounded out by a sentence which, while still calmly expository, nevertheless begins to reveal its author's anxiety; and a following question again expresses his characteristic search for meaning: "All this was accomplished in an instant by a kind of fire out of the heavens called lightning, or a thunderbolt, accompanied by a crashing sound. For what purpose?" Annihilation he might be able to accept, but only if he could convince himself of its ultimate rightness as part of a greater design. "*For what purpose?*"—throughout the rest of the long entry Thoreau wrangled with the implications of that question. At first the lover of wildness exulted in this "Titanic force, some of that force which made and can unmake the world," and in the fact that "the brute forces are not yet wholly tamed." But the exultation is fleeting, promptly undercut by the next question: "Is this of the character of a wild beast, or is it guided by intelligence and mercy?" And an observation that "the ancients" regarded the thunderbolt as the means by which Jove "punished the guilty" introduces a central motif of the entry.

Thoreau comments that the association of such a "manifestation of brutish force" with ideas of "vengeance, more or less tempered with justice" is a "natural impression" in the minds of men in any period of history. He goes on to disavow this impression as superstition, and to sound what he probably regarded as the controlling theme of the passage: "Yet it is our own consciousness of sin, probably, which suggests the idea of vengeance, and to a righteous man it would be merely sublime without being awful." Nevertheless, at other points, he appears to accept the verdict of "the ancients." His debate on the advisability of erecting lightning rods involves a complex cluster of ideas: first the question of their literal effectiveness, then, of the user's psychological motivation, and finally, a suggestion that such safeguards will be disdained by "the righteous man," who will be safe in any case! One tends to assume that Thoreau here meant a transcendental safety: that the brave and the good—who can regard "the lightning itself . . . with serenity, as the most familiar and innocent [of] phenomena" in nature—cannot suffer any ultimate injury to the personality, or the soul.* But in fact he *says* that the refusal to employ lightning rods suggests that

impunity in respect to all forms of death or disease, whether sickness or casualty, is only to be attained by moral integrity. There runs through the righteous man's moral spinal column a rod with burnished points

---

* Thoreau's attitude on much of this is close to that of Melville in his short tale "The Lightning-Rod Man"; Melville's narrator is in fact an epitome of Thoreau's "righteous man." Found delighting in the sublimity of a mountain thunderstorm at the story's beginning, he ends by thrusting the lightning-rod "salesman" out of his house, declaring that "The hairs of our heads are numbered, and the days of our lives. In thunder as in sunshine, I stand at ease in the hands of my God. False negotiator, away!" The lightning-rod man himself (explicitly identified with Satan) is both a purveyor of fear and, like Melville's Confidence Man, a dealer in spurious devices and counsels of "security." If Thoreau read this story (which first appeared in *Putnam's Magazine* in 1854, well after the date of his Journal entry) he might have pondered especially one detail of Melville's portrait of the lightning-rod man—his hysterical insistence that in time of thunder one should "of all things . . . avoid tall [i.e., upright and fearless] men." "Do I dream?" Melville then has his narrator exclaim, "Man avoid man? and in danger-time, too" (Herman Melville, *Selected Tales and Poems*, ed. Richard Chase [New York: Rinehart and Company, 1957], pp. 151–58).

to heaven, which conducts safely away into the earth the flashing wrath of Nemesis, so that it merely clarifies the air. This moment the confidence of the righteous man erects a sure conductor within him; the next, perchance, a timid staple diverts the fluid to his vitals.

Since neither the rod nor the lightning itself ("flashing wrath") is invested with any consistent metaphorical significance, the one word "moral" modifying "spinal column" is hardly adequate to counteract the quite literal import of the neighboring sentences. At several points Thoreau's failure to qualify his statements as having to do only with moral "safety" makes it easy to conclude that he believed in divine retribution in a direct physical form. "There is no lightning-rod by which the sinner can finally avert the avenging Nemesis," he asserts, quite in the vein of Jonathan Edwards, or of a lesser, more literal Puritan preacher. And the passage's last sentence declares that "men are probably nearer to the essential truth in their superstitions than in their science" (J, IV: 155–58; 1852).

Apparent in this passage is the familiar ambivalence of feeling toward humanity which I have been stressing. The glowing eulogy of "the righteous man" occurs side by side with the harsh condemnation of "the sinner" (defined, by implication, as "he who receives injury because he feels guilt and therefore fear"); and despite that harshness, there are repeated instances of the communal "we": "If we trust our natural impressions"; "so mixed are we"; "We are ashamed of our fear." Here also, however eloquent the sentences on the righteous man's serenity, is ample evidence once again of Thoreau's deep anxiety about death. In fact, in its rapid vacillations between common-sense rationalization and transcendental affirmation or primitive awe, this seems to me one of the few really confused passages in all the Journal's fourteen volumes.

Another manifestation of brutish force in nature—the storm at sea—stirred Thoreau to equally complex, if not confused, reflections, some of which are familiar to readers of Cape Cod, generally considered his least complex and most cheerful book. In its first chapter, "Shipwreck," he describes the fate of an Irish immigrant ship, the St. John, bound in 1849 from Galway to Boston and sunk at "Grampus Rock" near Cohasset with the loss of almost all her company. Thoreau and Channing, setting out for the Cape, had learned in Boston of the wreck, and immediately "decided to go by way of Cohasset"—along with several hundred others, including anxious relatives, shipping officials, salvagers, and curious sightseers. Thoreau made no effort to explain or justify his own and Channing's motivation, which was, of course, pure curiosity— or perhaps not so "pure," but containing an element of morbid fascination. And he remarked without comment on the other sight-seers who were "flocking" and "streaming" toward the shore— although there is irony in the detail that these included several "sportsmen in their hunting-jackets, with their guns, and game-bags, and dogs." Further on, he noted, but not censoriously, the presence on the beach of a number of local farmers, busily har-vesting the mounds of seaweed that the storm had brought in: "Drown who might, they did not forget that this week was a valuable manure." The huge common grave, newly dug in a church-yard, which they passed, the wagons loaded with pine boxes which passed them, the tangled corpses on the beach, and the corpses that were already boxed but now and again uncovered for iden-tification by grim searchers—all these are described in the clean expository prose, not markedly different from the best journalism, of which, among other modes of writing, Thoreau was a master. Perhaps he was able to maintain this level of detachment because, as he says, "I witnessed no signs of grief, but there was a sober dispatch of business which was affecting."

The nearest his own narrative comes to an expression of grief is in two references to a drowned child, who was being brought from Ireland to its mother by her sister. Child and aunt, having perished together, were assigned to one pine box, with the label "Bridget such-a-one, and sister's child." Thoreau reports (he was told later by a dweller near the beach) that the mother, who had rushed to the scene from Boston, did not herself long survive the sight of those two bodies in one coffin. There is obvious suffering in his terse rendering of this terrible drama. But the same para-graph also contains a very cool description of one of the drowned corpses—a description which is horrifying to most readers: "livid, swollen, and mangled ... the coiled-up wreck of a human hulk, gashed by the rocks or fishes, so that the bone and muscle were exposed, but quite bloodless,—merely red and white,—with wide-open and staring eyes, yet lustreless, deadlights; or like the cabin windows of a stranded vessel, filled with sand." This was the body of an Irish girl, "who probably," Thoreau remarks, "had intended to go out to service in some American family." That remark is the only indication that he felt any sense—as he put it in connection with another shipwreck—of the "life . . . connected with" that relic.

There follows a page on the non-human relics, fragments of the ship and its fittings which had come ashore, a sight which increased his "surprise at the power of the waves." And then, toward the end of the chapter, Thoreau proceeded to his personal reflections on the scene—which might help to explain that degree of coolness one feels in his earlier description of it. These reflections culminate in an affirmation which sounds more like Christian piety than anything else I can remember from Thoreau:

Why care for these dead bodies? They really have no friends but the worms or fishes. Their owners were coming to the New World, as Columbus and the Pilgrims did; they were within a mile of its shores; but before they could reach it, they emigrated to a newer world than ever Columbus dreamed of, yet one of whose existence we believe that there is far more universal and convincing evidence—though it has not yet been discovered by science—than Columbus had of this: not merely mariners' tales and some paltry driftwood and seaweed, but a continual drift and instinct to all our shores. I saw their empty hulks that came to land; but they themselves . . . were cast upon some shore yet further west, toward which we are all tending, and which we shall reach at last, it may be through storm and darkness, as they did.[10]

If this is an expression of the traditional Christian hope, it was probably never more firmly and attractively expressed. And whether the passage voiced acceptance of a doctrine or some more private transcendental or metaphorical assurance, it was not a flourish to please publisher or public but, like everything he wrote, a sincere statement of what Thoreau then felt.[11]

Before this final affirmative peroration occurs a paragraph which is in some ways more typical of its writer, more suggestive of his familiar *Journal* style, and more illustrative of his ambivalent feelings about human mortality:

On the whole, it was not so impressive a scene as I might have expected. If I had found one body cast upon the beach in some lonely place, it would have affected me more. . . . I saw that corpses might be multiplied, as on the field of battle, till they no longer affected us in any degree as exceptions to the common lot of humanity. Take all the graveyards together, they are always the majority. It is the individual and private that demands our sympathy. A man can attend but one funeral in the course of his life, can behold but one corpse.[12]

Given its context and the fact that it was intended for publication in its time, this seems the bravely shared thought of an honest man; and we of the overpopulated and terror-numbed twentieth century may nod agreement especially to the sentence about "corpses . . . multiplied, as on the field of battle, till they no longer affect us in any degree." But note how it is also reminiscent of Thoreau's 1843 letters to his mother and to Emerson about the crowds in New York City. And again the tone has a kind of toughness, almost bravado, that marks this as yet another of his attempts to "outface" death.

Although ultimately it involved only "one body cast upon the beach in [a] lonely place," ambivalence is clearer still in his commentary upon the other shipwreck in his experience. As with every other humane errand he was asked to perform, Thoreau had carried out as best he could, with good sense and little fuss, the melancholy task delegated to him by Emerson of searching out the remains of Margaret Fuller Ossoli, her husband and their child.* The strain of this more intimate encounter with death-by-drowning is revealed, however, in two *Journal* entries, some portions of which were later used in a letter to Harrison Blake and in *Cape Cod*. Some time soon after his July, 1850, trip to Fire Island, he wrote an undated meditation (beginning "I find the actual to be far less real to me than the imagined") whose main thrust resembles the serenely confident passage at the end of the *Cape Cod* chapter on the fate of the *St. John:*

Whatever actually happens to a man is wonderfully trivial and insignificant,—even to death itself, I imagine. . . . This stream of events which we consent to call actual, and that other mightier stream which alone carries us with it,—what makes the difference? On the one our bodies float, and we have sympathy with it through them; on the other, our spirits. . . . Our thoughts are the epochs of our life: all else is but as a journal of the winds that blew while we were here.

But in the midst of these philosophical reflections occur two sentences which are sharper in tone, and which suggest the anxiety

---

* Thoreau also attempted to identify for Charles Sumner, the abolitionist and later the liberal Massachusetts Senator, the body of his brother who died in the same wreck; and he reported fully to Emerson and the Fullers the little he was able to learn of Margaret's last hours (*Correspondence*, pp. 262–63; letter to Emerson, July 25, 1840).

latent in "even to death itself, I imagine": "I have in my pocket a button which I ripped off the coat of the Marquis of Ossoli on the sea-shore the other day. Held up, it intercepts the light and casts a shadow,—an actual button so called,—and yet all the life it is connected with is less substantial to me than my faintest dreams." * The assertion of the greater reality of the "spiritual" world amounts to a dismissal of the individual's corporeal existence—even to a slur upon the memory of that individual called the Marquis of Ossoli. Now another generalized statement repeats the theme of the preceding page, with a startling bitterness: "I do not think much of the actual. It is something which we have long since done with. It is a sort of vomit in which the unclean love to wallow." (One wonders how this "actual" differed in Thoreau's mind from the "real" to which he so often proclaimed a passionate commitment: "Be it life or death, we crave only reality.") Then comes a puzzling announcement—"There was nothing at all remarkable about them"—whose pronoun reference is made clear only in the next sentence: "They were simply some bones lying on the beach. They would not detain a walker there more than so much seaweed. I should think that the fates would not take the trouble to show me any bones again, I so slightly appreciate the favor" (J, II: 43–44; probably early August, 1850). Surely this has the sound of overprotestation. Both the abruptness with which these bones are introduced, and the insistent (and flippant) denial that they are at all interesting, suggest an obsessive preoccupation.

This suggestion is reinforced by the fact that Thoreau returned to the subject a few months later. And in this later entry he completely contradicts his earlier claim that the bones were insignificant. "I once went in search of the relics of a human body," he began, early in the following November, "which had been cast up the day before on to the beach, though the sharks had stripped off the flesh. I got the direction from a light-house." He related matter-of-factly how he proceeded for "a mile or two" and was

---

* This paragraph reappeared, in substance, in a letter of the same month to H. G. O. Blake—with the general meditations upon the spiritual versus the "actual" considerably abridged, but with the comment on the Marquis's button made even more emphatic: "all the life it is connected with is less substantial to me, *and interests me less* [my italics], than my faintest dream" (*Correspondence*, p. 265; letter to Blake, Aug. 9, 1850). (The italicized phrase was added in the letter; I have remarked above on Thoreau's tendency to magnify his misanthropic impulses when writing to Blake.)

able at a half-mile distance to discern the cloth-covered stake which, he had been told, was set up to mark the remains, and which formed the only interruption in a long, smooth expanse of sand. Five complex sentences are devoted to this optical phenomenon, and in each succeeding sentence one is able to sense more and more of the awe and dread that Thoreau had felt as—with a foreknowledge of what it marked—he approached that stake. Presumably these were the same bones referred to in the earlier passage which asserts their insignificance. But this passage, evidently written two or three months later, offers a much more detailed account of his actual experience of finding them, and therefore possibly a more accurate rendering of his feelings at that time— or of the shape and meaning which the experience later assumed in his mind:

As if there was no other object, this trifling sliver had puffed itself up to the vision to fill the void; and there lay the relics in a certain state, rendered perfectly inoffensive to both bodily and spiritual eye by the surrounding scenery. . . . It was as conspicuous on that sandy plain as if a generation had labored to pile up a cairn there. Where there were so few objects, the least was obvious as a mausoleum. It reigned over the shore. That dead body possessed the shore as no living one could. (*J*, II: 80; between Oct. 31 and Nov. 8, 1850.)*

The tone of these last sentences is difficult to define. The two beginning "It was as conspicuous" and "Where there were so few objects" are still ostensibly describing the optical illusion of a large

---

* Thoreau used a large part of this paragraph, with slight alterations, in chapter 6 ("The Beach Again") of *Cape Cod*. There it flows smoothly in a context which discusses, in yet greater detail, the optical illusion dwelt on here. But the slight alterations which it received on its inclusion in *Cape Cod* are extremely interesting. For one, Thoreau picked up a brief phrase, one only, from the troubled *Journal* passage of early August: "There was nothing at all remarkable about them." A new sentence follows: "But as I stood there they grew more and more imposing." In other words, in adapting this material for *Cape Cod*, Thoreau seems consciously to have attempted, with that short sentence, to reconcile the strikingly contradictory *Journal* entries of August and November. Still following the November entry, "They were alone with the beach and the sea . . . ," etc., the *Cape Cod* passage goes on; but then a significant new clause is worked in: "as if there was an understanding between them and the ocean which necessarily left me out, with my snivelling sympathies" (*Cape Cod*, pp. 107–8). I shall have occasion to recall that phrase, "snivelling sympathies," in my next and final chapter.

and distant object appearing smaller and nearer, or of a small and relatively near object suggesting a large structure seen at a distance. But if Thoreau had wanted only to emphasize the illusion of relative size, he would not necessarily have chosen for comparison the kinds of structures that he did choose. The cairn which results from the labor of a generation can be, like the mausoleum, a memorial to the dead, or a monument to some human achievement or aspiration. Both these images are potentially charged with emotion. And with the last two sentences the bones themselves take on an absolute significance. What is the meaning of the assertion that "that dead body possessed the shore as no living one could"? It seems to suggest that Thoreau was then overwhelmed by a sense of the mystery and the dignity of death. But perhaps it merely reveals his painful apprehension, amounting to a confession of his inability, this time, to outface the fact of death.

Another of Thoreau's encounters with human mortality, recorded in two entries in a later journal, also involved death in a sudden and violent form. An unspecified number of men were killed—and their bodies denuded, dismembered, and flung over a wide area—by the explosion of a powder mill complex located a few miles west of Concord. This time, the deaths were not caused by a "manifestation of brutish force in nature"—at least not directly so: one of the fascinating things about this *Journal* episode is the way in which Thoreau initially failed to make that obvious distinction, and then later drew a subtler conclusion.

In the first entry Thoreau's tone is as calmly analytical, at the outset, as it was in the beginnings of the passages on the lightning bolt and the shipwrecks. Seated at his desk, he had heard and felt the concussion of the explosion, and immediately deduced the cause to be either an earthquake or the detonation of a powder supply. Then, seeing a great column of smoke in the west, he "jumped into a man's wagon and rode toward the mills." Upon arriving at what remained of them, he found "perhaps thirty or forty wagons there." Again, as in his report of the Cohasset shipwreck, he did not comment upon this "flocking" to the scene of curious sightseers, nor upon his own impetuous rush to join them. But these two incidents clearly confirm what could also be deduced from the obsessive protractions and repetitions of other passages treated in this chapter: that Thoreau's dread of, and anger at, death could at times involve a fascination, a susceptibility to the sensational, which bordered on the morbid, although certainly there is

no vulgarity, no "cheap thrills" touch of enjoyment, in his handling of these subjects. In the case of the powder mill explosion,
though capable of an efficient reportorial assault on the subject,
he seems ultimately to have suffered acutely as a consequence of
his impulsive curiosity.

The second paragraph is primarily devoted to an analysis of
the progress of the explosions in chain reaction from building to
building, and of the damage resulting to structures and equipment.
At certain points one can well imagine its having been written by
some engineer called in to explain the calamity. In fact, the paragraph ends, as might such an expert's report, with a recommendation for the avoidance of similar calamities in the future. This
recommendation is contained in only one terse sentence, however—
"Put the different buildings thirty rods apart, and then but one
will blow up at a time"—whose very brevity and abruptness (with
two other short sentences immediately preceding it) perhaps betray
the shock under which Thoreau was laboring.

For it was just before these three breathless-sounding sentences that he confronted the toll in human life. Near the paragraph's beginning, he had remarked that three men were killed in
the first explosion, which occurred in the "kernel mill." He then
detailed the explosion of various other buildings and the scattering of their contents. Then, at last, he fully acknowledged the
presence of *death:*

I mistook what had been iron hoops in the woods for leather straps.
Some of the clothes of the men were in the tops of the trees, where
undoubtedly their bodies had been and left them. The bodies were naked
and black, some limbs and bowels here and there, and a head at a
distance from its trunk. The feet were bare; the hair singed to a crisp.
I smelt the powder half a mile before I got there. Put the different
buildings thirty rods apart, and then but one will blow up at a time.
(*J*, IV: 453–55; 1853.)

Even these details might be taken, at first reading, as the kind
which might be included in an analytical report. But surely there
is evidence of revulsion and pain in the very absence—I suggest
it was avoidance—of emotionally colored words and of moralizing.
This passage contains no hint of a moral judgment, not the slightest comment on the fact that this now demolished industry was
devoted to the manufacture of a powerful agent of destruction,
one of the basic components of war munitions. Yet it is hard to

believe that such a thought did not enter Thoreau's mind. This first account of the explosion occupies in all a little over two pages in the *Journal* entry for January 7, 1853.* It is preceded by two paragraphs on various winter phenomena, which were presumably interrupted when their author heard the explosion and felt its earthquake force. It is followed by three more paragraphs dealing with winter birds and with a book he was then reading by a Canadian naturalist. Considering the sequence of these paragraphs under the same date, one may wonder that Thoreau was able to concern himself with such matters after the holocaust he had witnessed—or, one may sense his grim determination to banish that scene from his mind. This latter possibility is reinforced, I think, by the seemingly unemotional quality of the description quoted above, by the abrupt and disjointed nature of its conclusion, and also, very subtly, by the statement that "the clothes of the men were in the tops of the trees, where undoubtedly their bodies had been and left them." The organization and economy of that sentence render it almost (grotesquely) comical; yet it is less impersonal than the rest. The humanness of those men is here recognized (whereas the two neighboring sentences contain a mere tally of "limbs . . . bowels . . . a head . . . a trunk"—along with iron hoops and broken glass), and *they* are implicitly distinguished from "their bodies" as—much more explicitly—were the victims of the shipwreck.

A two-page entry for the next day, January 8, contains only scientific data. But the entry for the ninth ("To Walden and Cliffs") begins with a paean to the "telegraph harp." This vibrating sound—"the undecayed oracle," at times a kind of muse for Thoreau—had received no mention in the *Journal* during the previous two months, and in the two before that it had been mentioned only briefly. This passage, however, reveals Thoreau's

---

* If my earlier conjectures about certain passages in the manuscript notebooks are at all valid, then the manuscript original of this passage (Morgan MA 1302, no. 19, Morgan Library, New York) offers further evidence of its having been written under extreme pressure, perhaps in something like a state of shock. It abounds in scribbled insertions (in ink, and probably made at the time of the passage's first inscription), in words and phrases heavily crossed out, in odd omissions (which the published *Journal*'s editors filled in intelligently, but without in every case bracketing their additions)—and is in fact by far the messiest, most nearly illegible passage that I encountered up to this date (that is, among the first nineteen notebooks).

response to the "harp" at its most intense: it is "revelation...
everlasting truth"; "I never hear it without thinking of Greece....
It allies Concord to Athens, and both to Elysium. It always intoxi-
cates me, makes me sane [—a typically Thoreauvian juxtaposi-
tion].... This wire is my redeemer. It always brings a special
and a general message to me from the Highest." Dated in 1853,
this paragraph is one of the relatively few latter-day expressions—
and from this time they are fewer and fewer—of that kind of
mystical ecstasy which Thoreau described with some frequency in
the earlier journals. But here the tone is less ecstatic than desperate. The desperation, hinted at among the phrases already quoted—
"makes me sane,... is my redeemer," and "brings a special...
message"—becomes overt at other points: "It is something as en-
during as the worm that never dies. Before the [word missing] it
was, and will be after.... How the Greeks *harped* upon the words
immortal, ambrosial!... I get down the railroad till I hear that
which makes all the world a lie." The conclusion supplies an explanation for the desperate tone: "Day before yesterday I looked
at the mangled and blackened bodies of men which had been blown
up by powder, and felt that the lives of men were not innocent,
and that there was an avenging power in nature. Today I hear
this immortal melody.... Are there not two powers?" (*J*, IV:
458–59).

Here at last is Thoreau's recognition,—so notably absent from
the January 7 entry,—of the moral implications of the explosion.
The men who perished there were not innocently employed. The
misuse of elements in nature for destructive purposes has called
forth "an avenging power," so that in a sense this incident was
as much a "manifestation of brutish force in nature" as were the
lightning, the gale and the crashing waves. How it was that the
humming of the telegraph wire could dissipate the horror of that
scene, "make all the world a lie," and restore Thoreau's sanity—
this question is probably beyond scholarly elucidation, though it
may not be wholly beyond our intuitive grasp. Thoreau continually
sought this kind of experience, and he was acutely sensitive to
sound. In its context the question "Are there not two powers?"
implies the recognition of a healing and invigorating as well as
an "avenging" power.

But Thoreau had not yet finished with that troubling subject.
Four and a half months and two journal notebooks later he noted
that "the news of the explosion of the powder-mills was not only
carried seaward by the cloud which its smoke made, but... by

the fragments which were floated thither by the river." It seems that George Melvin, at the end of their trek to find the pink azalea, had shown him some of these charred remains as they returned through the river marshes. One can sense Thoreau's renewed distress in his elaborate imaginings of the fragments' watery travels:

And some, no doubt, were carried down to the Merrimack, and by the Merrimack to the ocean, till perchance they got into the Gulf Stream and were cast up the coast of Norway, . . . or who can tell what more distant strand?—still bearing some traces of burnt powder, still capable of telling how and where they were launched, to those who can read their signs. . . .

Mingling with the wrecks of vessels, which communicated a different tale, this wreck of a powder-mill was cast up on some outlandish strand. . . . Shouldered by whales. Alighted on at first by the muskrat and the peetweet,—and finally perhaps the stormy petrel and the beach-birds. It is long before Nature forgets it. (*J*, V: 211–12; June 1, 1853.)

Here is another of Thoreau's great geographical panoramas, as stylistically exciting, and as moving, as the paragraphs on Walden ice mingling with the Ganges, or the topography of Cape Cod ("all America behind it" and *"plus ultra . . . ultra"* beyond), or the Esquimaux walking under the northern lights. Here the tone is somber throughout; the grammatically incomplete "Shouldered by whales" sounds like the tolling of a great deep bell; every detail prepares for the mournful conclusion, "It is long before Nature forgets."

But midway through the ever-expanding geographical survey (just after ". . . to those who can read their signs") the focus is suddenly, shockingly narrowed:

To see a man lying all bare, lank, and tender on the rocks, like a skinned frog or lizard! We did not suspect that he was made of such cold, tender, clammy substance before.

Note the elliptical structure of the first sentence—it follows a Thoreauvian pattern (beginning with an infinitive and ending with an exclamation point) which always signals intense emotion. And note the "we" of the second sentence. It is a guarded "we," not so much the communal, as it is the impersonal, editorial "we"—a means by which Thoreau momentarily gained anonymity for himself and a little distance from his subject. These sentences are the heart of the passage, the terrible concentrated image which (however it might be with "Nature") Thoreau could not forget, and which gave a grim significance to the global wanderings of those blackened bits of wood. What was his attitude here? Of course there is revulsion in the simile—"like a skinned frog," and in the adjectives "lank . . . cold . . . clammy." There is an echo, once again, of the remark that the sight of so many "herds" of people in New York City made him feel "less respect for flesh and bones" and suspect them to be "more loosely joined, of less firm fibre than the few he had known." And yet the expressive ellipsis, "To see a man . . . !" plainly conveys the shock he had felt: *"a man"* ("the crowning fact!") come to this, suddenly flung "on the rocks, like a skinned frog or lizard." And the word "tender," used twice— I suggest that it conveys both the sense of "delicate, highly vulnerable" *and* of a fugitive tenderness on Thoreau's part. The second sentence can, I think, most accurately be read as follows: "We [I, behind an impersonal mask] did not suspect [had always tried to avoid recognizing] that he [we, I, Mankind] was made of such cold [Ugh!], tender [vulnerable, *and* worthy of tenderness], clammy [repulsive] substance.

In these sentences Thoreau seems to have gathered up all his intense and ambivalent feelings about human mortality. Here, fully acknowledging the shock of that confrontation with the basic fragility of human flesh, he tacitly admitted, also, his prior attempts to evade or to minimize such a confrontation. Along with the familiar shrinking, or disgust, there is a touch of the familiar indignation. The words which express simple physical revulsion may carry a note of scorn as well, of disdain for the corpse of that anonymous workman, "lying on the rocks," who was killed at a questionable occupation. Nevertheless, the opening exclamation clearly voices, not only shock and indignation but also a sense of identification. This workman is Mankind, Everyman, and the "tender, clammy substance" of that broken body was identical, Thoreau knew well, to his own.

And yet evidence from the *Correspondence* and the anecdotes of friends shows that Thoreau approached his own death, at the early age of forty-five, serenely and even cheerfully. No doubt he drew support from the loving attentions of those friends, especially Channing, Alcott and Ricketson. And surely he was also aided by his realism, and his well-known "stoicism," just as these in turn must have been strengthened by his painful struggle, over the course of more than two decades, with the idea of death.

Ten

"... To Men in Their Waking Moments"

ULTIMATELY for Thoreau the thought of death—whether confronted or circumvented—served always to underscore the
never-taken-for-granted fact of life. "I did not wish to live what
was not life," we remember from the pivotal "What I Lived For"
chapter of *Walden*, "living is so dear." Here a common and ma-
terialistic phrase (one imagines Thoreau's having heard it often
from his mother or from other Concordians: "Things are too ex-
pensive: the cost of living is so dear these days") became a central
motif for his major work: "*living* is so dear"—so rare, so fleeting,
so precious. "Wherever I sat, there might I live," he mused, contemplating a retired farm, a sun-dappled hillside, or a swamp. And,
of his response to those who inquired how he could manage to live
(exist) on a vegetable diet, he wrote: "I am accustomed to answer ... that *I* can *live* on board nails [my italics]. If they cannot
understand that, they cannot understand much that I have to say." [1]

If at times, as in these quotations and in some of the death-
confronting passages just examined, he seems chiefly to have been
asserting his intention to live *his* life fully, or to have recoiled in
disgust from the spectacle of other men's deaths, there is abundant
evidence elsewhere of his wish both to preserve and to revitalize
the lives of others. In chapter 7 above, in proposing that *Walden*
be viewed as the finest result of Thoreau's determination to "serve
the public good," I suggested that its central theme is the necessity of "renewal," or the difference between mere existence and
life. Regarding *Walden* in this way, we see that its tenth chapter,
"Baker Farm," occupies a crucial place in the book's overall thematic scheme. For in this chapter Thoreau told of one specific

effort which he made to render another human being aware of that difference and help him to alter the quality of his life. It was an effort doomed to failure, one is likely to feel less than halfway through the chapter. Yet to think this is neither to accept unquestioningly Thoreau's conclusions about that human being, nor to dismiss the advice he gave. With only some slight alterations in the message, in the listener's circumstances or his receptivity, it might have been a qualified success. At any rate, the interest lies in Thoreau's account of the effort, and in his reaction to the failure.

This chapter is preceded by the extended lyrical one entitled "The Ponds," the central chapter in the book, and followed by the meditative "Higher Laws." "The Ponds" celebrates Thoreau's mystical relation to Walden and two neighboring ponds ("great crystals on the surface of the earth, Lakes of Light"); but near its end an angry paragraph describes the changes that had recently occurred in the Walden area. "Of all the characters I have known," this paragraph begins, "perhaps Walden wears best, and best preserves its purity. Many men have been likened to it, but few deserve that honor." It then details the ravages of the railroad, and the fact that "the woodchoppers have laid bare first this shore and then that, and the Irish have built their sties by it." [2] "Their sties": the word may slide by unnoticed in a casual reading, but *Journal* readers will remember its comparison of "the mass of men" to "pigs in a litter." In "Baker Farm," nonetheless, within a few pages of his reference to the Irish "sties," Thoreau is discovered attempting the education of an Irishman—"honest, hardworking, but shiftless" John Field. Caught in a thunderstorm on his way to fish in Fair-Haven Bay, on the river, he had sought shelter in Field's tumble-down shanty. Thoreau recorded the episode in the *Journal* on the evening of that same day, but since he further elaborated upon it in *Walden,* I shall concentrate chiefly on that version.

Sitting where the shanty roof leaked least, regarded shyly by perspiring Mrs. Field and her children, and boldly by the scrawny chickens that shared their cramped quarters, Thoreau heard the brief story of John Field's "arrangement" (in Thoreau's eyes a self-enslavement) with a neighboring farmer. The description of Field as "honest, hardworking but shiftless" comes early in the passage, along with a tribute to the "bravery" of his wife, a tribute which blends sympathy and humorous detachment. She is "brave to cook so many successive dinners ... with round greasy face, ... still thinking to improve her condition one day; with the never absent mop in one hand, and yet no effects of it visible anywhere." A similarly mixed feeling is evident in the description of "the wrinkled, sibyl-like, cone-headed infant that sat upon its father's knee as in the palaces of nobles, and looked out from its home in the midst of wet and hunger inquisitively . . . not knowing but it was the last of a noble line, and the hope and cynosure of the world, instead of John Field's poor starveling brat." In the *Journal* Thoreau added to this sentence: "or, I should rather say, still knowing that it was the last of a noble line and the hope and cynosure of the world" (*J*, I, 384; 1845). This significant addition renders the entire *Journal* passage more sympathetic in tone. Was it omitted from *Walden* for aesthetic reasons—to avoid the repetition—or because Thoreau's attitude toward the Fields had hardened in the intervening time? At any rate, there is no ambivalence (it is no surprise to observe) in the two brief references to Field's little "broad-faced" son, who "worked cheerfully at his father's side" in the bog, "not knowing how poor a bargain the latter had made." Perhaps it was chiefly for his sake (for he seems, in sturdiness and cheerfulness, to resemble Johnny Riordan) that Thoreau undertook to "wake up" and advise John Field.

"I tried to help him with my experience," he went on, "telling him that he was one of my nearest neighbors, and that I too, who came a-fishing here, and looked like a loafer, was getting my living like himself; that I lived in a tight light and clean house, which hardly cost more than the annual rent of such a ruin as his commonly amounts to. . . ." The message was "simplify, simplify"; it consisted, as *Walden* readers will remember, of detailed recommendations about diet, clothing and occupations as well as housing—ultimately about a reassessment of values, a reordering of priorities, and its tone was consistently earnest and frank, neither overdelicate nor condescending. ("For I purposely talked to him as if he were a philosopher, or desired to be one.")

Field listened respectfully. But the kind of life that Thoreau proposed was utterly new and strange to him. Although both he and his wife looked wistful at the suggestion that, could they but reorganize and simplify, they might all spend their days in fishing and huckleberrying—and simply in thinking—they still "appeared to be wondering if they had capital enough to begin such a course with, or arithmetic enough to carry it through." And so, "alas!" Thoreau concluded, "the culture of an Irishman is an enterprise to be undertaken with a sort of moral bog hoe." * ³ "Alas" appears three times in the course of one page as this passage draws to conclusion; and in describing his departure Thoreau felt constrained to add a heavily facetious account, which does not appear in the *Journal*, of his asking for a drink and at last receiving a dipper full of alarmingly murky water.

The next paragraph contains the second of Thoreau's two confessions in *Walden* that he had experienced doubts about his chosen mode of life, and specifically about his retreat to the woods:** "As I was leaving the Irishman's roof after the rain, bending my steps again to the pond, my haste to catch pickerel, wading in retired meadows, in sloughs and bog-holes, in forlorn and savage places, appeared for an instant trivial to me who had been sent to school and college...." The word "trivial" is the key here. What is obviously meant would more commonly be expressed by the term "inappropriate," or possibly "degrading." But "trivial" evidently included both these connotations for Thoreau.

He used the word twice in just this way in his agonized and self-defensive *Journal* account of the forest fire that he and Edward Hoar had accidentally started when, on a fishing trip, they stopped to cook their lunch—a fire which "burned over a hundred acres," mostly in timber, and left in its wake much bitterness between Thoreau and his fellow townsmen. That passage abounds in hos-

---

* I could be accused of an unscholarly partiality if I failed to comment on this sentence. Why "an Irishman" rather than simply "John Field" or "such a man as John Field?" That statement stands at one extreme among the varying attitudes expressed by Thoreau toward the ever increasing numbers of Irish immigrants who were settling in New England in this period. This study has already cited instances of amusement, sympathy, and exasperation, and some instances in which all of these are blended, in Thoreau's reactions to various of the Irish in his sphere. The fact of their exploitation at Yankee hands was recognized in one of *Walden's* most memorable puns, in which the railroad "sleepers," wooden cross-ties, became the human—Irish— "sleepers" whose lives were expended in building the railroad. I think it is fair to say that Thoreau's occasional exasperation and scorn were never simply a reflection of an unthinking Yankee prejudice (which surely existed all around him), but were reactions to specific situations in which certain Irishmen appeared to him gullible, dishonest, "shiftless," etc.—as indeed, often, did "the mass of men." Still, his use of the generalized "an Irishman" in this sentence is disturbing, and we recall "their sties." (For a somewhat fuller discussion see Frank Buckley, "Thoreau and the Irish," *New England Quarterly Review* 13: 389–400.)

** The other such confession is in chapter 5, "Solitude"; see above, p. 2.

tility, and in ambivalence. "I could not help noticing that the crowd who were so ready to condemn the individual who had kindled the fire did not sympathize with the owners of the wood," he asserted,

but were in fact highly elate and as it were thankful for the opportunity which had afforded them so much sport; and it was only half a dozen owners, so called, ... who looked sour or grieved, and I felt that I had a deeper interest in the woods, knew them better and should feel their loss more than any or all of them.

Yet on the preceding page there is an explicit disclaimer of such feelings:

... I have done no [purposeful] wrong therein [he told himself as he watched the flames spreading], and now it is as if the lightning had done it. These flames are but consuming their natural food. (It has never troubled me from that day to this more than if the lightning had done it. The trivial fishing was all that disturbed me and disturbs me still.)

And again, two pages beyond: "To be sure, I felt a little ashamed when I reflected on what a trivial occasion this had happened, that at the time I was no better employed than my townsmen" (J, II: 23–25; 1850). No doubt all the collective censure which Thoreau had suffered, and was to suffer for some time to come, is mirrored in this "no better ... than my townsmen." And the repetition on that occasion of "trivial" confirms one's impulse to take seriously the little crisis of self-doubt described in *Walden's* "Baker Farm": as he left the Fields, such a "savage" life as he then led, and such a primitive method of obtaining food, seemed to him ("for an instant") *trivial* (unworthy, degrading) for a college graduate— or for the literary man that Thoreau elsewhere proclaimed himself to be. Perhaps he also felt a need still to assert his own difference from John Field. After all, to an outsider his ascetic life at Walden might not have seemed so different from Field's impoverished one.

The doubt was soon banished, however, and was succeeded by a lyrical rededication to his peculiar life-style: "but as I ran down the hill toward the reddening west, with the rainbow over my shoulder ... my Good Genius seemed to say,—Go fish and hunt far and wide day by day,—farther and wider,—and rest thee by many brooks and hearth-sides without misgiving. Remember thy Creator in the days of thy youth. Rise free from care before the dawn, and seek adventures.... Grow wild according to thy nature. . . ." [4] The 1845 *Journal* entry which summarizes the visit to John Field also contains references both to the feeling of doubt and to the surge of reaffirmation that followed it, but both are described at greater length in *Walden*. It is possible, of course, that in *Walden* Thoreau exaggerated his doubts in order to rebut them with a passionate statement of his personal credo. I am inclined to think, however, that his doubts were very real, and that they were brought on by his sense of having failed in his mission to John Field, a neighbor, a flesh-and-blood fellow man, encountered in what Thoreau hoped would be "a waking moment." The chapter's conclusion definitely supports this interpretation. For after having described his recovery of confidence (which might well have served for a conclusion) Thoreau suddenly exclaims, "O Baker Farm!"—and John Field once more enters the scene. On an impulse he has foregone "bogging" for the day and hurried to join Thoreau on the water. There his "bad luck" in fishing (as in everything else) leads him to change his seat in the boat, but then "luck changed seats too": "Poor John Field!" In deploring the man's defeatism, and his "thinking to live by some derivative old country mode in this primitive new country," Thoreau's tone is a mixture of compassion, extreme impatience, and amused resignation.

The chapter's last sentence has a density comparable to that of the two "Gone-to-Seed" passages discussed above, a density which I think reflects its author's complex feelings throughout this experience:

Poor John Field!—I trust he does not read this, unless he will improve by it, . . . With his horizon all his own, yet he a poor man, born to be poor, with his inherited Irish poverty or poor life, his Adam's grandmother and boggy ways, not to rise in this world, he nor his posterity, till their wading webbed bog-trotting feet get *talaria* to their heels.[5]

Not surprisingly, the long "sentence" beginning "With . . ." is grammatically incomplete,—another elliptical cluster of thoughts set down as a sentence. It says in effect that Thoreau has given up on John Field. Although its initial phrase—"With his horizon all his own"—suggests the possibility of change, the rest imply that Field's case is hopeless; *talaria* are the winged sandals of Hermes. Yet the extravagance, the syntactical eccentricity and cumulative, run-on character of this conclusion—with its striking range of images, from the colloquial "Adam's grandmother and boggy" to the learned *talaria*—all these indicate plainly that Thoreau was not reconciled to this failure, did not cheerfully give up on John Field.

Many of the misanthropic statements in the *Journal* and in *Walden* are the result of similar disappointments.

Undoubtedly, some of Thoreau's misanthropy was bound up with what has been called his egotism. One can conclude from the *Journal* that he did have, much of the time, a reasonable regard for himself (to which it should be added that he probably understood himself better than many men do). And from this self-regard apparently there did grow a kind of diffidence, a chip on the shoulder, as I have suggested earlier. For this self-regarding man was an eccentric, who had chosen to disregard, in effect to flout, many of the conventions of his time and his community. Most certainly some of his hostile feelings sprang from real or fancied criticisms and condescensions on the part of others—as we have seen in the report of the forest fire, in the complaint that the community never asked him to "do anything quite worth the while to do," and in his references to the Apollo-Admetus myth. Nevertheless, a great deal more of the misanthropy that Thoreau expressed arose from his having entertained the same kind of hope, or attempted something like the same kind of help, for some individual—or for "the mass of men"—as for John Field, and having suffered something of the same frustration.

A study of this man's life—the essential, interior life of Henry David Thoreau as it is disclosed in his writings—reveals at least two striking paradoxes. It reveals the paradox of one who, for two years, sought solitude in the woods, who eloquently preached self-reliance and independence, yet who felt, all his life, a deep need for human intimacy and true community. And it reveals the paradox of one who consistently criticized "reformers," but was himself the most earnest of would-be reformers—taking that word in its fundamental denotation, as he liked to take words: one who all his life passionately desired to "wake up" and to educate other people, to help them to re-form their lives.

I have suggested that the passage in which Thoreau described his sense of "a certain doubleness" in himself is important to our understanding of his ambivalence about other individuals and about humanity (see pp. 111–12 above). Chiefly it helps us to recognize his complexity of mind, his ability (perhaps at times an excessive tendency) to "look at the other side"; and his ability to see himself with some detachment, which is perhaps the first step toward achieving a sympathy with others. But this does not wholly explain those extreme and rapid alterations which we have been observing in his attitudes toward other people. In discussing the extremes of misanthropy and of humanism found in the *Journal*, I suggested that we may have ultimately to postulate a kind of pendulum swing in Thoreau's feeling: an inevitable recoil from an idealization of another individual, or of humanity, to an expression of hostility, and a similar recoil from some sourly misanthropic stance to a suddenly compassionate and accepting one. This hypothesis makes sense, I think, as far as it goes. It rests on a recognition of the intensity of Thoreau's emotions. Whatever else may be said of him—and with due acknowledgment of the stoicism he cultivated—it must be said that he was a passionate man.[6]

Much of the misanthropy encountered in Thoreau's writings can be traced to his appraisal of the evils in institutions and the injustices in society, to his disappointment—reasonable or unreasonable—in individuals he had admired (such as Emerson) or whom he had unsuccessfully tried to help (such as John Field), and finally to a less personal but still strongly felt disappointment in many of the men and women he saw around him—gone-to-seed farmers, complacently anti-intellectual and anti-poetic villagers, cautious citizens who unthinkingly condemned John Brown. Such great expectations as he sometimes expressed for humankind could only result in disillusion. Just as he was angered by the thought of death, of individual extinction, so he reacted in anger to Man's self-diminishment, his cowardice and hypocrisies, his blind materialism and his failures of imagination. To say this is not to deny that Thoreau's expectations and standards of conduct were sometimes inordinately stringent. Nor is it an attempt to excuse all of his severities, his sometimes savage denunciations of individuals or of "the mass of men"—it is not an effort to "rehabilitate" or "white-wash" his reputation. It is an effort to explain as best I can the seeming contradictions upon which this study has focussed.

I have been talking chiefly about motivation, about certain possible origins which we might call "social" for the expressions of misanthropy and the ambivalences we find in Thoreau. But there is also, after all, the matter of his character, one facet of which was that stringency just referred to, an unwillingness to compromise in what he considered matters of "Principle." Another important facet was what Emerson called his stoicism. Thoreau often sounds tough because he *was* tough, he had schooled himself in toughness ("I am no piece of crockery that cannot be jostled without danger of being broken"); and he was realistic, a man for whom the word "fact" took on an ever-increasing power. His own yearning for a perfect intimacy, whether of love or friendship, could not easily be appeased; the kind of sympathy he desired—informed, active, inviting reciprocity and containing no element of condescension—was rarely available. Yet there is little or no conscious pathos in his recognition of this fact. There are instances in Thoreau's *Journal* of tersely expressed bitterness, tight-lipped confrontations with loneliness and failure, but never of any supine wallowing in self-pity. The toughness I have spoken of was remarked upon, at some time and in one fashion or another, by all of Thoreau's friends. It was this quality which led Emerson, in the "Biographical Sketch," to speak of "somewhat military in his nature, not to be subdued." *[7] And the toughness, the "true mettle" and "habitual equanimity" which he sought to attain himself, he coveted also for others. So in the poem "Manhood" he praised "the mature soul ... who ... has proudly steered his life with his own hands." So, describing the plans of "brave and resourceful" Kate Brady, he added that "I would by no means discourage, nor yet particularly encourage her, for I would have her so strong as to succeed in spite of all ordinary discouragements."

Strength, maturity, realism, and resilience—these are the qualities of Thoreau's "hero," and these are the human attributes which are celebrated in *Walden*. "Why should we knock under and go with the stream?" its readers are asked in chapter 2; "Let us not be upset and overwhelmed.... Let us settle ourselves, and work and wedge our feet downward through the mud and slush of opinion, and prejudice, and tradition, and delusion, and appearance ... till we come to a hard bottom ... which we can call reality,** and say, This is, and no mistake. ..." And, in the final chap-

---

* Any serious reader of Thoreau must at some point have reflected on this small paradox: that though he adhered more and more, as he grew older, to a pacifist ideal, felt keenly the futility of armed conflict, he nevertheless continued from time to time to employ military imagery—and finally, near the end of his life, found himself in sympathy with John Brown's desperate effort.
** We should not overlook the word "call"—"which we can *call* reality"—

ter, Thoreau writes: "In sane moments we regard only the facts, the case that is. . . . However mean your life is, meet it and live it; do not shun it and call it hard names." [8]

Near the end of *Walden*'s chapter 17, "Spring," there is a sentence on "Compassion": Thoreau says it is "untenable ground," and that "its pleadings will not bear to be stereotyped." [9] A conscious and prolonged luxuriating in feelings of sympathy, an exhibition of pity, would always seem to him spurious or self-indulgent. This was implied when, in the *Cape Cod* shipwreck passage, he spoke of "my snivelling sympathies," and surely it is the central import of the *Journal* entry that we examined in chapter 1, which asks "what is my sympathy good for?" Compassion, the *Walden* sentence goes on, "must be expeditious"—must be active, effective, and speedily so. Therefore Thoreau could not merely admire the fortitude of little Johnny Riordan, nor rest content with writing a poem about him, but he must carry a new cloak to Johnny Riordan, and, moreover, make of this charitable errand a genuinely neighborly visit, stopping to chat and inquire about Johnny's progress in school. Therefore, his *Journal* could not at all contain his painful sympathy for John Brown, awaiting death in a Southern jail, and he rang the bells of Concord town, sent personal announcements to many of its citizens, and (disregarding the Abolition Committee's protest that his action was "premature") delivered a passionately partisan speech which, Emerson tells us, was "heard by all respectfully, by many with a sympathy that surprised themselves." [10] An appearance of callousness in Thoreau is almost always the result of frustration, a sense of helplessness: wrongs that could not be righted, suffering that he could not alleviate, he would not willingly mourn.

But, as my second chapter and the last two have made clear, he could not always choose not to mourn. Thoreau's stoicism was not a seamless coat of mail. There were situations which it could not cover, many times when it deserted him. We have seen how, in the privacy of the *Journal*, he could let himself voice his long-

---

in reading this passage. Intent on the necessity of cutting through prejudice and convention, Thoreau still was careful to suggest that ultimately each individual has to define "reality" for himself or herself; and this "call reality" is a reminder that Thoreau's own definition would always include the experience of poetry, the perception of moral courage, and the possibility of mystical ecstasy.

ings for human intimacy ("What if we feel a yearning to which no breast answers? I walk alone. . . . I knock on the earth for my friend. . . ."), and also how he could be all but overpowered by compassion, although powerless to render help.

The fact that compassion could be for him a painful emotion is explicitly confessed, along with a self-protective impulse, in the first of the *Journal* references to Johnny Riordan: "The thought of its greater independence and its closeness to nature diminishes the pain I feel when I see a more interesting child than usual destined to be brought up in a shanty" (*J*, II: 116–17; 1850). Similar confessions of experiencing pain and of seeking relief from it are implicit in many other passages: for example, in the unfinished letter to Ricketson describing George Minott's last days, in the paragraphs on Bill Wheeler, the Breed family, Hugh Quoil, the victims of the powder-mill explosion, and in the gone-to-seed passages. In all of these (except for the aborted letter—and there seems little doubt that it was unfinished precisely because of Thoreau's fear that his emotion was getting out of hand), the expressions of sympathy were, sooner or later, repudiated or undercut. As a result, these passages (along with the *Walden* chapter on John Field) became extremely complex stylistically, often breaking grammatical conventions, and their tone seems unusually intense and remarkably changeful.

What I have come to feel, in the course of this study, is that the contradictions and ambivalences in Thoreau, far from proving his coldness, are instead all traceable to the strength of his emotions, and that ultimately his profound humanism and his need for loving personal relationships were the source—that is, their frustration was the source—of his misanthropic outbursts, as well as of the stoicism and self-sufficiency for which he is famous. The ideal of stoic self-reliance was indispensable to his development— perhaps to his survival—because he was also a realist: his splendid respect for *fact* precluded his clinging to any illusions about other people, or about the human race. Yet the realization of that stoic ideal was continually threatened by his needs and his sympathies.

Thoreau is a great writer, his work is inexhaustibly interesting to succeeding generations, because in him this depth of feeling was combined with a uniquely restless intelligence, which never relaxed its hatred of the facile and the insincere. It was this combination, and with it the range of his commitments (to Nature, to Humanity, and to a perception of truth which for him transcended them both) which gave to what he wrote its classic stature and—whatever may be said of the geographical and social "limitations" of his life—its breadth. And it was the frequent conflict of these commitments, and the more frequent conflict of his needs and his sympathies with his stoic sense of reality, that everywhere imparted to his style such tension and such force.

Notes

Introduction

1. Thoreau, *The Correspondence of Henry David Thoreau*, ed. Walter Harding and Carl Bode (New York: New York University Press, 1958), p. 413.

2. Perry Miller, ed., *Consciousness in Concord: The Text of Thoreau's Hitherto "Lost Journal," 1840–41, Together with Notes and a Commentary* (Boston: Houghton Mifflin Co., 1958).

3. "From its inception the *Journal* was anticipating the books. What was squeezed out of experience referred not to the experience from which it came but to the project for which it was designed" (Miller, p. 110). How could so eminent a scholar take responsibility for such a statement as that? In his attempt to illustrate this point Miller's exhibit A is a comparison of two passages on "a maiden"—presumably Ellen Sewall—who went boating with Thoreau in 1840. In the *Journal* she was said to have been in a row-boat, and "in the stern"; when the passage was introduced into the *Week* the boat became a sailboat and the maiden sat "in the prow"—in both versions, "nothing but herself between the steersman and the sky." Miller's comment is that if Ellen "could be moved at will from stern to prow, to meet a literary convenience . . . we may divine that here is one more instance of . . . collecting material out of limited experience, in which the predominant emotion is not a passion for anybody but a greed for tidbits" (p. 86). It can be argued, however, that Thoreau's "using" this passage from the *Journal* "meant" that he liked to dwell on the memory of that experience, just as easily as that "she is a literary prop, to be utilized—consciously, oh so consciously!—to furnish interest within a limited angle of vision" (Miller, ibid.). Of course his moving the maiden from stern to bow was a "literary convenience"—as are all such choices that a writer makes. Perhaps Thoreau considered a sailing craft more picturesque than any other for this context. Does that necessarily convict him of calculating coldness? But this tends to quibbling. My real quarrel is with Miller's dogmatism, and with his gloatingly disparaging tone—which is well illustrated in "greed for tidbits."

4. Thoreau, *The Journal of Henry D. Thoreau*, edited by Bradford Torrey

and Francis H. Allen, in fourteen volumes, and comprising volumes VII–XXX in Thoreau, *The Writings of Thoreau* (Boston: Houghton Mifflin Co., 1906), III: 239. (Volume numbers given these notes follow the I–XIV independent numbering of the journals.)

This same edition of the *Journal* was reissued, with a new foreword by Walter Harding, by Dover Publications, New York, 1962. This publication, which has the same volume and page numbering as the 1906 edition, has been invaluable in the preparation of this study.

Future citations from the *Journal* will usually be documented parenthetically in the text. *The Journal* will henceforth be abbreviated as *J*, and references are to volume and page.

5. Joseph Wood Krutch, *Henry David Thoreau*, American Men of Letters Series (New York: William Sloane Associates, 1948), pp. 119–20. For another example of a positive response to Thoreau's craftsmanship and to the *Journal* as "a work of art," see Walter Harding, foreword to the Dover Publications reprint of the 1906 edition of the *Journal*. (See below, note 22, chapter 4.)

6. Miller, *Consciousness in Concord*, pp. 78, 110, 206 n.

7. One counterweight to this influence is Odell Shepard's "Unconsciousness in Cambridge," a review of Miller's *Consciousness in Concord*, *Emerson Society Quarterly* 13 (1958), pp. 13–19. Remarking on the "excessive length" of Miller's introduction and footnotes, Shepard continues: "Those pages are made to seem much longer and more numerous than they are, moreover, by frequent inaccuracies of statement, by assertions unproved, and unprovable, by confusions and inconsistencies of thought, by the dragging-in of matters wholly adventitious, and by the use and abuse of violent language.... The prevailing tone of his commentary is the tone of contempt, varied now and then by patronizing commiseration" (pp. 14–15). Among other things, Shepard devotes some space to Miller's handling of Thoreau's attitudes about friendship, love, and sex, and the allegations and insinuations of insincerity and hypocrisy on Thoreau's part which are quite clearly present in Miller's study. Although his indignation at Miller's treatment of Thoreau leads this critic, in turn, into a few rather intemperate outbursts, I would say that his assessment of the "inaccuracies and excesses" in *Consciousness in Concord* is quite just.

One. *Thoreau*, le Misanthrope

1. Ralph Waldo Emerson, "Biographical Sketch," printed as an introduction in Thoreau, *A Week on the Concord and Merrimack Rivers* (Boston: Houghton Mifflin Co., Sentry edition, 1961), pp. xii–xiii. See also Harding and Bode, eds., "The History of Thoreau's Published Correspondence," in Thoreau, *Correspondence*, p. xiii.

2. See for example Ralph Waldo Emerson, *The Journals of Ralph Waldo Emerson*, ed. W. H. Gilman, Alfred Ferguson, et al. (Cambridge: Harvard University Press, 1960–), X: 343, XIII: 183, XIV: 76: "If I knew only Thoreau I should think the cooperation of good men impossible. Must we always talk for victory, and never once for truth, for comfort, and joy?... Always some weary, captious paradox to fight you with, and time and temper wasted"

(Feb. 29, 1856). Sherman Paul also notes Emerson's participation in this judgment of Thoreau as a misanthrope, in *The Shores of America* (Urbana: University of Illinois Press, 1958), p. 24.

3. Thoreau, *Walden*, 1854 (Princeton: Princeton University Press, 1971), chapter 1, pp. 9–10, chapter 7, p. 164, chapter 18, p. 325.

4. Ibid., chapter 5, p. 131, chapter 18, 329.

5. This passage appears almost intact in Thoreau's speech, "A Plea for John Brown," given in Concord October 30, and elsewhere. (Thoreau, *Writings*, IV: 434–35.)

6. Thoreau, *Correspondence*, pp. 515—16; letter to Lowell, June 22, 1858.

7. "As for taking Thoreau's arm, I should as soon take the arm of an elm tree" Emerson, *Journals*, X: 343. In Emerson's "Biographical Sketch" of Thoreau, 1862, we find this remark attributed to "one of his friends": "I love Henry ... but I cannot like him; and as for taking his arm, I should as soon think of taking the arm of an elm-tree" ("Biographical Sketch," p. xiii).

8. In the *Journal*, the statement follows Thoreau's account of his having set fire to the woods, some years before, which involves several pages of self-justification, and some remarks on the reactions of his fellow-townsmen. It appears also in *Walden*, chapter 8, where the reference is to his being jailed by "those who represented the state" (pp. 171–72).

9. Thoreau, *Correspondence*, p. 107; May 23, 1843.

10. Ibid., pp. 110–12; June 8, 1843.

11. Ibid., p. 142; Oct. 1, 1843.

12. See his letter to Harrison Blake of Dec. 6–7, 1856, in Thoreau, *Correspondence*, pp. 444–45. The quotation from the editors is taken from pages 445–46.

13. Thoreau, *A Week*, pp. 358–61.

14. See Sherman Paul, *The Shores of America* (Urbana: University of Illinois Press, 1958), chapter 4, "A Walker in the city," for an interesting discussion of this subject. The scattered evidence of a positive, or at least neutral Thoreauvian response to the city was well summed up by John C. Broderick in his dissertation, "Thoreau's Principle of Simplicity, as Shown in His Attitudes toward Cities, Government, and Industrialism" (University of North Carolina, 1953). While acknowledging the generally negative character of Thoreau's response, Broderick argues that his attitude did shift as he grew older, becoming more complex and to some degree more tolerant toward specific cities and toward the advantages of urban living. In support of this he cites Thoreau's *Journal* account (it is lively, though less than "enthusiastic," as he claims) of his visits to New York and Philadelphia in 1854 (*J*, VII: 73–76), and a *Journal* passage of 1853 in which he congratulated himself on the "room there is in Nature," his ability to enjoy rural "retirement and solitude," yet still draw upon the resources of the village—lyceum, library, book-store, and frequent trains to Boston. (*J*, IV: 478–79, quoted in Broderick, pp. 55, 74). In general, Broderick's thesis is that Thoreau could only admire the city/community (or government, or industry) insofar as it contributed to the total well-being of the individual instead of tyrannizing over him and thwarting his growth. This well-being would be defined in terms of the principle of Simplicity—a determination of the most basic needs

for individual growth and fulfillment—which would always include a direct contact with wild Nature. (See especially Broderick's chapters 2, pp. 102–10, and 6, pp. 284–95.) His argument here parallels my own in my discussion of Thoreau's "sense of community," below, in chapter 5.

15. Thoreau, *Journal*, in Perry Miller, *Consciousness in Concord* (Boston: Houghton Mifflin Co., 1958), p. 149; Aug. 8, 1840. Miller points out that the findings of " 'Oriental' pageants" in sunset skies had long been "a cliché of romantic poetry." Such an image may have held fresh significance, however, for a young writer who already had some experience of oriental literature. And in any case his choice of "cliché" would seem significant in this present context, with its specification of a city—where men's lives are "as poetical" as is the pastoral life!

Two. Friendship and Love

1. Thoreau, *Correspondence*, pp. 85–144. Cf. letters to Richard Fuller, Jan. 16, 1843; to Elizabeth Hoar, May 15; to Mrs. Thoreau, May 11 and Aug. 29; to Helen Thoreau, May 23 and July 21; to the Emersons, July 8; to RWE, Oct. 17; and to Lidian Emerson, May 22, June 20, and Oct. 16.

2. Ibid., p. 124; July 8, 1843.

3. Ibid., p. 125. See also Henry Seidel Canby, *Thoreau* (Boston: Houghton Mifflin Co., 1939), p. 160.

4. Thoreau, *Week*, pp. 285, 293, 283.

5. Ibid., pp. 277, 281, 284.

6. Perry Miller, *Consciousness in Concord* (Boston: Houghton Mifflin Co., 1958), pp. 95–96.

7. *Week*, pp. 301–2. (Also, earlier, *J*, I, 348.)

8. In *Walden*: "If a man does not keep pace with his companions, perhaps it is because he hears a different drummer. Let him step to the music which he hears, however measured or far away" (p. 326).

9. *Correspondence*, pp. 189 (Nov. 14, 1847); 200 (Dec. 29); 207 (Feb. 23, 1848); and 225 (May 21).

10. Miller, *Consciousness in Concord*, p. 82.

11. Joel Porte, *Emerson and Thoreau: Transcendentalists in Conflict* (Middletown: Wesleyan University Press, 1966), chapter 5, "Thoreau's Quarrel with the Transcendentalists," p. 96.

12. Sherman Paul, *The Shores of America* (Urbana: University of Illinois Press, 1958), chapter 6, p. 272. Paul speaks at the same time of the "anguish" of his loss of rapport with Lidian.

13. Miller, *Consciousness in Concord*, p. 94.

14. Canby, *Thoreau*, pp. 350–51.

15. Thoreau, *Walden*, p. 270. Walter Harding notes in *The Variorum Walden* that this last phrase is taken from "an Old English ballad, 'The Children in the Wood' ": "But never more could see the man / Approaching from the town" ([New York: Washington Square Press, Inc., 1962], p. 309).

Three. Seven Friendships

1. Ralph Waldo Emerson, "Biographical Sketch," in Thoreau, *Week*, p. xix–xxxiv.

2. Ralph Waldo Emerson, *The Journals of Ralph Waldo Emerson*, ed. Edward Waldo Emerson and Waldo Emerson Forbes (Boston: Houghton Mifflin Co., 1909–14): X, 357; June 1871.

3. Thoreau, *Correspondence*, p. 317; Jan. 1, 1854.

4. Ibid., p. 373; letter to Mrs. Elizabeth O. Smith, Feb. 19, 1855. See below, p. 60, for a *Journal* account of Thoreau's meeting with this lady in 1851.

5. Ibid., pp. 371 (Feb. 7, 1855), 399 (Nov. 8, 1855), and 435–36 (Oct. 20, 1856).

6. Ibid., pp 537–38 (Jan 1, 1859), 616 (May 11, 1861).

7. The published *Correspondence* carries only one real letter from Channing to Thoreau, a witty, affectionate one of 1845, which advised him that "I see nothing for you in this earth but that field which I once christened 'Briars' [beside Walden Pond]; go out upon that, build yourself a hut, and there begin the grand process of devouring yourself alive." A note of 1843 requested Thoreau's supervision of renovations to a house Channing had taken in Concord—a commission faithfully performed; and there is a later, undated scrap which yet gives us the flavor of that relationship: "Dear H. How would you like to go up to Holt's point to-day or will you. . . . / Yrs W E C" (pp. 61, 96, 653).

8. Ellery Channing, *Thoreau, the Poet-Naturalist* (Boston: Roberts Bros., 1873), p. 23.

9. Thoreau, *Correspondence*, p. 609; Mar. 22, 1861.

10. Thoreau, *Correspondence*, pp. 595–97; letter to Blake, Nov. 4, 1860.

11. Here a comment of Perry Miller's is surely apt: "There must have been something so pontifical in Blake as to call out this tone; Emerson's letters generally convey a sweet informality which makes them a joy to read, but the moment he addressed Blake, he too became oracular" (Miller, *Consciousness in Concord* [Boston: Houghton Mifflin Co., 1958] p. 227). (The comment occurs in a back-of-book footnote; in the corresponding text Miller contented himself with hitting at Thoreau's "pomposity" and "absurdity.")

12. Thoreau, *Correspondence*, pp. 297 (Feb. 27, 1855), 303 (Apr. ?, 1853), 330 (Aug. 8, 1854).

13. Ibid., pp. 266 (Aug. 9, 1850), 299 (Feb. 27, 1853), 385 (Sept. 26, 1855).

14. Miller, *Consciousness in Concord*, p. 89; see also p. 227, n. 29.

15. Thoreau, *Correspondence*, pp. 476–77; Apr. 17, 1857.

16. Ibid., pp. 444–45 (Dec. 7, 1856), 401–2 (Dec. 9, 1855), 476–77 (Apr. 17, 1857), 491–92 (Aug. 18, 1857).

17. Ibid., pp. 442–44; 1856.

18. Ibid., p. 384; Sept. 26, 1855.

19 Ibid., p. 311; Dec. 19, 1853.

20 Ibid., p. 490; Aug. 18, 1857.

21. Some of this passage is carried over into *Walden*, chapter 14 ("Former Inhabitants and Winter Visitors"), p. 269.

22. See also J, V: 141 (May 10, 1853), 365 (Aug. 10, 1853). In the latter entry he reported that the Abolition Society had refused Alcott's offer of his services, "very much to their discredit. . . . Such a connection . . . would confer unexpected dignity on their enterprise. But they cannot tolerate a man who stands by a head above them. They are as bad—Garrison & Phillips, etc.— as the overseers and faculty of Harvard College. They require a man who will train well *under* them."

23. Thoreau, *Walden*, chapter 14, p. 241.

24. Thoreau, *Correspondence*, p. 436; Oct. 20, 1856.

25. Thoreau, *Correspondence*, pp. 341–42 (and note); Oct. 1, 1854.

26. Ibid., p. 477, Apr. 17, 1857. See also pp. 383 (Sept. 26, 1855), 536 (Jan. 1, 1859): "Glad to hear that you had called on R[icketson]," Thoreau wrote to Blake on the latter date, "How did you like him? I suspect that you did not see one another fairly."

27. See letters of March 28 and April 1, 1857, Ibid., pp. 470, 472, and also a note to these letters, in Thoreau, *Writings*, VI *Letters*, ed. Franklin B. Sanborn, pp. 305–6.

28. Thoreau, *Correspondence*, pp. 479–80.

29. Ibid., p. 393; Oct. 16, 1855.

30. Ibid., pp. 593-94 (Ricketson to Thoreau; Oct. 14, 1860), 599–600 (Thoreau to Ricketson; Nov. 4, 1860).

31. Ibid., p. 608; Feb. 27, 1861.

32. Ibid., pp. 609–10; letter to Ricketson, Mar. 22, 1861 (see below, pp. 68–69 and note 18 to chapter 4, for the background of this letter); p. 536; letter to Blake, Jan. 1, 1859.

33. Ibid., p. 403; Dec. 25, 1855.

34. Ibid., p. 371; Feb. 7, 1855 "I wish," Thoreau wrote, "that I could believe that the cause in which you are embarked is the cause of the people of England."

35. Ibid., pp. 480–83; May 26, 1857.

36. Ibid., pp. 484 (letter to Blake, June 23, 1857), 525 (letter to Ricketson, Nov. 6. 1858).

37. Ibid., pp. 448–55; Dec 16, 1856. Cholmondeley was then returning from the Crimea, and sent the letter from Rome.

38. Ibid., p. 477 (Apr. 17, 1857, letter to Blake); and see also p. 470 (Mar. 28, 1857, letter to Ricketson).

Four. Other Relationships

1. Thoreau, *Correspondence*, pp. 401–2; Dec. 9, 1855.

2. Ibid., 427–28; July 12 and July 17, 1856.

3. Thoreau, *Journal*, in Perry Miller, *Consciousness in Concord* (Boston: Houghton Mifflin Co., 1958), p. 193.

4. See J, X: 15–16 for a sympathetic reference to Elizabeth Hoar, and see also above, note 1 to chapter 2.

5. For a fuller discussion of Thoreau's complex attitudes toward women, see Mary E. Moller, "Thoreau, Womankind, and Sexuality," *ESQ: A Journal of the American Renaissance* 22 (1976): 123–48.

6. Richard Lebeaux, *Young Man Thoreau* (Amherst: University of Massachusetts Press, 1977), pp. 45–46.

7. Thoreau, *Correspondence*, p. 546; Feb. 12, 1859.

8. See Sherman Paul, *The Shores of America* (Urbana: University of Illinois Press, 1958), chapter 8 (especially pp. 383–84). And see Lebeaux, *Young Man Thoreau*, chapter 6, which offers a penetrating analysis of Thoreau's need and love for John, and of his deep sense of guilt, arising from their rivalry over Ellen Sewall, and intensifying after his brother died. Lebeaux believes that Thoreau's fondness for singing the ballad of "Tom Bowling," or "Bow-

line," and his handling of the shipwreck passage in *Cape Cod* (which I explore also, below, chapter 9), reflect his memory of John and of that terrifying death. "He had lost a brother, and he would never fully recover from that loss. His life was forever transformed" (p. 204).

9. Thoreau, *Correspondence*, pp. 36–38; Jan. 21, 1840. See also pp. 15 (Oct. 27, 1837), 39–40 (June 13, 1840), 127–28 (July 21, 1843).

10. Ibid., pp. 108–10; May 23, 1843; also Thoreau, *Poems*, pp. 151–52.

11. "Farewell," Thoreau, *Poems*, p. 215.

12. Franklin B. Sanborn, *Henry D. Thoreau*, American Men of Letters Series (Boston: Houghton Mifflin Co., 1886), pp. 259–60. See also Ellery Channing, *Thoreau, the Poet-Naturalist* (Boston: Robert Bros., 1873), pp. 52–53.

13. See for example Thoreau, *Correspondence*, pp. 187–188 (Oct. 24, 1847), 438–40 (Nov. 1, 1856), 581–82 (July 8, 1860).

14. See, for example, *J*, V: 204 (May 31, 1853), 226 (June 6, 1853).

15. Thoreau, *Correspondence*, p. 135; Aug. 29, 1843.

16. *J*, IV: 194 (July 6, 1852); III: 337 (Mar. 6, 1852).

17. *J*, III: 41; VIII: 150–51 (1856); IX: 288 (1857).

18. Thoreau, *Writings*, VI, *Letters*, ed. Franklin B. Sanborn, pp. 374–75. (Editorial note, p. 375.) The "very different letter" which Thoreau sent to Ricketson—which mentions bluebirds (and gives the date of their first sighting as Feb. 26, said to be "one day earlier than your date"), but which does not mention Minott—is cited above, page 57. Harding and Bode did not include the draft letter in their edition of the *Correspondence*.

19. Thoreau, *Walden*, chapter 6, pp. 144–50.

20. Thoreau, *Week*, p. 21.

21. Thoreau, *Walden*, chapter 11, "Higher Laws," pp. 211–16.

22. For example, Sherman Paul, discussing Thoreau's response to New York City, goes on to say that "The city, the strange surroundings, were exciting to a man of perception. (His descriptions of cabmen, immigrants, and Lucretia Mott [*Letters*] reveal a superb skill: he had the makings of a social novelist, but not a fictive imagination—the moral pressures of New England that turned him to the natural fact robbed us of a novelist. His descriptions, nevertheless, indicate a greater sense of society and people and a greater compassion than has usually been accorded him.)" (*The Shores of America*, pp. 144–45.)
Early in his long essay on Thoreau, Perry Miller remarked that the *Journal's* "innumerable side glances at the town ... amount to a sort of hilarious gazette," and that such things as "the character of George Minott or John Goodwin have become as much a creation of literature as Queequeg" (*Consciousness in Concord*, p. 29).
In his foreword in the 1962 Dover reprint of the *Journal*, Walter Harding twice speaks of it as "a work of art"—containing "character sketches, tales, descriptions, humor, pathos, argumentation, exposition—God's plenty of it and incomparably good" (p. vii). As for Thoreau's "disdain for the popular fiction of his day," the *Journal's* 1906 editor, Bradford Torrey, had written (with, as Harding says, "a certain condescension") that "A bit of boyish play now and then ... or a dose of novel-reading of the love-making, humanizing (Trollopean) sort, could one imagine it, ... might have done him no harm" (pp. l–li in the Dover reprint).

23. See Thoreau, *Cape Cod*, in *Writings*, IV: 80–101.
24. Thoreau, *Week*, pp. 80–81; *J*, III: 166, 37–38.
25. Thoreau, *Walden*, pp. 153, 96.
26. See, for example, *J*, II: 72, 291, 314; III: 150, 364.
27. *J*, II: 21 (May or June, 1850); IV: 114 (June 25, 1852); II: 184 (Apr. 30, 1851).
28. *J*, V: 488 (Nov. 7, 1853); III: 160–61 (Dec. 29, 1851).

Five. Communitas

1. Sherman Paul, *The Shores of America* (Urbana: University of Illinois Press, 1958), p. 143.
2. Thoreau, *Walden*, "The Village," pp. 171, 167.
3. In Richard Lebeaux's book treating Thoreau's earlier years one can find once again a rather extreme statement of the more traditional view: "Even at this early stage of development Thoreau perceived nature as an escape from, or an alternative to, a community and family which disapproved of him, shamed him, did not understand him" (*Young Man Thoreau* [Amherst: University of Massachusetts Press, 1977], p. 73). It is clear from a number of *Journal* citations in my present chapter that Thoreau's relationship with the Concord community underwent a deepening of appreciation on both sides during the fifties. Yet Lebeaux's "Even at this early stage ..." implies only an unremitting and growing hostility between them from the early forties onward. As we have seen, even in the forties the situation was not so simple as that.
In his introduction, Lebeaux makes another statement which I must question: "Thoreau clearly has limitations as one who, by his words, thoughts, and deeds, can guide or lead us today. For instance, I have deep reservations about his relative disinterest in, and apparent devaluation of, human relationships and 'social facts'; ..." (p. 7). (Here Lebeaux is borrowing a term from Quentin Anderson, "Thoreau on July 4," *New York Times Book Review*, 4 July 1971, which adds up to much this same view.) In chapter 7 ("Experience; and Phil-anthropy") below, I have offered argument and evidence, chiefly from the *Journal* and *Walden*, to counterbalance this view. To the degree that we are all somewhat cynical, and selfish (and lazy, which Thoreau was not), we can understand and to some extent identify with that particular "struggle" (to adopt a word used later by Lebeaux) which he was often caught up in: between the private good—growth, "redemption" (to adopt Frederick Garber's word)—and the public. And we can, in fact, be "guided" in the area of social responsibility, be inspired by Thoreau—not only by his affirmations in *Walden*, "Civil Disobedience," "Life Without Principle," and, on behalf of the preservation of wild nature, in "Walking" and many others of his works, but also by the very seriousness of the struggle itself.
But passages in which Lebeaux underestimates his subject are rare. Stressing the "powerful psychological and social obstacles" against which Thoreau had to contend, he argues effectively that the fact (and surely this is a fact) that "his strengths were born partly out of struggle with weaknesses should

increase rather than diminish our admiration of his accomplishments" (p. 87). My reservations about this useful book have to do only with its author's occasional failure sufficiently to document the positive as well as the negative attitudes, i.e., the degree of ambivalence, which Thoreau expressed about community—humanity—(as about his family and other close associates) in his *Journal*, from its very inception to its close.

Six. Thoreau's Humanism

1. Humanism: in this study, the word denotes "devotion to human welfare: interest in and concern for man ... ; a doctrine or set of attitudes ... centered upon human interests or values." (Webster, *Third International Dictionary*, definitions two and three.) Although one reader, citing historical Renaissance Humanism, has questioned my application of this word to any aspect of Thoreau's thought, I find it indispensable for conveying these ideas. (Incidentally, although—or because—he was a mystic, Thoreau does of course share an important anti-ecclesiastical position with the Renaissance Humanists.) Frederick Garber also uses, and stresses, this word, in discussing Thoreau's perceptions of the limitations of Nature. Quoting an 1859 *Journal* passage (*J*, XII: 90–92) on Indian arrowheads (also quoted on page 110 in the present study), Garber comments that, in Thoreau's view, "one gets closer to the essence of a man by examining his artifacts, 'this work of his bones,' than by poring over the bones themselves. *The latter have little part in the most important business of a man, his task of humanizing the face of the earth* [my italics].... Ultimately [Thoreau] is after what the stones reveal of the work of consciousness upon nature.... These are the oldest crops of the mind. *Thoreau, the inveterate humanist* [my italics], could not take part in such cultivation (whether of turnips or arrowheads) as though he were the first man in that place to do so. He knows that when he is disturbing the earth he is stirring up other men as well...." (*Thoreau's Redemptive Imagination* [New York: New York University Press, 1977], pp. 144–45).
2. Thoreau, *Journal*, in Perry Miller, *Consciousness in Concord* (Boston: Houghton Mifflin Co., 1958), p. 209; Jan. 7. 1841.
3. See for example, *J*, I: 391 (1845?); II: 373 (1851); III: 5 (1851); IV: 114 (1852); VI: 185 (1854); and see *Correspondence*, p. 46; letter to Lucy Brown, Sept. 8, 1841.
4. Thoreau, *Correspondence*, p. 74; Jan. 16, 1843.
5. Thoreau, *Correspondence*, pp. 302–3 (April 10, 1853), 299 (Feb. 27, 1853).
6. *J*, I: 310 (1842); *Walden*, chapter 11, p. 220.
7. Thoreau, *Writings VI, Letters*, ed. Franklin B. Sanborn, p. 208.
8. One of these is Perry Miller, two of whose relevant comments I have cited above (pp. 22 and 34 n). And see *Consciousness in Concord*, pp. 81–96. Another critique which exaggerates the negative side in treating this aspect of Thoreau is the more recent "Scatology and Eschatology: The Heroic Dimensions of Thoreau's Wordplay," by Michael West (*PMLA* 89 [1974] pp. 1043–64). West remarks, reasonably I think, that "Thoreau remained haunted by a profound ambivalence toward the body" (p. 1046). But while

it is useful in documenting the degree of Thoreau's interest in the human body and its functions, especially as this interest is reflected in puns and other kinds of "wordplay," West's article seriously distorts Thoreau's attitudes toward women, and thereby his overall view of human sexuality. (See especially p. 1051; and see also Mary E. Moller, "Thoreau, Womankind, and Sexuality," *ESQ* 22 (July, 1976), pp. 137, 148 nn.).

9. *J*, II: 3 (1850); *Walden*, chapter 11, p. 221; *Letters*, ed. Sanborn, p. 204.

10. F. O. Mattheissen, *American Renaissance* (New York: Oxford University Press, 1941), pp. 91, 88.

11. Joel Porte, *Emerson and Thoreau: Transcendentalists in Conflict* (Middletown: Wesleyan University Press, 1966), chapter 6. The parenthetic quotation is from *Walden*, chapter 2, p. 97.

12. Moller, "Thoreau, Womankind, and Sexuality."

13. The year 1852 is the fullest (by about twenty pages) in the *Journal*; by this time his *Journal* had become a major element in Thoreau's life. The volumes for this year contain richly varied subject matter. There are many pages of sensitive reporting on nature observations and excursions—but it was after 1852 that the journals began to serve increasingly for field notes. In 1852 Thoreau was still suffering his alienation from the Emersons; these notebooks contain many emotional passages, and much evidence of "the hand put forth"—a desire for communication and intimacy. They also contain many lively character sketches and narratives; they also display as extreme contrasts of misanthropy and phil-anthropy as can be found anywhere. And by 1852, then at work on *Walden*, Thoreau had perfected his style, his literary craftsmanship. As the editors of the *Correspondence* remark in their introduction to this year, "now he could drive his pen ahead with the efficiency of a well-trained professional author. There is little waste motion to be noted in the manuscripts that survive..." (p. 275). This is as true of the manuscript journals for this period as of the letters.

Seven. Experience and "Phil-anthropy"

1. Thoreau, *Walden*, chapter 12, p. 227.

2. Thoreau, *Journal*, in Perry Miller, *Consciousness in Concord* (Boston: Houghton Mifflin Co., 1958), p. 211; Jan. 10, 1841.

3. Thoreau, *Poems*, p. 225.

4. Carl Bode, personal communication.

5. Thoreau, *Walden*, chapter 11, p. 216.

6. Stanley Cavell, *The Senses of Walden* (New York: Viking Press, 1972), pp. 5–6. Farther on, citing the widespread view of *Walden* as "a transcendental declaration of independence," Cavell questions "From *what* is Thoreau supposed to have declared his independence?" (pp. 7–8). "Clearly not from society as such," he answers; "the book is riddled with the doings of society. From society's beliefs and values, then? In a sense—at least independence from the way society practises those beliefs and values. But that was what America was for; it is what the original colonists had in mind" (p. 8).

7. Thoreau, *Walden*, chapter 2, p. 84 (this sentence appears also as the epigraph at the head of the book); and chapter 4, "Sounds," p. 127.

8. Thoreau, *Walden*, pp. 4, 324.
9. Ibid., 4, p. 111; 2, p. 88. Thoreau says that the second sentence—"Renew thyself...."—was "engraven on the bathing tub of king Tching-thang."
10. Ibid., "Where I Lived and What I Lived For," pp. 90–91, 97–98.
11. Ibid., "Economy," p. 17.
12. Ibid., pp. 10, 45, 118, 140, 268.
13. Ibid., p. 323.
14 Ibid., chapter 18, "Conclusion," pp. 323–24.

Eight. *"A Certain Doubleness"*

1. Thoreau, *Walden*, p. 164.
2. J, I: 403–4; 1845–47. A shorter version of this poem appears in Thoreau, *Poems*, pp. 161–63.
3. Thoreau, *Correspondence*, p. 66; letter to Isaiah Williams, Mar. 14, 1842. Here is the statement's context in the letter: having explained that John's illness arose from "the slightest apparent cause—an insignificant cut," Thoreau added, "but nature does not ask for such causes as man expects—when she is ready there will be cause enough. I mean simply that perhaps we never assign the sufficient cause for anything—though it undoubtedly exists." He then went on to speak of John's calm, his "serenity and playfulness ... to the last," adding that, whether or not Williams himself had known John, "no eulogy of mine would suffice." The sentence in question—"For my own part...."—concludes the paragraph.
4. Thoreau, *Walden*, chapter 2, p. 84. Walter Harding's Variorum edition (New York: Washington Square Press, Inc., 1962) restored the quotation to the head of the book, as it appeared in the original 1854 edition, although many other editions have failed to place it there. Harding remarks in a note (p. 255) that this omission is unfortunate, since the quotation incorporates the "awakening and morning theme," which is "a basic image," and "sets the mood for the entire book."
5. Thoreau, *Walden*, chapter 1, p. 78.
6. One very long sentence (though not the longest) from Faulkner's "The Bear" is reminiscent of Thoreau in its central idea and of the "Gone-to-Seed" passage especially in its manner:
"All right. Escape.—Until one day He [God] said ... just *This is enough* and looked about for one last time ... upon this land this South for which He had done so much with woods for game and streams for fish and deep rich soil for seed and lush springs to sprout it and long summers to mature it and serene falls to harvest it ..., and saw no hope anywhere and looked beyond it where hope should have been, where to East, North and West lay illimitable that whole hopeful continent dedicated as a refuge and sanctuary of liberty and freedom ..., and saw the rich descendants of slavers ... passing resolutions about horror and outrage in warm and air-proof halls: and the thundering cannonade of politicians earning votes ... to whom the outrage and the injustice were as much abstractions as Tariff or Silver or Immortality ..., and He could have repudiated them ..., except that out of all that empty sound and bootless fury one silence ... just one simple

enough to believe that horror and outrage were first and last simply horror and outrage and crude enough to act upon that . . ." (William Faulkner, "The Bear," in *Go Down, Moses* [New York: Random House, Inc., 1942], pp. 283–84). This "one" simple enough to see horror and outrage as they really are and crude enough to act upon his insight turns out to be none other than Thoreau's hero John Brown. And it was his action, the speaker implies, which caused God to "turn his face . . . once more to this land"— in the hope of its learning through suffering. Here also are biblical echoes; and the name of the speaker is Isaac, the central personage in "The Bear," who in this passage becomes a kind of Jeremiah. Nor do we need Faulkner's own explicit avowal of it to realize how his prose style, like Thoreau's, was profoundly influenced by the sonorities and rhythms of the Old Testament, King James Version.

7. Thoreau, *Walden*, chapter 14, pp. 257–64.

Nine. The Problem of Death

1. "Insolent familiarity": Perry Miller used this apt phrase (p. 67) in his discussion of Thoreau's attitudes toward death, although he did not cite the "Plea for John Brown" passage. (See Perry Miller, *Consciousness in Concord* [Boston: Houghton Mifflin Co., 1958], chapter 6.)

2. *J*, XII: 437–38 (Oct. 22, 1859); and, with the order of sentences slightly rearranged, "A Plea for Captain John Brown," *Writings*, IV: 434–35.

3. In addition to Miller's chapter 6, see also, for example, Sherman Paul, *The Shores of America* (Urbana: University of Illinois Press, 1958), pp. 296–97 and 383–85. Miller stressed the revulsion felt by Thoreau whenever he contemplated death, and especially burial, and his frequent efforts to "circumvent" such confrontations. Paul has suggested that both Thoreau and Emerson were so profoundly shaken by the deaths (within the same month) of John Thoreau and Emerson's little son, that they were obliged thereafter to appear "unfeeling" to many observers: "death had chilled them, and it seems that they were only able to maintain their faith [in life] by closing off forever the channels of grief" (p. 383). (I have pointed out, however, how feelingly Thoreau could write, in the privacy of his *Journal* and of letter drafts, of the deaths of his sister, his father, George Minott, and John Brown.) Paul also makes a point—in what I think is one of his best passages–about the error of those who would deny that Emerson and Thoreau possessed "a sense of evil, . . . as if anyone, especially men of such acute sensibility, could avoid it, could mount their hope on any less substantial foundation [than a full recognition of suffering, evil and death in the world]." Thoreau, he goes on, might have been content "only to report his ecstasy . . . one day well spent in Nature"; but he was "more concerned with telling how ecstasy was earned, and [how] . . . in the absence [of certain conditions considered "necessary" by others] one deliberately remade his life" (p. 296).

4. Thoreau, *Walden*, p. 98.

5. It was in the same connection that, at least once in the *Journal*, Thoreau ranged himself with those dreary men who, he said, could not die—were

dead-in-life. In the late forties he wrote that he felt himself as far from the scene and time of their river voyage together as was John, "who has finished the voyage of life." "Am I not most dead," he asked, "who have not life to die, and cast off my sere leaves?" (J, I: 455).

6. This is quoted, I think, in every biographical study of Thoreau, and probably first in that by F. B. Sanborn, who identified the visitor as Parker Pillsbury, an earnest abolitionist with whom Thoreau had corresponded now and then during his last years (Henry D. Thoreau, American Men of Letters Series [Boston: Houghton Mifflin Co., 1886], p. 314). Joseph Wood Krutch took great pleasure in this and the other famous retort made by the dying Thoreau to solicitous friends. Although they might have spared the sick man their platitudinous questions and urgings, he says, these "challenges" resulted in "two memorable sayings." —The second of these was prompted by an orthodox relative's asking Thoreau whether he had "made his peace with God." One can imagine a variety of replies to such a question—annoyed, pious, fearful, flippant, defiant, or hypocritical. "But only Thoreau," says Krutch, "could have answered, as he did, that he was not aware that he and God had ever quarreled—thus making "one of his last sayings one of his most characteristic." Krutch finds this "a tremendous statement... in some sense innocent," which once again underlines Thoreau's "deep satisfaction in his life" (Henry David Thoreau, American Men of Letters Series [New York: William Sloane Associates, 1948], pp. 245–46).

7. Quoted by Hawthorne in his journal after Melville had visited him in England in the fifties. "[He] informed me," Hawthorne wrote, "that he had 'pretty much made up his mind to be annihilated'; but still he does not seem to rest in that anticipation,..." (Nathaniel Hawthorne, English Notebooks, ed. Randall Stewart [New York: Oxford University Press, 1941], p. 432; Nov. 20, 1856).

8. The feeling Thoreau expressed here closely resembles that described by Whitman in the first section of "This Compost."

9. Thoreau, Journal, in Miller, Consciousness in Concord, pp. 188–90; Dec. 14, 1840. See also a—considerably milder—meditation upon burial customs and, in particular, burial monuments, in the Week (pp. 176–79). Miller also discusses a few work sheets for the Week, discarded by Thoreau, which reveal the same complexity of feeling about death, the same intense revulsion, as that displayed in the 1840 and the 1853 Journal passages (pp. 68–70).

10. Thoreau, Cape Cod; Writings, IV, pp. 5–13.

11. Richard Lebeaux has pointed out that during this sojourn on the south shore Thoreau visited Ellen Sewall Osgood and her husband who lived nearby. Assuming that this visit must have called up memories of John Thoreau, of his rivalry with Henry for Ellen's affection, and of the brothers' river voyage together not very long before John's death, Lebeaux suggests that Thoreau probably had John in mind when he wrote this confident affirmation of the soul's immortality. (Young Man Thoreau [Amherst: University of Massachusetts Press, 1977], pp. 199–204.)

12. Thoreau, Cape Cod, Writings, IV, pp. 11–12. "Can anyone doubt," Lebeaux asks, "that the 'funeral' and corpse Thoreau had in mind were John's? Certainly no-one else's death had affected him so profoundly" (Young Man Thoreau, p. 201).

Ten. ". . . To Men in Their Waking Moments"

1. Thoreau, *Walden*, chapter 2, pp. 90, 81; *J*, I: 64–65.
2. Thoreau, *Walden*, chapter 9, pp. 199, 192.
3. Ibid., chapter 10, pp. 204–7.
4. Ibid., p. 207.
5. Ibid., 208–9.
6. And the most basically wrong-headed aspect of Perry Miller's long essay is that it manages, much of the time, to represent Thoreau as a cold, an emotionally limited man. (At certain other times Miller acknowledges the fact of Thoreau's having had emotions by the use of such terms as "spasm," "frenzy," "lustful," and in such phrases as "he was thus internally compelled to vomit forth the cancer of his guilt.") This particular phrase refers to Thoreau's *Journal* account of the forest fire brought about by himself and his fishing companion. Miller introduces his discussion of the fire episode in this way: "In April, 1844, five months after he had fled [note "fled"] back home from New York, Henry Thoreau, master of woodcraft, set fire to the Concord woods [this sentence suggests that the setting could have been deliberate; and note "Concord woods," which suggests simultaneous combustion of every tree lot in the township, instead of the fire's actual origin in a fringe of dried grass at the river bank] and almost destroyed the town [a wild overstatement, of course]." Miller next acknowledges the fire to have been an "accident"—in these words: "Thoreau's biographers mention this accident, as they must, for the memory of it still remains in Concord [otherwise, he implies, biographers would not mention it], furnishing proof positive that he was not only shiftless but dangerously irresponsible" (Perry Miller, *Consciousness in Concord* [Boston: Houghton Mifflin Co., 1958], p. 119). "Proof" for whom? I will forbear further comment on that sentence, and rather refer my reader to Odell Shepard, who deals quite efficiently with the "unscholarly" and sledgehammer quality of these statements, and also with the side question of Concord opinion ("Unconsciousness in Cambridge, *Emerson Society Quarterly* 13 [1958]: 13–19).
7. Ralph Waldo Emerson, "Biographical Sketch," in Thoreau, *Week*, p. xii.
8. Thoreau, *Walden*, chapter 2, pp. 97–98, 327–28.
9. Ibid., chapter 17, p. 318.
10. Emerson, "Biographical Sketch," in *Week*, p. xvi. A few days after his Concord speech (Oct. 31, 1859), Thoreau wrote to Blake urging that meetings be organized on Brown's behalf in Worcester, and offering to give his own speech there. He did deliver it there, and also in Boston, during the month of November (Thoreau, *Correspondence*, p. 563).

Library of Congress Cataloging in Publication Data
Moller, Mary Elkins, 1929–
Thoreau in the human community.
1. Thoreau, Henry David, 1817–1862.
2. Humanism in literature. 3. Authors, American
—19th century—Biography. I. Title.
PS3053.M6   818'.3'09   [B]   79–22549
ISBN 0–87023–293–2